Modern Critical Views

Modern Critical Views

STEPHEN KING

Edited and with an introduction by
Harold Bloom
Sterling Professor of the Humanities
Yale University

FINKELSTEIN
MEMORIAL LIBRARY
SPRING VALLEY, N.Y.

CHELSEA HOUSE PUBLISHERS
Philadelphia

Library of Congress Cataloging-in-Publication Data

Stephen King / edited and with an introduction by Harold Bloom.
        p. cm.— (Modern critical views)
    Includes bibliographical references and index.
    Summary: A collection of critical essays discussing the work of the
prolific horror writer Stephen King.
    ISBN 0-7910-4780-6 (hc)
1. King, Stephen, 1947-   —Criticism and interpretation.
2. Horror tales, American—History and criticism. [1. King,
Stephen, 1947-   —Criticism and interpretation.   2. Horror
stories—History and criticism.]   I. Bloom, Harold.   II. Series.
PS3561.I483Z878   1998
813'.54—dc21   97-49605
                                                                         CIP
                                                                          AC

Contents

Editor's Note

This book offers a selection of the better criticism available upon the work of the popular American novelist Stephen King. I am grateful to Tenley Williams for assistance in the editing of this volume.

My Introduction broods upon the significance of King's enormous popularity, as American society moves towards the Millennium. This anthology then begins its chronological sequence of commentary with Chelsea Quinn Yarbro's account of King's relation to fairy tales, with *Carrie* as a version of Cinderella, and *The Shining*, *The Stand*, *The Dead Zone*, and *Firestarter* all analogized to mythic archetypes.

Ben P. Indick sees King in the tradition of Gothic fiction, with particular debts to Poe, Bram Stoker, and Lovecraft. Poe is also the spirit animating Clive Barker's tribute to King. Allegory, as a pervasive mode in King, is examined generally by Bernard J. Gallagher, and in the particular form of machine-human conflicts by James Egan.

The intense distinction between adults and children in King is seen by Anthony Magistrale as a central thematics of "innocence betrayed." In another essay, Magistrale traces Hawthorne's influence upon King. Clare Hanson, influenced by Julia Kristeva, reads King's fiction as the obverse of romance, and as a mode of abjection designed to distance males from the image of the mother.

The Shining is examined by Jeanne Campbell Reesman as an extension of the American literary naturalism of Frank Norris, Theodore Dreiser, and Jack London. Katherine K. Gottschalk confronts the horror of Annie Wilkes, the terrible mother-goddess of *Misery*, while Jonathan P. Danis also pursues mythic patterns, King's visions of childrens' rites of passage in *Carrie* and elsewhere.

Karen A. Hohne strenuously applies Bakhtin to King's *Skeleton Crew*, after which Linda Badley associates King's belated "nod to feminism" with similar gestures in Clive Barker and Anne Rice.

Needful Things is judged by Sharon A. Russell to be a considerable advance in the horror genre. Edwin G. Casebeer, examining the whole of what he calls King's "canon," finds a "quest" motif that mirrors the "accommodations" accomplished by King's vast audience.

Introduction

In a brilliant study, *Nightmare on Main Street* (1997), the critic Mark Edmundson attributes the immense popularity of Stephen King to our universal Gothic obsessions as we approach the Millennium. Edmundson is very shrewd in surmising a quasi-religious source for the latest wave of American Gothic:

> Yet if I were pressed to submit one reason for the contemporary proliferation of Gothic, that reason would in a certain sense be religious. Though most of us Americans claim to believe in God, few of us seem able to believe in God's presence. That is, we do not perceive some powerful force for good shaping the events of day-to-day life in accord with a perceptibly benevolent master plan. Most of us don't have a story that we can believe about the way God's designs are unfolding among us. Whatever God is up to, he is not busying himself unduly with worldly events.
>
> Many of us have, I think, turned from hope in benevolent religion to fascination with the Gothic. There is something to gain in accepting the harsh belief that the world is infested with evil, that all power is corrupt, all humanity debased, and that there is nothing we can do about it. With the turn to contemporary Gothic—no-fault, dead-end, politically impotent though it may be—we recover a horizon of ultimate meaning. We recover something of what is lost with the withdrawal of God from the day-to-day world. With the Gothic, we can tell ourselves that we live in the worst and most barbaric of times, that all is broken never to be mended, that things are bad and fated to be, that significant hope is a sorry joke, the prerogative of suckers. The Gothic, dark as it is, offers epistemological certainty; it allows us to believe that we've found the truth.

1

On this persuasive account, our lust for Gothic is a parody of Gnosticism, which is a major strand in the American Religion. Stephen King is not at all Gnostic, whether in religious persuasion or in temperament. Edmundson notes a Wordsworthian strain in King: he exalts children, and severely distrusts adults. I suspect that Mark Twain and not Wordsworth is the source: many of King's heroes are very diffuse versions of Huckleberry Finn. Though King manifestly derives from many major storytellers in the American tradition, he has much the same relation to them that television and film scripts frequently possess: a waning out of imaginative energies. I find King very hard to read, even when I can discern redeeming social values in his narratives. There are depths beneath depths, and clearly King is preferable to the sadistic Anne Rice, whose fictions are profoundly unhealthy, and whose style is even more tedious than King's. Nothing intrinsic in King's work is nearly so important as the overwhelming fact of his popularity. Like television, motion pictures, and computers, King has replaced reading. Hundreds of thousands of America schoolchildren, who will read nothing else that isn't assigned, devour King regularly. They turn to King as their parents resort to Danielle Steel and Tom Clancy. I see no point in deploring this, and yet we ought not to deceive ourselves: the triumph of the genial King is a large emblem of the failures of American education.

I will confine this brief Introduction to just two of King's works, *Carrie* and *The Shining*, equally famous, and clearly representative of his achievement, whatever that is. With great effort, I have just reread both, after an interval of some years. The narrative line of each book has a certain coherence and drive; the prose is undistinguished, and there is nothing much that could be termed characterization or inwardness, or even vivid caricature. And yet there is an imagistic strength in both tales, by which I do not mean individual images, but rather the heaping-up of events to constitute giant or central images. King's most authentic continuity with Gothic masters like Mary Shelley in *Frankenstein*, and Poe in his stories, is his ability to concentrate upon what the reader is compelled to see. *Carrie* and *The Shining* have nothing to match Mary Shelley's grand vision of the daemon's (or monster's) self-immolation as an arctic funereal pyre, or Poe's nightmare evocations of the shades of deceased beauties. And yet Carrie at the Prom, first humiliated as a scapegoat, and then horribly triumphant as a fiery avenger, is a marvelous culmination of popular melodrama. She will not survive as a figure of American literature, but she seems to have entered our folklore, as the apotheosis of the wallflower, and a caution to many. Similarly, the image of a mother and her boy pursued by a crazed husband-father, himself victimized by demons, outlasts the tired tracts of *The Shining*'s prose. A

prolix storyteller, generally trapped by his own facility, King nevertheless
has a kind of archetypal power of the image.

As I understand what I have learned to call the American Religion, no
American truly feels free unless she is alone, and no intensely spiritual
American believes that she is part of the creation. Though he has a secular
sensibility, King implicitly endowed the boys of his earlier novels with the
conviction that the best part of their selves was older and wiser than the corrupt adult world, whether manifested by individuals or by institutions. A
perpetual contrast between youthful value and mature depravity enabled
King to fashion a sequence of persuasive images of sympathetic horror. In his
recent work, this most popular of writers has retreated from boyish protagonists, perhaps out of an uneasiness at repeating himself. Yet the later books
rarely sustain the enormous images summoned up by *Carrie* and *The Shining*.
I cannot locate any aesthetic dignity in King's writing: his public could not
sustain it, nor could he. There is a palpable sincerity to everything that he
has done: that testifies to his decency, and to his social benignity. Art unfortunately is rarely the fruit of earnestness, and King will be remembered as
a sociological phenomenon, an image of the death of the Literate Reader.

CHELSEA QUINN YARBRO

Cinderella's Revenge:
Twists on Fairy Tale and Mythic Themes
in the Work of Stephen King

Most children have a taste for the gruesome; comic books and Saturday morning cartoons reflect their fascination with mayhem. This is not new to this culture or this century, as a quick glance at children's books, to say nothing of those books traditionally called "The Classics," will show. The myths and fairy tales that are progenitors of most literature are tales of the most dastardly, violent, despicable, treacherous behavior, and require hero-ic, though often unpleasant remedies. This is the source of much of the suspense in literature, and it is an easy thing to assume that the need for suspense generates the need for ghastly deeds and events in modern fiction, horror and otherwise. Judging from the recurring popularity of the scarey/gothic/supernatural/horror/shudder tale, it may well be that the case is the other way around–suspense is the means to achieve the *frisson* that is sought by the reader.

No contemporary writer is more in tune with this literary resonance than Stephen King, and the great general appreciation of his work is ample proof of this. King knows how to evoke those special images that hook into all the archetypal forms of horror that we have thrived on since earliest youth. He often puts menace in stodgy settings: not for him the "Once upon a time in a land far away from here" approach to a story. He shows us the beloved malignant forms not in castles and caves but high schools and con-dominiums. He does not rely on the exotic for his tension, but the mundane,

From *Fear Itself: The Early Works of Stephen King*. © 1993 Underwood-Miller Inc.

everyday world. Yet the figures he puts there are known and familiar to any-one who shivered in blissful fright at those ominous words: "Who's been sleeping in *my* bed?" He has not turned away from the Handsome Prince, or the Poor Woodcutter, or the Little Mermaid; he has transformed them, but we recognize his characters as old friends (we always knew they were).

Nowhere is this more apparent than in *Carrie*. Although Carrie lacks the Ugly Step-sisters, she has more than enough to contend with in her mother, who is so rejecting and unlike her that Carrie's mother serves the function of a step-mother better than most real ones could. Carrie is, as is only mythically proper, the ugly duckling, caught up in a home that is no shelter and protection to her, but a terrifying prison where she is at the beck and call of a mother who neither understands her nor wishes to, because of her own warped personality and rigid religious thought. Carrie is not in a position to find comfort from her peers, because in a very real sense, they are not her peers; they mock her for her manner and appearance, their derision not unlike the Step-Sisters. It is not a fairy-Godmother and mice who come to her rescue, but a classmate feeling guilty who lends Carrie her Prince Charming to alleviate her shame for the dreadful way Carrie has been treated. There are conditions to her gift, as all fairy tales have condi-tions. In this case, she will not have a pumpkin coach and mice footmen to return, but she will have to give back Prince Charming, who is not truly her own. So far the material is not unlike the story we all read when very young. But just as the original mythic versions of the story have been softened over the centuries, so this story returns to the more somber tale. In one of the original versions of Cinderella, when she is given the chance to be revenged upon her family, she has their noses and hands cut off. Carrie goes further than that; she wrecks the entire town in a display of psychokinesis that smacks of Jovian rage. It is the right of the Queen of the Fairies to punish erring mortals, and Carrie, being psychically gifted, reflects not only the beautiful and beneficent nature of fairy-folk, but their malignancy and caprice as well. This is not the Cinderella of later days when virtue and humility were supposed to be their own rewards, but an earlier manifestation of that figure, taking much more than an eye for an eye. Although destroy-ing herself, Carrie exacts a terrible price for such riddance.

To say that Stephen King deliberately set out to do a modern-day Cinderella story with a nasty end would be both silly and misleading. Few writers are quite so academic in their approach to their work, and certainly King is no different in this respect. But he has the same resonances as the rest of us, and for that reason it is not strange that he would use a very strong archetypal conflict for his little morality play. Certainly the miseries of high school are as agonizing as anything suffered by sweeping ashes from the hearth and running errands for an ungrateful and unfeeling family. The anguish Carrie feels has been experienced by almost anyone who endured high school America this century. The plight of honest servants is not as strong a subject for most of us because few of us have been or have been raised with servants. King has taken one set of intolerable circumstances—servitude—and substituted another that is equally ghastly—high school.

However, in some respects, with this and several other of his works, where he might have had his greatest strength, King reveals a telling weakness. Part of the Cinderella myth is concerned with the proper programming of women in western European society, and a good case can be made for Carrie that she was treated as she was because she was a girl, not a boy. I find it hard to believe that no one in that book ever was troubled by the neglect Carrie was subjected to because as a girl she was expected to submit to the will of her mother. No one pointed out that the girls in the school were treating her badly, and that as girls they had an interest in how Carrie was abused. And there was a tendency to avoid the uncomfortable feeling that perhaps some of the other girls might have made as sweeping devastation of the town if they had the chance because of the frustrations being female often evokes. No other girl is able to stand up for Carrie, though most of them must surely have had some difficulties in high school that might cause anger, if not on the scale of Carrie's wrath, at least as intense as hers. There was no element of sympathy invoked with the horror.

In *'Salem's Lot* there was a more obvious archetype to deal with: the vampire. Again, the setting is ordinary to the point of dullness, and the townspeople are not foreign and strange, but very familiar. King takes the most movie-land Lugosiad, 20th-century baroque representation of the vampire menace and introduces him with all the trimmings to this ordinary little town. This is the malignant version of the Prince from Another Land; instead of showing wonders he brings death and the most vile resurrection to people unprepared to deal with them. In this book, there is a deliberate recognition of the *reality* of fairy tale and mythic figures in the life of children, for it is the children who have the quickest understanding of the source of danger that has come to town. They are the most unusual prey and they appreciate the risks being taken. The fact that to all intents and purposes the vampire wins only adds to the mythic power of the story, since it not only emphasizes the power of the Undead but avoids the glib reassurances that are often found at the end of the most hair-raising penny dreadfuls. Unlike Stoker, King is not afraid to let the evil figure triumph when he logically would win, given the book's circumstances. The malign Prince (a title that is given to vampires somewhat less often than "Count") is the victor because he has not only the power mythically conferred on him, he also has the tactical advantage that most of the townspeople do not believe in him and take no precautions whatever to protect themselves from his predations. Myths and fairy tales abound with cautionary tales of the men who learned, but learned too late, and paid for their ignorance and obstinacy with any combination of their lives, their souls, and their fortunes. By the time King is through with it, 'Salem's Lot is a ghost town in every ironic sense of the word, and much of this comes about through the stubborn resistance of the townspeople to the notion that they might be dealing with a great danger.

The dubious advantages of gods or demi-gods living among mortals is one of the most persistently recurring themes in myth. Certainly a vampire figures as demi-god, as well as highly ambivalent archetype. Giving such a creature haven, no matter how unwittingly, openly invites disaster. Fairy tales far more often warn of entertaining demons unaware, than angels. King has a fine sense of the hazard and plays upon it, mixing in just enough social paranoia to make the course of the action compelling, and far more important, convincing.

In *The Shining*, King comes closer to a fairy tale setting; that huge pile of an empty hotel in the isolated mountains of Colorado is as exotic a locale as the castles of medieval romances. In this case, however, the unused and dangerous house is also a metaphor for Jack's mind, filled with closed rooms that may contain things he does not wish to look at. Who can blame him? Those are the very forces that at last destroy him. This castle is inhabited by dangerous spirits—Jack and his family—and is therefore slated for destruction. Castles of evil wizards almost always fall, and often through the use of the owner's own twisted powers. King's skill in story-telling disguises this so that the reader is more caught up in the victimization of the family than in the manipulations of the mind that is the source of the trouble. In this context it is not important whether the things Jack sees are actual or invented or past events in the hotel's history. Jack's state of mind calls these demons forth, just as the fate of his son Danny is to be the blessed spirit or pure soul that sees the fall from grace and all that it entails and can do little or nothing to prevent or change the destruction taking place, within the house and within his father. Sadly, this complex mythic element was one of many aspects of the book that the subsequent film did not develop. What could have been a tremendous accomplishment of the psychological sense of reality would also have sustained the cinematic version.

But back to that lamentable flaw in King's perceptions. It is disheartening when a writer with so much talent and strength and vision is not able to develop a believable woman character between the ages of seventeen and sixty. Jack's poor, troubled wife has little to do but worry about her child and husband. She takes action only when the danger is so omnipresent and so obvious that to deny its existence would be true madness. While King effectively shows a gifted and intelligent child and a ruined human being of a father, he is stymied by a woman. Why does she remain inactive for so long? Is she one of those who freezes when frightened? Is she blinded by love? Is she in fear of retribution or retaliation? With the general excellence of King's work and solidness of characterization, this blind spot is particularly disappointing. In a less accomplished writer it would be unnoticeable or understandable, but Stephen King is too good to make this kind of mistake. While it is true that there are fewer mythic figures of the sort that makes for the best of stories, King has shown a great capacity for invention and mythic appreciation, and it is unfortunate that this is one area where he has not yet shown the range and force that are the hallmarks of his work. Perhaps in balance I should point out that few writers have been able to show the relationship of fathers to their children, and to integrate that relationship with the development of the plot so effectively, as King has.

Of all King's work, the most clearly mythic in structure and intent is *The Stand*. Here King is using the post-catastrophic landscape as the setting for a final confrontation of Good and Evil. Beginning as a survival novel, it quickly shifts into gear for a proper Armageddon, complete with a very diabolical symbol of evil going to and fro in the earth and walking up and down in it.

The mythic derivations are so demanding that the narrative develops along lines that allow for little ambiguity; the one character, Nick, who is the embodiment of ambiguity, is eliminated before the final confrontation of the book, so that the lines are clearly drawn from the first to the last of that confrontation. Since there were substantial cuts in this work, it is not entirely fair to criticize it in the same light as his other works, which are intact. With much material missing from *The Stand*, many of the usual subtleties are not present that would increase the strength of the work. The post-disaster landscape in which *The Stand* takes place has many mythic resonances that add to the focus of the work, so that the action is already highly colored by the setting and location. King has a keen sense of the power of environment evinced in *The Shining*, but it took *The Stand* to bring this perception into full flower. King presupposes a world in ruin which makes it possible to achieve a world cleansed of evil and destruction. This is not unlike the Hindu teachings of the Dance of Shiva which occurs on the Burning Ground. Shiva is spirit, free from the degradation of the flesh. Shiva dances on the Burning Ground, trampling the dwarf of ignorance and beating the drum which is the pulse of time. The pacing of the evil being in *The Stand* through the ruined world is not unlike the dance of Shiva on the Burning Ground. While this may not have been King's specific intention, there are enough similarities to make the Burning Ground a persuasive reality for the setting of *The Stand*.

There is also the question of the figure of God, who in this case is the answer to the riddle: "Well, to begin with, She's black." King has taken the figure of an elderly black woman, Mother Abagail, who acts as deity and compassionate judge in the middle-to-middle-end of the book. She serves both as oracle and god, and for that reason has strengths far beyond her immediate characterization. King shows an appreciation of the extended power of the individual in this woman, and leans on her heavily to keep positive characters moving against the negative ones.

After *The Stand* comes *The Dead Zone*, which is in many ways King's most successful book. King does not often deal with Everyman so clearly as in *The Dead Zone*. To pit a man, something of an innocent, against the casual brutality of his villains shows an increasing depth to King's work. Johnny is out of synch with the rest of the world, as is Everyman, and has to deal with his uncanny awareness of evil as best he can. At first this is merely inconvenient and awkward, but as the presence of the evil grows stronger and attracts reinforcements, Johnny is made more and more aware of the need for action. This is not unlike the story of Grimm's Everyman, Faithful John, who to avert great travail must act in ways that will earn him the punishment and the odium of his peers and superiors. Like Faithful John, Johnny does as his conscience and perceptions require, and he is prepared to pay the price. As Johnny with his paranormal gift devotes his attention to the needs of mankind, so Faithful John, in overhearing the ravens talking, realizes that if he is to be a worthy servant, he must ignore the immediate commands of his Prince and dedicate himself to preserving the Prince's family. Faithful John becomes a stone statue for his efforts; Johnny is almost a murderer; both of them set aside considerations of personal safety and the good opinion of those around them for the greater good of their countries. Selflessness is not a virtue often espoused in literature these days, but pitting selflessness against the Neo-Nazi destruction in *The Dead Zone* shows how that choice must be clearly made by all of us at one time or another, with or without the benefit of psychic insight. As Faithful John had the ravens, so Johnny has his precognition, and both of them are required to pay the price of what they and they alone understand to be a deadly threat. As fairy tales often deal with the question of moral responsibility, so Stephen King often broaches the subject through his characters, in situations where moral and civic good must be weighed against personal advantage. This sort of double bind is not only the stuff that great fairy tales are made of; they are also the issues that make for compelling literature of any time, any culture, any century.

In *Firestarter*, King once again returns to children, to one special child for his focal point. Charlie is one of those very wise children who populate myths, in a special niche all her own. Charlie is a mutant, which gives King the chance to change the usual rules of childhood in order to show the persuasive strength of the gifted kid more sharply. This is the fairy child, the changeling, brought into the Twentieth Century and into modern parlance. Charlie is not just a bright little girl: she is a kid with the power to (dare I say it?) rule the world. We know from relatively early in the story that Charlie is able to make a great many changes in the world around her with relatively little danger to herself. What brings her into hazardous positions are the expectations of others.

Like a great many of the demi-gods of mythology, Charlie is tested by circumstances and escapes peril through the use of her inborn abilities, not unlike the infant Hercules or the child Jesus (see the *Apocrypha*, Infancy Books I and II). As is often the case, the single biggest threat that this wonder-child faces comes from the king, or in Charlie's case, the government, the modern equivalent. The minister of the king, or the men of the Shop who attempt to use and subvert Charlie, have their parallels in fairy tales and myths, in the sinister figures of plotting viziers and zealous lieutenants, in treacherous dukes and malignant guardians. That one of them is basically well-intentioned but misled is a device often found in Greek myths, most familiar as the minister to the King of Arcadia who acts on his king's orders, unaware that he has only half of them, and thereby makes several fatal mistakes. Charlie, in remaining true to her father, also remains true to herself, for in myths and fairy tales the denial of family and heritage is one of the most reprehensible and damning of actions, for which there is rarely any forgiveness; if pardon comes at all, it is after the expiation of suffering and trial. In myth and fairy tale, the wonder-child must never deny his or her humanity, for that leads to destruction and the utmost rejection. King was canny in *Firestarter* because he pitted Charlie against a wonder-child gone wrong, a wonder-child who had denied his heritage and his past in a way that Charlie had not and could not. Rainbird is her mythic antithesis, the demi-god who perverted his gift. In true mythic fashion, he is now the servant of the king, who has the mark of his betrayal on his face. Most failed demi-gods are scarred or crippled in some way, and Rainbird is no different.

Firestarter, in the grand tradition of heroic fairy tales, starts with an ordeal and persecution, and ends with implied revenge of a sort that every demi-god from Brunhilde to Samson to Loon Brother understands: justice will triumph or the world will end.

King's iconography is not that of Medieval and Renaissance Europe, nor that of ancient and Imperial Rome, but rather of the late 20th century America. Some of the changes are obvious—chariots and horses become automobiles and motorcycles, hymns and prophecies are transformed into popular songs, demi-gods into mutants and medically-altered people. Again, it would be too simplistic and absurd to say that this is done academically or deliberately, but the structure of much of King's writing draws on those archetypes, and it is no disservice to his work to examine it in this light. Even much of King's style is mythic and fairy-tale-like in tone. In general, his narrative style is low key and conversational, as if he were speaking to you, quite literally telling you a story. This conversational tone allows him to use these archetypes most effectively, since almost all of them come from the oral traditions. Today's tall tale is tomorrow's immortal myth. King has hooked into this sequence in a way that makes his writing doubly persuasive, giving it the force of good story-telling and neatly paranoid plot, and adding to it the whole weight of those well-known figures from our past. From the stories heard in childhood comes part of the impact he creates.

Cujo is perhaps the farthest from this fairy-tale world of any of King's work, but there is still that persistent sense of a larger reality. Plenty of myths warn that those creatures you trust may not be all that trustworthy. The whole book has a miasmic sense of uncertainty, as if the characters were already on their way to madness and despair before the horror actually hits them. There is something particularly hideous about rabies; few of us can think of that disease without a very real shudder. In this case, it serves as an evil spell, a malignant force that accelerates and enhances a decline that is in progress before the terrifying events begin. That the instrument of destruction is "man's best friend" is not only appropriately ironic, it serves to point up the assumptions of the characters in general, so that the fear engendered extends beyond the immediate threat.

King has a real appreciation and sympathy for monsters, so that even at their worst, they never go beyond the bounds of a rough kind of compassion. In *Cujo* he uses this more directly than in his other work, by making his monster—poor old sick dangerous beast that he is—pitiable. At no time does Cujo cease to be the dog we were all made to like; he is as much a victim as anyone else in the story. Fairy tales are full of monsters with wounded human eyes, the most obvious being Beauty's Beast. Although Cujo is not in that metaphor, there is much of the Beast tragedy touching him, just as it touches all those possessed and transformed creatures in myth—the Ondine does not intend to drown her Knight, she seeks only to love him; the Fool does not mean to send all the tsareviches over the precipice, but he knows no other answer to give them and they have no chance to question him; there need be no malign intention for things to go terribly wrong. In many ways, Cujo keeps the readers' sympathy because he is so much an object of terror (and the power, in this case from a disease, he has is no more in his control than anyone else's).

Just as myth and fairy tales are much concerned with the use and misuse of power, so King often balances his critical moments on that issue. When all the trappings are gone, King shows the difference between strength and tyranny, between persuasion and manipulation. He often makes sure that his characters have powerful gifts, but turns the plot on how those gifts are to be used, including the power of fear. In this, he is drinking from the same potent well as Euripides, Racine and Cervantes, who also drew heavily on the myths and folk tales of their people and cultures. It would be misleading to say that there must necessarily be a mythic correlation between popular fiction and the mythic archetypes of a society, but writers, being products of their society, will tend to be sensitive to these constructs and use them. Almost all horror fiction, no matter who writes it, relies on these earlier images to some degree to create the environment required to move its readers. That King is especially sensitive to these archetypes is evinced in the quality of his work and its wide popularity.

With Stephen King, you never have to ask "Who's afraid of the big bad wolf?"—You are. And he knows it.

BEN P. INDICK

King and the Literary Tradition of Horror and the Supernatural

As one of the most successful writers in the history of the horror tale, Stephen King has constructed his work on a sure knowledge of the fiction of his predecessors. References to authors and titles abound in the pages of his novels. Even more important, he has absorbed and utilized those qualities which characterize the different types of stories in the horror genre. In his own distinctive style are mirrored the major traditions he has inherited.

The ghost in fiction is at least as old as the Graeco-Roman era, but Pliny the Younger's chained ghost is merely a plaintive creature seeking proper interment. Chaucer's "Nun's Priest's Tale" tells of a traveler who dreams of seeing his companion's wounded and bleeding body, but the purpose is to help him discover that murdered friend. With the Witches of *Macbeth* and the ghosts within *Hamlet* and *Macbeth*, Shakespeare added a sense of fright to Elizabethan theatre, in which the ghosts' purpose was largely the furthering of the mechanics of the play.

It was the dawning era of Romanticism which gave birth to the supernatural story as we know it: an anti-rationalism accepting essentially unknowable and hidden aspects of nature. A very real world was busy exploring, geographically and industrially; in response, poets and story-tellers looked for mystery, and found it in strange islands and weird creatures of imagination. For Horace Walpole, a devotee of Medievalism, what better period could there be than that era called the Gothic?

Others obviously agreed. The novel Walpole wrote in 1764, *The Castle*

From *Fear Itself: The Early Works of Stephen King.* © 1993 Underwood-Miller, Inc.

of Otranto, precisely caught the mood. He populated his decaying castle with an array of noble lords, helpless females, scheming villains and a battery of supernatural forces, all of whom were manipulated through real as well as fantastic dangers directly menacing the heroes. The story itself was frequently absurd and the plot melodramatic. The narrative style was ponderous and the dialogue, which would influence a century of stage melodramas to come, was formal and stilted. (A friar speaks: "The will of heaven be done! I am but its worthless instrument. It makes use of my tongue to tell thee, prince, of thy unwarrantable designs. The injuries of the virtuous Hippolita have mounted to the throne of pity.") The style did not bother the reading public. The book became a best-seller. Its weaknesses are excusable, for it was, after all, the *first* Gothic novel. Issued under a nom-de-plume, the novel's enormous success quickly persuaded the author to have his true name appended.

Walpole's ingenuity resulted in an endless flow of similarly inspired Gothic novels, which offered better characterizations as well as more sensational fears. Moral tone was usually present, to justify the excesses. Thus, Clara Reeve concludes in *The Old English Baron* (1777): "All these . . . furnish a striking lesson to posterity, of the overruling hand of Providence and the certainty of RETRIBUTION." Sometimes, as in the very popular *The Mysteries of Udolpho* (1794) by Ann Radcliffe, weak explanations for the supernatural events were offered; fortunately for her readers, these rationalizations came too late to dilute the action.

Sensationalism reached early heights in Matthew Gregory "Monk" Lewis' work, particularly his lurid *Ambrosio or the Monk* (1795). To the mysterious knights and swooning maidens of his predecessors, he added explicitly personal terms of fear with strong sexual overtones and violence. Lust, matricide, incest and murder are ladled up with many fantastic elements, upon none of which he wastes a word of rationalization.

The style and manner of the Gothic would begin to appear in fiction distinguished by grace and honesty in writing. Charles Dickens used ghosts effectively if sentimentally in *A Christmas Carol* (1843) and quite unsentimentally in such stories as "The Trial for Murder" (1865). Charlotte Brontë employed the essence of the Gothic form powerfully in her non-fantastic novel *Jane Eyre* (1847) with the castle, the mysterious owner and his dark secret, and a suffering but courageous heroine. Her sister Emily eschewed the trappings but retained the potency of ghostly images with her ill-starred lovers of *Wuthering Heights* (1847).

While the broad outlines of the original Gothic style withered, the supernatural elements, particularly the ghost story, prospered. The 19th and

20th centuries have been rich with lastingly effective examples of the genre. The external ghost as limned by Montague Rhodes James (1862–1936) in "Oh, Whistle, and I'll Come to You, My Lad," wherein a figure composed of the crumpled linens of a bed suddenly rises, remains potent. Algernon Blackwood (1869–1951) made equally feasible the presence of a Satanic mystery and willing human followers in "Ancient Sorceries." The tradition of the ghostly tale is well exemplified in the stories of such writers as Henry James, Edith Wharton, Mary E. Wilkens Freeman, J. S. Le Fanu, E. F. Benson and H. R. Wakefield. Their prose is characterized by subtlety and avoidance of the sensational.

The castle of the Gothic novel, with its ghostly accoutrements, would survive in humbler form as The Haunted House, beloved alike to fictioneers and spiritualists. Perhaps the most distinguished modern example is Henry James' *The Turn of the Screw* (1898), a subtle work with ghosts so tenuous that the reader must decide whether or not they truly exist. A half century and many haunted houses later, the form still retained its potency in *The Haunting of Hill House* (1959) by Shirley Jackson. Ira Levin's *Rosemary's Baby* (1967) utilizes a huge apartment house, gothic in its architectural details, as a fine counterpoint to his lively New York scene. Peter Straub fills a mansion with a ghost's vindictive terror in *Ghost Story* (1979). Stephen King himself displays a splendidly classic haunted house in *'Salem's Lot* (1975) and the haunted house to end all haunted houses, the craggy Overlook Hotel of *The Shining* (1977).

But the Gothic held little validity for serious writers of the 19th century. In the hands of Edgar Allan Poe (1809–1849) for the first time the point of view was significantly altered. The weird tale would not merely provide fear for the characters of the story, but would provide *the reader* the greater fear of self-identification. "The Tell-Tale Heart," "The Cask of Amontillado," "The Fall of the House of Usher" have no Satan, no externally influential force, no abstract presence of Evil to direct the characters. The vengeance that is so much a part of Poe's fiction always stems directly from the actions of his actors, and they must later bear full responsibility for their acts. Their own decisions will finally destroy them.

In this sense, Poe's writing is of true psychological content; the grotesque behavior actually represents the normal distorted by emotion to the extreme. Even his allegorical tales follow a line of inevitability and deterministic logic. His weird stories are as rational as his detective stories, and his use of the fantastic must be understood as the ultimate extension of this logic. As a poet, his language was both natural and important to him; his favored themes of murder, retribution and dissolution are couched in a florid and gorgeous tapestry of words so evocative of mood and place that in themselves they heighten the tension. The characters are intense, humorless, compulsive and expressive.

This vein of psychological insight which Poe added to the supernatural tale was exploited by others. Fitz-James O'Brien (1828–1862) wrote what was basically science fiction to create terror in "What Was It?": an invisible, inimical creature is discovered in a hotel room and is finally beaten to death. Guy de Maupassant (1850–1893) offered a more subtle approach in "The Horla." His narrator is threatened also by something unseen; it may be of extraterrestrial origin, or it may indicate his own growing madness. Ambrose Bierce (1842–?) had insight as sharp as Poe, tempered by cynicism. The psychological power of his stories derives from the eternal hope of his characters, who eventually discover it to be a futile snare. Fate, to Bierce, is not only blind but cruel.

The inner psychiatric maze Poe opened lies at the heart of the Victorian world of Wilde's *Dorian Gray* (1891) and Stevenson's schizophrenic *Dr. Jekyll and Mr. Hyde* (1888), each a study of internal evil. May Sinclair, Walter de la Mare, Oliver Onions and numerous others continued the tradition. With one notable exception, the Vampire Tale, the course of the weird tale would not change again until the advent of H. P. Lovecraft.

In 1816 at Lake Leman, Switzerland, three travelers had a ghost-story writing contest. They were Lord Byron, John William Polidori, his traveling companion, and Mary Wollstonecraft Shelley, wife of the poet. Mrs. Shelley's *Frankenstein* would become immortal; Byron's "Fragment" would be completed by Polidori as "The Vampyre, A Tale," the first popularization of the vampire theme. Byron later disowned any part of it, professing to dislike "Vampires," but no doubt the attribution to him helped the work, as it achieved great popularity in print as well as in a stage adaptation.

The first modern treatment of the vampire theme, in plot, writing and characterization, is "Carmilla" (1872), a novella by Joseph Sheridan Le Fanu. Its turns, plot surprises, and sexual undertones hint at the potentials of the vampire novel. Yet none of his successors surpassed the sensitivity of Le Fanu, as expressed in his concluding lines: "To this hour, the image of Carmilla returns to memory with ambiguous alterations—sometimes the playful, languid, beautiful girl; sometimes the writhing fiend I saw in the ruined church; and often from reverie I have started, fancying I heard the light step of Carmilla at the drawing-room door."

Bram Stoker's *Dracula* (1897), a novel written entirely in the form of letters and journals, scarcely had a "light step." The trappings of the Gothic novel are notable here: the sepulchral castle, the brave heroes, the weak, helpless women, and a frightful, nearly insuperable villain. Yet the book soars beyond the limitations of the Gothic and its own self-imposed style of narrative. The action is continuous, and the book is packed with excitement and sexual allure (satisfying a Victorian preoccupation, yet remaining within the bounds of propriety). Stoker combined genuine pathos with a satisfactory psychological development in the characters. Innocent at the outset, they suffer deepening fear and a sense of guilt because of their increasing, if involuntary, complicity and debasement. The combination of these elements renders *Dracula* truly the first "Neo-Gothic" novel, indebted to the romantic past, yet contemporary in its characterizations and mores. It is interesting that Count Dracula himself has very few actual lines to speak in the book (he can only be quoted by others) yet emerges unforgettably.

In the Twentieth century H. P. Lovecraft reached into space and Time to give horror new dimensions. If Poe was the Newton of the weird tale, Lovecraft was its Einstein, bringing it into the Atomic Age. Horror in his writings arises from the helplessness of his protagonists before the awesome forces they have called up or else inadvertently encountered. These mysterious entities antedate Man, are extraterrestrial in origin, and survive, hidden and dormant, yet possessing limitless power. The pantheon of "gods" associated with Lovecraft represent more, however, than a "mythos" of squirming, tentacled creatures: they are inimical forces which taint man and his earth. This taint is an irreparable demeaning of the self and the ego, and the initial horror is in the realization of it. This leads to the final horror, which is death or capitulation, *the surrender of one's humanity.*

II

That King was aware of his genre and its beginnings is clear from the numerous references to writers and titles in so much of his writing. In *Carrie*, an interviewer on the west coast is described as having "an odd, pinched look that is more like Lovecraft than Kerouac out of Southern Cal." The first paragraph of Shirley Jackson's *The Haunting of Hill House* is utilized to hint at the horror of the Marsten House in *'Salem's Lot*. A passage from Poe illuminates the living-dead nature of the final state of the doomed Lot, while Poe's "Masque of the Red Death" is inspiration for and encapsulation of *The Shining*, and is subliminally referred to in its climactic pages.

H. G. Wells, Washington Irving, Algernon Blackwood, J.R.R. Tolkien, Bram Stoker and others roam his pages. Even King himself is present, when, in *The Dead Zone*, a hysterical woman accuses his hero of having started a fire "by his mind, just like in that book *Carrie!*"

The Dead Zone is, significantly, a tribute to one of King's most important inspirations, Ray Bradbury. Bradbury's early weird fiction had initiated
the use of a natural vernacular and ordinary individuals in their own homes
and small towns. The knowledge that horror could be local and the victim a
common man produced a more personal fear in the reader. King's novel not
only owes much of its carnival ambience to Bradbury's *Something Wicked This
Way Comes*, but it acknowledges the debt in mentioning the title and author,
and, in another reference, yet another Bradbury title, *Dark Carnival*. (It even
features a character who sells lightning rods, an occupation much discussed
in Bradbury's first chapter!)

The heroes of *The Shining* and Lovecraft's "The Shadow Over
Innsmouth" bear valid comparison. Each carries within him the seeds of his
fate. For Lovecraft, it is the taint of the decadent subhuman followers of the
fish-god Dagon; in King, it is Torrance's connection with the evil essence of
the hotel: "It laid its Jack Torrance hands on the valve . . . 'I WIN!' it cried."
The "it" is Torrance, lost forever to the hotel.

King's references to other writers in the field are not strictly in emula-
tion. He has succeeded because he has forged his own style. Nevertheless,
there are influences upon his thinking and his writing, and these may be
examined, as follows:

1. The Poesque

King is not about to become a poet, however much he enjoys quoting poets
and lyricists. The feverish prose of Poe is antithetic to King's terse and rapid
narration, although he is capable of expressive imagery: " The womb of his
young wife had borne a single dark and malignant child" (a metaphor for
cancer in *The Stand*); "The skeletal fingers danced and clicked on the dark air
like marionettes" (the convulsive, final gesture of the vampire in *'Salem's Lot*);
"Overhead, the moon rode the sky, a cold sailor of the night" (a moment of
foreboding mood from *The Dead Zone*). Such passages are uncommon.
Action, not metaphor, moves King's stories. Even in *The Shining*, which is so
directly affected by atmosphere adapted from Poe, the writing is devoid of
any self-conscious attempt at beautiful prose.

Poe's influence lies in the psychological honesty of his writing, which
discarded worthless labels of Virtue and Villainy, and in the subsequent burden of introspection which Poe gave his heroes. King, always a story-teller
first, is not above having villains to spice the action; however, with the

exception of a fantasy villain such as Barlow, the vampire of 'Salem's Lot, there is a measure of explanation for such destructive individuals as Greg Stillson and Frank Dodd of *The Dead Zone*, in early maternal acts of harshness and even cruelty. (In a sense King offers us the opportunity of seeing Dodd, the compulsive rapist, from another view, in his short story "Strawberry Spring." Here the narrator is a compulsive murderer much like Dodd, but is sensitive and aware of his acts—too late. It is pure Poe.) King's more normal characters such as Larry Underwood (*The Stand*) and Charlie McGee (*Firestarter*) tend to deliberate their future courses of action carefully, rueing past actions which resulted in grievance to others. The heroine of *Carrie*, no more mature than most of her fellow teenagers, nevertheless tries to understand herself and particularly her mother. Her destructive acts come only because she has no way to respond emotionally and intellectually.

The psychic powers of Carrie, Johnny Smith (*The Dead Zone*), Danny Torrance (*The Shining*) and Charlie McGee are thus in no way employed for *deus ex machina* pyrotechnics. To some degree they are a curse to the characters, who must try to control the powers, and to understand that they can never be a magic carpet of escape. It is the Fantastic made Real, instead of being accepted as simply fantastic. This is the triumph of Poe.

2. The Vampire Tale

Stoker's *Dracula* opens in the romantic, Gothic-inspired setting of the hills of Transylvania. King's 'Salem's Lot, his major contribution to the vampire genre, is set, characteristically for the author, in a typically small New England town. Its inhabitants are stereotypical; major characters receive individual chapters, titled for themselves, the others are covered broadly by chapters titled "The Lot." In a sense this repeats the individual epistolary and journal-entry division of *Dracula*.

Stoker wastes little time establishing his fantasy; Jonathan Harker quickly realizes he is a prisoner of the Count and then almost at once encounters three female vampires. When Dracula deprives them of feasting on the hapless Harker, he gives them instead a bag "which moved as though there were some living thing within it." They vanish with the bag, and "Then," writes Harker, "the horror overcame me, and I sank down unconscious."

King likewise moves quickly into the horror of his story, although not revealing at once the presence of vampirism. Hints of terrifying acts mount in the brief sub-chapters, usually commencing prosaically and concluding ominously. Only pages after a child has vanished, a "dark figure" appears at the cemetery, bearing the body of a child. An obscene prayer to a "Lord of Flies" is offered, along with the body. The subsequent lone line, "It became unspeakable," is the commencement of a crescendo of horror, which quickly becomes very explicit.

Once the presence of a vampire is suspected, the balance of Stoker's baggage is brought out, the garlic, the crucifix, the heroine who has been despoiled by the vampire and must be given the ritual absolution, the great Vampire himself. King actually attempts to avoid linking the fate of the vampire to the counter-power of Christianity; to a priest of insufficient faith, the vampire Barlow says "The Catholic Church is not the oldest of my opponents . . . I was old when it was young . . . My rites were old when the rites of your church were unconceived." Nevertheless, the crucifix remains a potent weapon for young Mark against a vampire, who hisses "as if scalded" when confronted with it.

At the climax, King's monstrous Barlow must die as did Stoker's Count, each still helpless at sunset, with the strength of immortality moments away, each in his coffin. King, however, is true to his own emotional style. Whereas Stoker's hero, Jonathan, sweeps a knife across the helpless but vindictively staring body, and causes it to "crumble into dust"; King's Ben Mears is far more physical. Barlow, conscious, screams: "Let me GO!" Mears must climb into the coffin, knees planted on the vampire's chest for a solid perch to hammer in a stake. "Here it comes, you bastard . . . here it is, leech" and he "brings down the hammer again and again," while the dying Barlow, blood gushing wildly, screams through a graphically described dissolution into dust.

King's villain manages more mayhem than Stoker's, and furthermore leaves his flock of Un-Dead behind him in the Lot, where fire may finally destroy them. (Perhaps not. In a related short story, "One for the Road," from King's collection, *Night Shift* (1978), a family traveling through the Lot during a blinding snowstorm experiences vampirism in a terrifying and poignant way.)

The credibility of so fantastic a tale in a setting so mundane is remarkable.

Nevertheless, *'Salem's Lot* must remain a footnote to its inspiration, *Dracula*. By choosing to portray a town's entire population, described individually to a great extent, King is forced to utilize readily recognizable types; the result is predictability in hero, heroine, villain. Without the fully rounded individuality which creates memorable characterizations, the danger of overkill and eventual ennui in the reader's mind is strong. Only King's most powerful allies, relentless pace and devastating shock, prevent this.

Finally, King cannot escape the sense of pastiche. Aware of this, he has his hero muse: "One was taught that such things could not be; that things like Coleridge's 'Cristabel' or Bram Stoker's evil fairy tale were only the warp and woof of fantasy. Of course monsters existed . . . hijackers . . . mass murderers . . . ." It is true enough, but still cannot disguise the essential imitation. *'Salem's Lot* becomes one more of the Un-Dead in the train of the evil Master.

3. H. P. Lovecraft

Except in deliberate pastiche of Lovecraft's style and thematic material, King seldom emulates a writer he obviously knows. The influence of Lovecraft is in his creation of horror wherein the fantastic element has a basis in scientific reality. The intrusion in such fiction of purely imaginative elements (ghosts, elves, demons and the like) would destroy the fabric of truth which sustains it.

Lovecraft's book of formulae, "The Necronomicon," is no mere medieval rune-book, nor are the powers it is capable of summoning such fantasies as Asmodeus or Beelzebub. The powers are "like some monstrous intrusion from outer space—some damnable, utterly accursed focus of unknown and malign forces." In his "The Colour Out of Space" such a force appears on a New England farm, no more tangible than an eerie color, but leaving desolation and death in its wake, "a frightful messenger from unformed realms of infinity beyond all Nature as we know it." These forces are real, and the horror which results from their intrusion into mundane life is real.

King employs no extra-terrestrials and no arcane books. Novels such as *Carrie, The Shining, The Dead Zone* and *Firestarter*, however, are dependent on reader acceptance of various extra-sensory abilities, a theme as unproven as any of Lovecraft's imaginings. Like the latter, King must establish a scientific basis for credibility. It is entirely the opposite of such outright fantasy as "The Turn of the Screw" and *Ghost Story*, which need offer no such basis in reality.

King asks no indulgence from his readers; he offers "evidence" to make the remarkable powers acceptable. By setting Carrie a few years into the future, King is able to refer to articles, books and the work of governmental commissions of inquiry which have already acknowledged Carrie's telekinetic powers. One such book, *The Shadow Exploded*, states "It is now generally agreed that the TK phenomenon is a genetic-recessive occurrence." By comparing it to the genetically transmitted disease of hemophilia, King makes it an apparent fact.

Johnny Smith of *The Dead Zone* has precognitive powers. We learn that he suffered an injury as a child which gave him "a very new human ability, or a very old one. " A "tiny part" had "awakened." In an epilogue, a physician states that Smith "had an extremely well-developed brain tumor," and then, in a letter written to his father, Smith writes that this tumor was probably part of the accident which was coincident with the beginnings of his "flashes."

In *The Shining*, the boy Danny Torrance possesses telepathic/precognitive powers. No scientific basis is offered other than the cook Hallorann's explanation that it is shared by him and others. "I call it shinin' on, the Bible calls it having visions, and there's scientists that call it precognition." In this instance, the strength of Danny's visions is so intense that the reader accepts the explanation. (Inasmuch as this novel is actually a ghost-tale, it operates within emotional rather than rational parameters.)

With *Firestarter*, King develops his strongest scientific basis for a psychic power. The terrifying ability of Charlie McGee to create fires is the result of chemicals administered to the young man and woman who would become her parents. The altering of their germ-plasms results in a unique child. If it is a stage beyond drugs such as Thalidomide, which affects an embryo, it is nonetheless credible.

4. The Ghost Story

The Shining, inspired by Edgar Allan Poe's allegorical "The Masque of the Red Death," is Stephen King's consummate ghostly tale. The palace of Poe's Prince Prospero becomes the Overlook Hotel, and his "assembly of phantasms" is played by the vast number of shades who have occupied its many rooms and left behind their evil essence. In time they will hold their "gay and magnificent revel, " but they are peripheral to the heart of the novel. This is the conflict of a man bent on self-destruction and his son, a telepath, who sense the horror of the hotel and the evils which will come upon them.

The story is constructed with extreme care, inexorably moving toward the terrible climax which it continually foreshadows. Almost at once the boy's apprehensions create a foreboding fear, which is enhanced by his mother's distrust of her unstable husband. With the episode of the wasps, badly stinging the boy when, by all rights, the wasps should have been dead, the family further disintegrates with fears and doubts. The abrupt fantasy is in the tradition of M. R. James, as Reality is unhinged and disbelief is challenged.

Torrance's encounter with the hedge animals of the topiary, apparently alive and threatening, is subtle in its psychological significance (*"NO NO I WILL NOT BELIEVE THIS NOT AT ALL!"*) It is, after all, a delusion which might happen to anyone. An hallucination, thinks Torrance, "a bad scare but it was over now." It is, in its implications, quite in the spirit of that other James, Henry.

It is the beginning of Torrance's breakdown, his absorption into the Hotel, and the Supernatural will now complement the final playing out of the family conflict. A rotting corpse of a woman in a bathtub appears not only to the sensitive child but to his father, who refuses to acknowledge it. Torrance is now able to discover the deceased caretaker and bartender as well as the many revelers of the Hotel's past.

The horrors mount swiftly, ghostly as well as human, as the man deteriorates, until the *Walpurgisnacht* of the climax. For an instant the blood-red presence of Poe's Red Death, in the *persona* of the Hotel itself, promises to "hold illimitable dominion over all," but it dies of its own weakness and evil. "The party was over."

The Shining is a tour de force, dependent like any good ghost story and supernatural tale upon neither science nor explanation, but only on its own inner logic and compelling narrative voice.

5. The Gothic

The ancient Greek philosophers preached the virtues of moderation. Their playwrights knew better. Scandal, murder, hair-rending and railing against the gods sold tickets.

King is not a philosopher. He knows how to sell tickets. He manages in his novels to encompass the desolation of a school, most of its students and much of the town as well by one distraught girl. He turns a village into a nest of vampires. He unleashes an army of ghosts, then utterly destroys their huge home. He polishes off New York City's teeming millions as well as 90% of the world's population. He uncovers a nuclear bomb and explodes it, but tops that by finding a child who has the ability of "creating a nuclear explosion simply by the force of her will."

King revels in excess on more private levels as well: the public menstruation of Carrie, followed by its reflection in her drenching with pig's blood; Frank Dodd as raincoated rapist, killing and dying with frightening violence; bodies literally torn to pieces by the monsters of *The Mist*.

Nevertheless, excess is only one element King inherited from the Gothicists. There is another, far more important. For Stephen King, who remembers shuddering through monster films as a child and claims he still cannot sleep without at least one light glowing in the house, the indispensable mainspring in his stories is Fear. Its origins may be psychological, physical, or even supernatural, but the fear itself is real, and his horror stories succeed because his readers share it.

Walpole's school had foundered when fear lost its rationality. Drs. Van Helsing and Freud rediscovered it beneath Prince Albert coats. King has put it into the shopping basket, next to the tomato sauce, the Sanka and the Tab. Fear has become a commonplace, no longer the evil dispensation of noble or supernatural villains. No one can be trusted, not teenaged school kids, not a cop or a prosaic motelkeeper, not even a small baby. It is a world with neither security nor stability.

We all live in Otranto.

CLIVE BARKER

Surviving the Ride

The tygers of wrath are wiser than the horses of instruction.
—William Blake: *The Marriage of Heaven and Hell*

First, a confession: I have no thesis. I come to these pages without an overview to propound; only with a substantial enthusiasm for the work of Stephen King and a *potpourri* of thoughts on fear, fiction, dreams and geographies which may bear some tenuous relation to each other and to King's fiction.

Theoretical thinking was never a great passion of mine, but ghost-trains are. And it's with a ghost-train I begin.

It's called—ambitiously enough—*L'Apocalypse*. To judge from the size of the exterior, the ride it houses is an epic; the vast, three-tiered facade dwarfs the punters who mill around outside, staring up with a mixture of trepidation and appetite at the hoardings, and wondering if they have the nerve to step out of the heat of the sun and into the stale darkness that awaits them through the swinging doors.

Surely, they reassure themselves, no fun-fair ride can be as bad as the paintings that cover every inch of the building suggest: for the pictures record atrocities that would have turned de Sade's stomach.

They're not particularly good paintings; they're rather too crudely rendered, and the gaudy primaries the artists have chosen seem ill-suited to the subject matter. But the eye flits back and forth over the horrors described here, unable to disengage itself. In one corner, a shackled man is having his head sliced off; it seems to leap out at us, propelled by a geyser of scarlet

From *Kingdom of Fear: The World of Stephen King*. © 1986 Underwood-Miller, Inc.

blood. A few yards from this, above a row of arches that are edged with canary-yellow lights, a man watches his bowels being drawn from his abdomen by a Cardinal in an advanced state of decomposition. Beside the entrance booth, a crucified woman is being burned alive in a chamber lined with white-hot swords. We might be tempted to laugh at such *grand guignol* excesses, but we cannot. They are, for all the roughness of their presentation, deeply disturbing.

I've never ridden *L'Apocalypse*. I know it only as a photograph, culled from a magazine some dozen years ago, and treasured since. The photograph still speaks loudly to me. Of the indisputable glamour of the horrible; of its power to enthrall and repulse simultaneously. And it also reminds me—with its sweaty-palmed punters queuing beneath a crystal blue sky for a chance at the dark—that nobody ever lost money offering a good ride to Hell.

Which brings us, inevitably, to the architect of the most popular ghost-train rides in the world: Mr. Stephen King.

It's perhaps redundant, in a book celebrating Stephen King's skills, for me to list his merits at too great a length. We, his readers and admirers, know them well. But it may be worth our considering exactly *what* he's selling us through the charm and accessibility of his prose, the persuasiveness of his characters, the ruthless drive of his narratives.

He's selling death. He's selling tales of blood-drinkers, flesheaters, and the decay of the soul; of the destruction of sanity, community and faith. In his fiction, even love's power to outwit the darkness is uncertain; the monsters will devour that too, given half a chance. Nor is innocence much of a defense. Children go to the grave as readily as the adult of the species, and those few Resurrections that circumstance grants are not likely to be the glory promised from the pulpit.

Not, one would have thought, a particularly commercial range of subjects. But in King's hands their salvability can scarcely be in question. He has turned the horror *genre*—so long an underdog on the publishing scene—into a force to be reckoned with.

Many reasons have been put forward for King's popularity. A common element in most of the theories is his *plausibility* as a writer. In the novels—though rather less in the short stories—he describes the confrontation between the real and the fantastic elements so believably that the reader's rational sensibilities are seldom, if ever, outraged. The images of power, of loss, of transformation, of wild children and terrible hotels, of beasts mythological and beasts rabid and beasts human—all are dropped so cunningly into the texture of the world he conjures—morsel upon morsel—that by the time our mouths are full, we're perfectly willing to swallow.

The net effect is akin to taking that ride on *L'Apocalypse*, only finding that the dummies on either side of the track, enacting over and over their appalling death scenes, closely resemble people we know. The horror is intensified immeasurably. We are no longer simply voyeurs, watching some artificial atrocity unfold in front of our eyes. We are intimately involved with the sufferers. We share their traumas and their terrors. We share too their hatred of their tormentors.

This is by no means the only approach to writing dark fantasy, of course. Many authors choose to plunge their readers into the world of the subconscious (which is, surely, the territory such fiction charts) with scarcely a glance over their shoulders at the "reality" the reader occupies. In the geography of the *fantastique*, for instance, Prince Prospero's castle—sealed so inadequately against the Red Death—stands far deeper in the world of pure dream than does the Overlook Hotel, whose rooms, though no less haunted by violent death, are far more realistically evoked than Poe's baroque conceits.

There are, inevitably, losses and gains on both sides. Poe sacrifices a certain accessibility by his method; one has to embrace the fictional conventions he has employed before the story can be fully savored. He gains, however, a mythic resonance which is out of all proportion to the meagre pages *The Masque of the Red Death* occupies. He has, apparently effortlessly, written himself into the landscape of our dreams.

King's method—which requires the establishing of a far more elaborate fictional "reality"—wins out through our commitment to that reality, and to the characters who inhabit it. It also earns the power to subvert our sense of the real, by showing us a world we think we know, then revealing another view of it entirely. What I believe he loses in the trade-off is a certain *ambiguity*. This I'll return to later.

First, a couple of thoughts on subversion. It has been argued, and forcibly, that for all the paraphernalia of revolution contained in King's fiction—the weak discovering unlooked-for strength and the strong faltering; the constant threat (or promise) of transformation; a sense barely hidden beneath the chatty surface of the prose, that mythic elements are being juggled here—that, despite all this apocalyptic stuff, the author's world-view is at heart a conservative one. Is he perhaps a sheep in wolf's clothing, distressing us with these scenes of chaos in order to persuade us to cling closer to the values that his monsters jeopardize?

I admit to having some sympathy with this argument, and I admire most those of his tales which seem to show the world irredeemably changed, with no hope of a return to the comfortable, joyless, death-in-life that seems to be the late twentieth century ideal. But if there is evidence that gives weight to such argument, there is also much in King's work which is genuinely subversive: imagery which evokes states of mind and conditions of flesh which, besides exciting our anxieties, excites also our desires and our perversities.

Why, you may ask, do I put such a high value upon subversion?

There are many reasons. The most pertinent here is my belief that fantastic fiction offers the writer exceptional possibilities in that direction, and I strongly believe a piece of work (be it play, book, poem) should be judged according to how enthusiastically it seizes the opportunity to do what it can do *uniquely*. The literature of the fantastic—and the movies, and the paintings—can reproduce, at its best, the texture of experience more closely than any "naturalistic" work, because it can embrace the complexity of the world we live in.

Which is to say: our minds. That's where we live, after all. And our minds are extraordinary melting pots, in which sensory information, and the memory of same, and intellectual ruminations, and nightmares, and dreams, simmer in an ever-richer stew. Where else but in works called (often pejoratively) *fantasies* can such a mixture of elements be placed side by side?

And if we once embrace the vision offered in such works, if we once allow the metaphors a home in our psyches, the subversion is under way. We may for the first time see ourselves as a *totality*—valuing our appetite for the forbidden rather than suppressing it, comprehending that our taste for the strange, or the morbid, or the paradoxical, is contrary to what we're brought up to believe, a sign of our good health. So I say—*subvert*. And never apologize.

That's one of King's crowning achievements. From the beginning, he's never apologized, never been ashamed to be a horror author. He values the *genre*, and if horror fiction is in turn more valued now than it was ten or twenty years ago it is surely in no small degree his doing. After all, the most obsessive of rationalists must find it difficult to ignore the man's existence: he's read on buses and trains; in Universities and Hospitals; by the good, the bad and the morally indifferent.

At this juncture it may be worth remembering that the dreams he is usually concerned to evoke are normally known not as dreams but as *nightmares*. This is in itself worthy of note. We have other classes of dreams which are as common as nightmares. Erotic dreams, for instance; dreams of humiliation. But it's only the dream of terror which has been graced with a special name, as though we recognize that this experience, of all those that come to us in sleep, carries some essential significance. Is it perhaps that in our waking lives we feel (rightly or wrongly) that we have control over all other responses but that of fear? Certainly we may use the word nightmare freely to describe waking experience ("the traffic was a nightmare," we casually remark), but seldom do our lives reach that pitch of terror—accompanied by the blood-chilling sense of inevitability—that informs the dream of dread.

In reading a good piece of horror fiction, we may dip into the dreaming state at will; we may even hope to interpret some of the signs and signals that nightmares deliver to us. If not that, at least there is some comfort in knowing that these images are *shared*.

(An aside. One of the pleasures of any fiction is comparing the intricacies of response with other readers, but this process takes on a wonderfully paradoxical quality when two horror enthusiasts are exchanging views on a favorite book or film. The gleeful detailing of the carnage, the shared delight, as the key moments of revulsion and anxiety are remembered: we smile, talking of how we sweated.)

There are many kinds of nightmare. Some have familiar, even domestic settings, in which commonplace particulars are charged up with uncanny and inexplicable power to intimidate. It is this kind of nightmare that King is most adept at evoking, and the kind with which he is probably most readily identified. It is in a way a natural progression from rooting outlandish horrors—*CARRIE*; *'SALEM'S LOT*—in settings so familiar we might occupy them, to making objects *from* those settings—a dog, a car—themselves the objects of anxiety. I must say I prefer the earlier books by quite a measure, but that's in part because the Apocalypses conjured seem so much more comprehensive, and I have a practically limitless appetite for tales of the world turned inside out.

The other kind of nightmare is a different experience entirely and it is not—at least in the conventional sense—about threat. I mean the kind of dream voyage that takes you out of any recognizable context, and into some other state entirely. The kind that lifts you up (perhaps literally; for me such nightmares often begin with falling that turns into flight) and whips you away to a place both familiar and utterly new, utterly strange. You have never been to this place in your waking life, of that your dreaming self is certain; but there are presences here familiar to you, and sights around every corner that you will recognize even as they astonish you.

What actually happens on these voyages will run from the banal to the Wagnerian, depending on the dreamer's sense of irony. But the way this second sort of nightmare operates upon your psyche is totally different from the first. For one thing, the fears dealt with in the first sort are likely to be susceptible to analysis. They are fears of authority figures, or terminal disease, or making love to Mother. But the second kind is, I believe, rooted not in the specifics of the personality, but in something more primitive; something that belongs to our response as thought-haunted matter to the world we're born into. The images that come to overwhelm us in this region are not, therefore, projections of neurosis: they are things vast; contradictory; mythological.

King can conjure such stuff with the best of them; I only regret that his brilliance as a creator of domestic demons has claimed him from writing more of that other region. When he turns his hand to it, the effect is stunning. *The Mist*, for example, is a story that begins in familiar King territory, and moves through a variety of modes—including scenes which, in their mingling of the monstrous and the commonplace work as high, grim comedy—towards a world lost to humanity, a world that echoes in the imagination long after the book has been closed. In the final section of the story the survivors encounter a creature so vast it doesn't even notice the protagonists:—

> . . . Its skin was deeply wrinkled and grooved, and clinging to it were scores, hundreds, of those pinkish 'bugs' with the stalk-eyes. I don't know how big it actually was, but it passed directly over us. . . . Mrs. Reppler said later she could not see the underside of its body, although she craned her neck up to look. She saw only two Cyclopean legs going up and up into the mist like living towers until they were lost to sight.

There is much more of breathtaking imaginative scope in THE STAND, and in a more intimate, though no less persuasive fashion, in THE SHINING and 'SALEM'S LOT. Moments when the terror becomes something more than a fight for life with an unwelcome intruder; when the horror reveals itself, even in the moment of causing us to recoil, as a source of fascination and awe and self-comprehension.

This is the root of the ambiguity I spoke of before, and to which I said I would return. *Wanting* an encounter with forces that will change our lives—that will deliver us once and for all into the regions of the gods ("I had a dream that I saw God walking across Harrison on the far side of the lake, a God so gigantic that above the waist He was lost in a clear blue sky."—*THE MIST*)—yet fearful that we are negligible things and so far beneath the concern of such powers that any confrontation will simply kill us.

Charting that ambiguity is, I would suggest, a function that the fantasy *genre* can uniquely fulfill. It is perhaps the liability of King's virtues that such ambiguity is often forfeited in exchange for a straightforward identification with the forces of light. King's monsters (human, sub-human and Cyclopean) may on occasion be *comprehensible* to us, but they seldom exercise any serious claim on our sympathies. They are moral degenerates, whose colors are plain from the outset. We watch them kick dogs to death, and devour children, and we are reinforced in the questionable certainty that we are not like them; that *we* are on the side of the angels.

Now *that's* fiction. We are not. Darkness has a place in all of us; a substantial place that must, for our health's sake, be respected and investigated.

After all, one of the reasons we read tales of terror is surely that we have an *appetite* for viewing anguish, and death, and all the paraphernalia of the monstrous. That's not the condition of the angels.

It seems to me vital that in this age of the New Righteousness—when moral rectitude is again a rallying-cry, and the old hypocrisies are gaining acolytes by the hour—that we should strive to avoid feeding delusions of perfectibility and instead celebrate the complexities and contradictions that, as I've said, fantastic fiction is uniquely qualified to address. If we can, we may yet keep from drowning in a wave of simplifications that include such great, fake dichotomies as good versus evil, dark versus light, reality versus fiction. But we must be prepared to wear our paradoxes on our sleeve.

In King's work, it is so often the child who carries that wisdom; the child who synthesizes "real" and "imagined" experience without question, who knows instinctively that imagination can tell the truth the way the senses never can. That lesson can never be taught too often. It stands in direct contradiction to the basic principles which we are suckled upon and are taught make us strong in the world. Principles of verifiable evidence; and of the logic that will lead, given its head, to terrible, but faultlessly logical, insanities.

I return again to the list of goods that King is selling in his fiction, and find my summary deficient. Yes, there is death on the list; and much about the soul's decay. But there's also *vision*.

Not the kind laid claim to by politicians or manufacturers or men of the cloth. Not the vision of the *better* economy, the *better* combustion engine, the *better* Eden. Those visions are devised to bind us and blind us. If we look too long at them we no longer understand what our dreams are telling us; and without that knowledge we are weak,

No, King offers us another kind of vision; he shows us adults what the children in his fiction so often take for granted: that on the journey which he has so eloquently charted, where no terror shows its face but on a street that we have ourselves trodden, it is not, finally, the stale formulae and the trite metaphysics we're taught from birth that will get us to the end of the ride alive; it is our intimacy with our dark and dreaming selves.

BERNARD J. GALLAGHER

Reading Between the Lines: Stephen King and Allegory

Without a doubt, Stephen King is the one popular novelist whose earnings and reputation have undergone a horrifyingly meteoric rise. In 1982 King pocketed two million dollars for all of his works (Gray 87); in 1986 he pocketed three million dollars alone as an advance on his novel, *It* (Bangor-Kanfer 74). In 1982 he had almost forty million books in print (Gray 87). In 1986 he had over sixty million books in print (Bangor-Kanfer 743). In 1982 *Time* magazine's Paul Gray claimed that King represented a threat to serious book lovers everywhere. In 1986 *Time* magazine's Stefan Kanfer and Cathy Booth-Bangor aim no poison darts at King and his works. At worst their breezy and irreverent style implies a critical attitude toward King and his works. At best, they attempt both to explain the tradition of horror fiction and to locate King within the context of that tradition.

Time magazine's shift in attitude, to some degree, reflects a corresponding shift in the halls of libraries, high schools, and colleges. I don't mean to suggest that King is about to replace Shakespeare. I do, however, want to suggest that a cultural phenomenon of such proportions deserves scrutiny. Moreover, I want also to suggest that a good number of the readers, fans, and critics of Stephen King, as do *Time*'s reporters, ignore what eventually may be regarded as the most important book in the King corpus, Stephen King's *Danse Macabre*. This book of quasi-criticism not only brings an interesting and sometimes incisive critical vision to the work of horror, it also reveals an implicit critical method which opens up a realm of interpretive possibilities for popular fiction, film, and television. What I propose to

From *The Gothic World of Stephen King: Landscape of Nightmares.* © 1987 Bowling Green State University Popular Press.

do, then, is to clarify King's discussion of critical method in his *Danse Macabre* and then demonstrate how this method might apply in both close readings of a particular text and in general interpretations of popular cinema and television.

The insight which King offers into the work of horror is based upon a bimodal or dualistic vision which insists upon the necessity of reading between lines. The first mode or level which King describes is the "gross out" level—i.e., that level at which a cultural norm is violated for shock effect (4). Examples of the gross out include Reagan's vomiting in the priest's face in *The Exorcist* or the monster in Frankenheimer's *The Prophecy* crunching off a helicopter pilot's head (4). The second and subtextual level—the between the lines, so to speak—he describes is the artistic level (4), that is, a second level at which horror novels seek to probe "phobic pressure points" (4) which address archetypal, "political, economic, and psychological rather than supernatural fears" (5). Examples of this second and artistic level include the fear of death implicit in *Ghost Story* (262), the xenophobia implicit in Christopher Nybey's *The Thing* (152), and "economic unease" in *The Amityville Horror* (142). This second level, according to King, gives the work of horror its "pleasing allegorical feel" (5).

At this point, things become much less straightforward. King offers us little help in defining and understanding what he means by "pleasing allegorical feel." On one occasion, King treats allegory as a "symbolic way" of saying "things that we would be afraid to say right out straight" (31), a way for readers to "exercise emotions which society demands we keep closely in hand" (31). On another occasion he refers to the preceding notion of allegory as subtext or the "liaison formed between" our fantasies and our real fears (129). On still another occasion he talks about "symbols" and "symbolic mirrors" in general (144). And on other various occasions, he mentions "archetypes" (57) and "mass dreams" (144). Clearly, the pleasing allegorical feel about which King speaks has little to do with the allegory of the Middle Ages. The phrase, as he applies it, does not offer a system of symbology that extends and operates in the fashion of *The Pearl* or *The Romance of the Rose*. It is not a multi-modal system of symbols which offers the possibility of simultaneous interpretations on the literal, moral, anagogical, and allegorical levels.

Instead, the "pleasing allegorical feel" about which King speaks is a peculiar kind of psychological allegory, for the readings between the lines to which King invites us invariably discuss the political, social, and economic anxieties of the contemporary individual. For example, *Carrie*, according to King, is actually a feminist novel which confronts a young woman's psychic conflict when she attempts to live as a strong and autonomous individual in a culture that would prefer to see her as a passive and powerless piece of femininity (172). Moreover, *The Amityville Horror*, according to King, is really a story of economic unease which traces the demise of a young couple who buy a home they can's afford (142).

Once we recognize that King's bimodal vision of allegory places extraordinary emphasis upon hidden psychological anxieties or upon reading between the lines, we begin to see that a surprising number of parallels exist between the structure of King's allegory and the structure Freud attributes to the dream. These parallels deserve our attention not so much because they correspond in an overly neat and academic way but because they help clarify King's interpretation of critical method and because they suggest the possibility that this critical method has universal applications.

Freud divides the dream into two basic levels of meaning just as King divides the work of horror into the levels of the gross out and subtext. The first and most obvious level of meaning in a dream, according to Freud, is the manifest or dream content-level (218). Physical experiences as recalled by the memory comprise this level. In other words, remembered movements, colors, sensations, and experiences compose the dream's first level of meaning. The second level of meaning in a dream, according to Freud, is the psychic or latent content level. Desires springing from the unconscious comprise this second level (218;238) These desires, of course, invariably involve the wish-fulfillment of an infantile sexual impulse (495).

Both the systems of Freud and King, then, are bimodal. Moreover, both men argue that their bimodal systems result from the need of the individual to generate a superficial level of meaning which will disguise or hide a deeper and more disturbing level of meaning. King writes that horror fiction allows us to say "things that we would be afraid to say right out straight" (31), and Freud argues that the psyche creates the manifest content of the dream to "evade censorship" and to allow the dreamer to continue to sleep while expressing his suppressed and potentially disruptive desires (485). The schemes of both King and Freud, then, operate on the assumption that the surface level in either the work of horror or the dream generates its symbolic structure in order to protect the individual from the internal conflicts which he finds disruptive.

This need to disguise the latent or deeper content of the work of horror and the dream, of course, serves to separate further the psychological allegories of Freud and King from medieval allegory. Medieval allegory did not exist as a means of protecting the individual from disruptive truths. Instead, it existed as a conscious artifice which allowed the individual to manufacture and to understand a multi-modal vision of life which emphasized both the physicality of the here and now and the reality and importance of the spiritual. The allegories of King and Freud, meanwhile, frequently result from the unconscious attempt of the contemporary individual to cope with and yet hide from disruptive wishes and experiences. In short, both men use the concept of allegory to explain a kind of psychological ambiguity which results from the individual's desire to remain relatively safe and comfortable when confronting any of the many unpleasant truths of the human condition.

Once we see that the bimodal visions of King and Freud arise from the beliefs of both men that individuals find it necessary to disguise the latent or allegorical contents of their works, we can find one more impressive parallel. The writer of the work of horror and the dreamer apparently rely on the same three basic principles of condensation, transference, and displacement (338) when choosing the material which will comprise both the manifest level and the disguise of the story or dream. King, of course, makes no direct reference to any of these terms, but he skillfully employs the concepts of condensation, transference, and displacement when he interprets the movie, *The Amityville Horror*. King begins his interpretation by employing the Freudian notion that the dreamer, (in this case you may substitute director), condenses or compresses into an everyday incident a hidden anxiety or wish. He argues that "everything which *The Amityville Horror* does well is summed up in" (143) a single scene which depicts a financial crisis: a brother-in-law loans $1,500 that he does not have to a newly-wedded bridegroom. On the basis of this scene alone, King goes on to argue that *The Amityville Horror* is really a movie about "economic unease" (142). In turn, King supports this hypothesis of "economic unease" by transferring to this everyday event—"Gee, honey I'm overdrawn at the bank"—an intensity which did not originally belong to it. Of course, this transference to an everyday event of intensity which does not belong to it is the very thing that Freud describes with his term, transference (338). In order to sustain this interpretation of "economic unease," King must also employ the Freudian concept of displacement, for he argues that the everyday incident of the overdraft at the bank holds a second and more important meaning than we would normally assign it (338).

Only three significant divisions, then, lie between King and Freud and their bimodal visions. The first and most obvious difference lies in how transference occurs in the work of horror. Normally, transference means that an individual has transferred to an everyday incident an intensity which does not belong to it. However, a work of horror apparently reverses this operation by using an unusually intense event as a way of obliquely referring to the horror inherent in an everyday act too disturbing to discuss openly. In effect, then, the work of horror provides a vehicle for the metaphoric expression of terror at some everyday event which normally masks its horribleness behind a mundane face. Second, King, unlike Freud, does not locate the Oedipal triangle and its obvious emphasis on sexual competition between the offspring and the parent of the same sex at the center of his allegorical system. Instead, he suggests, under the headings of archetype and symbol, that a variety of interpretations are available to the individual interested in the work of horror. There are the universal fears of death, sexuality, and dark nights, and there are everyday fears about money, complexion, politics, and the slightly odd next-door neighbor. Third, King, unlike Freud, does not reduce every work of horror to an infantile impulse. Consequently, the interpretive possibilities in King's system of allegory are less reductive than the interpretive possibilities in Freud's system.

In spite of the fact that King is not a Freudian, the parallels which exist between his critical vision and Freud's are important. The Freudian concepts of manifest and latent content, condensation, transference, and displacement help to define King's critical method of reading between the lines. More importantly, though, the similarities between King's method of interpreting the work of horror and Freud's universal method for interpreting dreams imply that King's critical method has applications extending far beyond the work of horror. In fact, King's method for reading between the lines may be applied with great success to popular fiction, film, and television.

For instance, we do not need to scrutinize Ludlum's *The Bourne Identity* too closely in order to discover that it possesses the "pleasing allegorical feel" about which King speaks. On the gross out or manifest level, the novel traces the odyssey of David Webb, alias Jason Bourne, who has experienced a total loss of memory while in the middle of a counter-insurgency spy mission designed to draw out and destroy the super assassin, Carlos. On the artistic or subtextual level, though, the novel explores the problem of human identity. In short, it asks the same question Christopher Lasch asks in his book, *The Minimal Self: Psychic Survival in Troubled Times:* has the invasion of "culture and personal life by the modern industrial system produced . . . a loss of autonomy . . . [and] a tendency to confuse self-identification with the exercise of consumer choices" (41–42). Lasch's answer is a resounding yes. According to him we live in a narcissistic culture, that is, a culture in which the individual, like the Narcissus of Greek Myth, can no longer clearly distinguish between himself and his environment. Ludlum's answer to the question is also a resounding yes; and he, too, suggests that the individual who is self-reliant has at least a slight chance at independence and personal identity.

We can easily begin to support the notion that *The Bourne Identity* symbolically explores the problems of personal identity in an indifferent, or perhaps even hostile, technological world by first identifying, as did King and Freud, the incidents and characters in which everything the novel does well is "summed up" (King 143). And without a doubt, the novel's protagonist, David Webb, provides us with a perfect example of King's summing up and Freud's condensation. When Webb, alias Jason Bourne, nearly drowns at the outset of the novel, we encounter what I consider to be the key to understanding the story's subtextual discussion of the perils of personal identity.

> He felt rushing cold water envelope him, swallowing him, sucking him under . . . And there was heat, a strange moist heat at his temple that seared through the freezing water that kept swallowing him . . . he felt these things, acknowledging his own panic as he felt them. He could see his own body turning and twisting, arms and feet working frantically against the pressures of the whirlpool . . . yet strangely there was peace. It was the calm of the observer, the uninvolved observer, separated from the events. . . . Then another form of panic spread through him. . . . He could not submit to peace. Not yet. (14)

What you've just read, on the manifest level or the level of the gross out, is the description of the near-drowning of David Webb after he has been wounded and washed overboard into a stormy sea. This near drowning, however, takes on new significance when we read the comments made by Doctors Washburn and Panov. Washburn clearly establishes Webb as a sort of white Anglo-Saxon everyman when he describes Webb as "the prototype of the white Anglo-Saxon people seen everyday on the bitter cricket fields, or the tennis court" (22). At the conclusion of the novel, Doctor Panov expands Washburn's guess at Webb's everyman role when he says, "In a way, he's [meaning Webb] a functioning microcosm of us all. I mean, we're all trying to find out who the hell we are, aren't we?" (522) In short, Ludlum has condensed contemporary man into the character of David Webb.

Moreover, since the novel deals with the problems of an amnesiac everyman trying to discover his true identity, we also realize that the whirlpool and storm which threaten Webb represent much more than the far-reaching horrors of immediate drowning. At the subtextual level, in fact. these two elements of natural destruction actually serve as metaphoric expressions of the individual's desire to relinquish his personal identity. What tempts Webb is not the agony of drowning at sea but the peace that follows the abandonment of the struggle to survive. And what nearly kills Webb is not the sea itself but the calm detachment which renders him apathetic to his condition. Once we realize that the storm and the whirlpool have only drawn out attitudes that were already present, we also realize that the emphasis in this particular scene resides not in the physical presence of the sea but in Webb's psyche. And since Webb functions as an everyman, we also realize that we supposedly share in the same psychic weaknesses. Consequently, we can then see evidence of the transference to which King indirectly refers in his interpretation of *The Amityville Horror*, a way of intensely expressing our fears of losing our identities. Reading between the lines as King would, we also see, then, that a displacement has occurred and that Webb's temptations and near-drowning metaphorically express the contemporary American's temptations to abandon the struggle for personal identity in favor of the calm and peace of the unobtrusive and minimal self (Lasch 33–36).

Once we establish the subtextual concern of *The Bourne Identity* with the temptations and problems faced by the individual interested in developing an authentic personal identity, nearly every incident in the novel refashions and repeats the opening crisis of the near drowning in Chapter 1. Indeed, Ludlum seems to run Webb through a checklist of institutions in order to demonstrate the inability of any institution to form an authentic personal identity. For instance, the novel opens with a "Preface" which offers two seemingly authentic news releases about the shadowy figure, Carlos. As we read through both releases, we see that in both instances these newspapers offer very little real information. In fact, the only thing about which we can be sure is that the newspapers are not sources of hard information or personal identity. Later on in the novel, Marie St. Jacque—the romantic interest—confirms our suspicions about newspapers when she says:

> Both [stories] are constructed out of lies, the first connected to the second by tenuous speculation—public speculation on a banking crises that would never be made public. . . . And that second story—the patently false statement that millions were stolen from Gemeinschaft—was tacked onto the equally false story that I'm wanted for killing three men in Zurich. (278).

Newspapers in Ludlum's *The Bourne Identity* are sources of misinformation and are, therefore, incapable of aiding the individual in understanding either himself or his world.

The Bourne Identity, however, is democratic in its criticism. It not only damns the press, it also damns the military industrial complex and the United States government. In spite of an incredible amount of planning and an equally incredible amount of secrecy, the United States Government's plan to trap Carlos falls apart because government officers, due to circumstances beyond even their control, can no longer make sense of what has happened to Webb (292). Not only did their scenario fail to consider the possibility of Webb's injury, it also failed to consider Webb as a human being. Consequently, they are invariably puzzled by Webb's actions, largely because he has forgotten the identity they manufactured for him and has begun to act according to a set of internal values that emphasize love and loyalty. Furthermore, once Webb begins to operate consistently on a set of values, he also begins to abandon his chameleon-like identity for an identity which is both personal and authentic.

Ludlum's criticism of institutions as potential sources of personal identity extends beyond newspapers and government to include even the sacred cows of banking and medicine. For instance, Webb begins his search for identity at a bank in Zurich, believing somehow that the factual nature of his relationship with the bank will help him overcome his amnesia. Ironically, just the opposite happens. Once in the bank, Webb mistakes his alias, Jason, for his real name. He also wrongly surmises that the codename, Treadstone, is the name of a business firm for which he works. He also mistakenly believes that Mr. Koenig, an employee of the bank is trustworthy. At the root of these three mistakes, however, we find one truly serious mistake, that is the assumption that a bank and money can somehow help him discover who he is. Although the newspapers, government, and Swiss Bank are all venerable institutions promoting the established order, they cannot then, provide our everyman with an authentic identity.

Doctors and medicine are also inadequate sources of the individual's identity—they are far too materialistic and quantitative. However, both Doctor Washburn and Doctor Panov seem to understand that their profession is limited and that the individual alone must be the source of his personal identity. Washburn warns Webb early on that the task he is about to undertake is not easy and that he alone must be the source of his identity. He says:

> "I think I know what's going through your mind. A sense of helplessness; of drifting without a rudder to put you on course. I've been your rudder, and I won't be with you; there's nothing I can do about that. But believe me when I tell you, you are not helpless. You will find your way." (35)

Washburn's metaphor of the ship and rudder, of course, harkens back to the opening metaphors of the sea and the whirlpool in chapter one, and his statement is essentially a reaffirmation of Webb's earlier decision to brave the storm and whirlpool rather than to abandon himself to the whims of circumstance. Panov, at the end of the novel, makes a similar kind of assertion. He says:

> I've too much respect for the human mind to deal you chicken soup psychology; there's too damn much of it floating around in the wrong hands. . . . It's true we can go in with a knife and reach the storm centers, reduce the anxieties, bring a kind of peace to him. Even bring him back to what he was, perhaps. But it's not the kind of peace he wants. . . . (522)

In other words, Washburn and Panov both recognize that authentic personal identity resides not in institutions but in the individual and his attempts to confront the turmoil of life. Indeed, Ludlum's novel, *The Bourne Identity*, and Christopher Lasch's book, *The Minimal Self*, both seem to advise us that authentic personal identity resides not in the lobotomized peace of a minimal and chameleon self but in the tension and struggle of the individual to balance his individuality against the claims that nature and society make upon him.

I have only managed to offer you a little of what Ludlum has sandwiched between the lines of his popular novel, *The Bourne Identity*. However, I believe it is sufficient to show how we can apply King's method of allegorical interpretation to popular works of spy fiction as well as to popular works of horror. I will now provide you with a few more samples of how we may apply King's method of allegorical interpretation to popular film and television. Without any particularly strenuous effort, we can find any number of popular American films that offer the same sort of political, economic, and social allegories that King found in horror fiction. The recently released summer film entitled, *Short Circuit*, for instance, offers three major subtextual or allegorical possibilities.

On the manifest or gross-out level, it traces the picaresque adventures of a military robot, who because of an unexpected jolt of lightning to his circuitry, leaves the confines of the factory and undertakes an educational journey into the surrounding countryside. On the subtextual level things become more complicated. First and foremost, the movie satirizes the technological mind that attempts to reduce the world to stimulus response or to a vision of input and output. Eventually, the technocrats in the film must learn from a misplaced flower child that life necessarily involves relationships and emotions.

Second, but hardly less important, the film satirizes the tendency of the military-industrial complex to turn everything bright and beautiful into an unthinking purveyor of destruction. The delightful little robot has value for the military so long as he is a mechanism without emotion. Once he begins to function as a human being and to remind the human beings in the movie about the importance of humor, love, and plain old silliness, he loses any value he has for the military. In short, the film offers a comic but critical commentary on the notion that a good citizen is a good soldier who does what his country asks without question.

Third, the film offers a humorous indictment of American materialism with its portrayal of the martini-drinking but ineffectual scientist turned administrator. Thus, this apparently harmless little film offers in its blithe way encouragement to the American who feels insecure in his social role and uncomfortable with the recent bellicosity exhibited by his government. The uneasiness of Americans, however, does not always translate into movies criticizing society. Indeed, popular movies seem to just as often serve to support the *status quo*. Consider, for instance, the not-so-recent film *Splash*.

A seemingly harmless and irrepressible comedy, *Splash* does everything within its power to set the women's movement back into the fifties. A brilliant woman-mermaid (she learns English in no more than a couple of weeks), conventionally beautiful with her long blonde hair and svelte figure, and sexually insatiable, pursues the male romantic lead, who is puckish but not particularly handsome or intelligent. Clearly, the mermaid represents essentially the same vision of woman that we could find in the *Playboy* magazines of the fifties. The movie, however, does soften its sexist edge when the male character willingly relinquishes his earthly life for a life of love beneath the sea. However, even this last gesture does little to mute the film's sexism; for it clearly implies that a fantasy life with a fantasy woman as defined by conventional male needs is preferable to real life with a real woman.

Without looking too hard, we can find the same political, economic, and social concerns manifested in the programming of the major networks. Both *V* and *The Dukes of Hazard* were filled with latent political criticism. On the manifest or gross out level, *V* recounted in serial fashion the struggle of the human race to throw off an oppressive race of aliens determined to drain the earth dry of its resources and to use earth's population as a food supply. On a subtextual level, however, the military attire of aliens in *V* clearly established a connection between them and the same military-industrial complex criticized in *Short Circuit*. Moreover, whenever the aliens, who presented themselves as physically flawless humans, harmed a human, they justified their actions with the claim that what they did was for the good of the human race. The more intelligent humans, of course, reserved judgement and watched cautiously. Ultimately, we, along with the cautious characters in the program, discover that scaly carnivores lurk underneath the faultless complexions of the aliens and that the only way they will ever serve mankind is on a platter garnished with parsley. *V's* warning was quite plain: be careful of whom you believe because governments and institutions are not beneath manipulating us for their own colossal and corporate ends.

By way of contrast, the *Dukes of Hazard* offers a light-hearted and comic look at politics. On the manifest or gross-out level this television program recounted in serial fashion the picaresque adventures of the Duke family. Invariably the Dukes would find themselves forced to somehow outwit Boss Hogg and his corrupt sheriff, Roscoe P. Coaltrain, without circumventing the very law that these two villains would brazenly and regularly break. Although the manifest level of this program might be described as humorous or comic, the assumptions behind it were hardly funny. It assumed that government was corrupt, that a wealthy few owned banks, law, land, and industry, and that these wealthy few, though bumbling and ineffectual, were nearly clever enough to deprive the poor, benighted, and golden-hearted but average guy of his happiness, wealth, and constitutional rights. The subtextual messages of both the *Dukes of Hazard* and *V*, then, were the same. The large and powerful should not be trusted.

Airwolf and *Knight Rider* offer a deadly social commentary on the relationship of technology to the individual and to society. On the gross-out or manifest level, both programs recount the adventures of two knight-errants who operate on the periphery of the law. Both programs also contain the obligatory romantic interest; Stringfellow Hawk and Michael Knight must invariably rescue a damsel in distress. Both programs offer an element of obligatory male comradery; Michael, Devon, and Reginald of *Knight Rider* offer the viewer a father, older son, younger son triangle, while Stringfellow and Dominic Santinni of *Airwolf* offer the viewer a less complicated father and son relationship. Both programs also cast women in supporting roles, Bonnie in *Knight Rider* and Katlynn in *Airwolf*, and attempt to offer a token of appeasement to the young feminists in the audience.

But none of these characters and their relationships are essential because both programs, on a subtextual level, are panegyrics to technology. It makes little difference whether or not the main characters are sufficiently intelligent to operate their machines; all it takes to solve a problem, according to these two programs, is the right kind of hardware. Drug rings, international spies, and crooks of all sorts are captured because their adversaries, our good guys, employ superior technology and possess true moral fiber. The bottom line of both programs is simple: technology is inherently good and works always in favor of the good. We, the audience, then, find these two programs appealing because they reassure us not only that the good guys will catch the bad guys but because they also assure us that the daily onslaught of high technology will solve our problems in the future.

It takes little imagination to realize that the list of popular films and programs to which we can apply King's method of interpretation could go on and on. Indeed, the possibilities for reading between the lines seem endless. Of more consequence, perhaps, is the realization that works of popular culture, if they are to be understood and appreciated for what they are, should be subject to continuously critical reading and viewing—the very kind of reading and viewing that King advocates in his *Danse Macabre*. Consequently, it seems to me that King is far too modest in his discussion of the existence of the subtextual or the allegorical in horror fiction. He may well have been able to argue that the pleasing allegorical feel found in horror fiction is also found in many popular American movies, novels, and television programs and that works of popular culture often provide a quiet forum in which the viewers and readers of America symbolically address serious concerns of the day.

JAMES EGAN

Technohorror: The Dystopian Vision of Stephen King

Stephen King has received considerable attention for his treatment of what Brian Ash calls the theme of a "darkening world" (Ash 86). Less familiar is the fact that, from the beginning of his career, King has concerned himself with the complex implications of science and technology, so much so that the horror he evokes often seems inseparable from the dangers of imperious science and runaway machinery of many sorts. The anti-technological slant of King's writing links it with one of the primary preoccupations of twentieth-century science fiction. Like many avowed science fiction writers, moreover, King shares the modern dystopian notion that calamity rather than enlightenment, peace, and security will result from the erroneous utopian premises of the technoscientific world view. Beneath the mayhem which permeates King's fiction lie interrelated, troubling questions about the power, extent, and validity of science and rationalism in contemporary society.

King, then, may be read as more than simply a writer of gothic horror fables. Douglas Winter points out that in 1954–55 King began to compose stories "emulating the science fiction that he read" (Winter 9). King's own analysis of the horror genre, *Danse Macabre* (1980), mentions Isaac Asimov, Arthur C. Clarke, and his favorite science fiction writer, John Wyndham. *Danse Macabre* likewise makes several important observations about science fiction, tales of terror, and kindred genres. Horror, King claims, explores fears "which exist across a broad spectrum of people. Such fears, which are often political, economic, and psychological rather than supernatural, give the best work of horror a pleasing allegorical feel" (*Danse Macabre* 18).

From *Extrapolation*, Vol. 29, No. 2. © 1988 The Kent State University Press.

Horror clearly can exceed the supernatural, and horror does not have to be nonscientific (*Danse Macabre* 30), for King stresses that science fiction and horror overlap, as do utopian and dystopian literature (*Danse Macabre* 30). Additionally, *Danse Macabre* offers a definition of technohorror which provides a useful perspective on his work. The sub-text of the technohorror film, King maintains, suggests "that we have been betrayed by our own machines and processes of mass production" (*Danse Macabre* 156). As examples of technohorror he cites the mutant and radiation movies of the 1950s; the more recent "vision of technology as an octopus—perhaps sentient—burying us alive in red-tape and information retrieval systems which are terrible when they work . . . and even more so when they don't"; and contemporary versions of an archtype: "the brilliant mind dangerously hypnotized by the siren song of technology" (*Danse Macabre* 159–60). Apparently, for King, horror can focus on major technological fears; the concern he voices in *Danse Macabre* over technological missteps rises to a clamor in his fiction (*Danse Macabre* 374).

Douglas Winter notes that the "technological horror theme is an obvious exploitation of the subversive tendencies of horror fiction" (Winter 82). These "subversive tendencies" have dystopian implications, though King does not explicitly discuss the contemporary assumption that technohorror sounds a dystopian cry of discontent. Paul Buhle's analysis of H. P. Lovecraft's fiction points out that horror has a dystopian ring because it calls into question "affirmative culture"; dramatizes the "increasingly empty faith in Progress" which has saddled society; implies a suspicion about the control mechanisms of the state; and articulates a fear that science and social knowledge are pushing aside humanity and nature (Buhle 120). King's work can, perhaps, best be characterized as a blend of anti-technological science fiction, gothic horror motifs and dystopian premises. This mixture of motifs and metaphors has distinguished precedents, for example, Shelley's *Frankenstein*, surely a prototypical horror story, but also an anti-technological, anti-utopian parable. A tenuous but definite link exists, moreover, between King's nightmare vision and the dystopian tradition of Zamiatin, Orwell, and Huxley.

Generally, King addresses what Harold Berger considers the "critical point in the interplay of man and science [when] man loses the savor of life or control of the course of events, or both." He articulates many of the primary fears generated by science and technology, especially mass anxieties about "man's survival, integrity, and compatibility with the natural universe" (Berger 6, 200). When read allegorically, much of King's work searches out a basic conflict: Can technological change be subordinated to human purposes? (Fogg 60). Specifically, King writes of malevolent machines, those which take on capacities their makers did not intend; of irresponsible and incompetent technology; of the monolithic, technocratic governmental apparatus; of the debilitating effects technology has on its users; of technology's ability both to cripple human awareness of the mystical and transcendent and to create illusory mythologies of its own; and of technology's ominous power to destroy the human race.

Malevolent machines stand out in King, who begins by focusing on devilish machines themselves and the threat they pose to civilization, then proceeds to an illustration of the complex, perilous relationship of the mechanical to the humanistic, placing particular emphasis on the destructive psychological interplay of machines and their makers. "The Mangler" (1972) features a mechanical antagonist, a Model-6 Speed Ironer and Folder, something which appears at first to be an ordinary piece of laundry equipment. A bizarre series of events, however, quickly differentiates the Mangler from ordinary industrial tools. Employees notice that the Mangler runs before anyone pulls the "on" switch. Soon it captures a victim and pulverizes her beyond recognition, and then a repairman loses an arm when the machine starts, apparently at its own command. These episodes lead detective Hunton, who has been investigating Model-6, to conclude that it is demonically possessed. Purely by accident it seems, the correct combination of magical ingredients fell into the Mangler and enchanted it. When Hunton tries an exorcism, however, he discovers that he has used the wrong formula, a mistake which multiplies the machine's power, allowing it to free itself from the laundry floor and pursue the now panic-stricken exorcist. In the closing paragraphs, Hunton waits, traumatized, for the "hungry" machine to devour him.

Anti-technology motifs permeate the story. The Mangler mimics the worst, not the best, qualities of its creators. As the fate of its first victim suggests, the Mangler has become a sadistic rapist and a murderer. The phallic-shaped machine leaves behind the bra and panties of the woman it has "mangled" with nearly orgiastic enthusiasm. Slowly, seemingly with pleasure, it pulls the arm of the repairman into its maw, though it apparently has the power to snatch him in an instant. Torture may be its objective. The Mangler likewise mocks naive, mechanistic assumptions about "machine" behavior. This machine operates itself rather than following human orders, takes the initiative, and acts unpredictably. Imagery completes the parody: the narrator consistently describes the Mangler as an animal which breathes like a dragon (80) and roars to life (82). Animism expresses a prominent anti-technological theme—the revenge of nature; clearly the Mangler displays many of the characteristics of a predator from the natural world. Finally,

King's parable articulates yet another anti-technological motif, one of the darkest fears of a technological age, that machines can fall under the control of an evil, transcendent will which must eventually have its way with humanity. The demonic images of the story lend credence to this fear—at the end Hunton waits, trembling, to be swallowed alive by an angry, smoke-belching devil, an image which recalls medieval woodcuts of sinners punished by being turned into the food of demons.

"Trucks" (1973), which involves a small group of people stranded at a truck stop on an interstate highway, widens the ripple of technological terror. "Trapped" better describes their situation than "stranded " because, outside the diner, driverless trucks of all sizes patrol like vicious, hungry watchdogs. A large freight-hauler, which repeatedly tries to crush the nameless narrator's car, chases him into the truckstop. Parallels with "The Mangler" are manifest. Machines have revolted, pursuing their former masters the way a huge prehistoric animal might have hunted game. Yet "Trucks" seems a more foreboding story than its predecessor for several reasons. The Mangler was but one machine; now a remnant of humanity discovers that the entire world has apparently been taken over by machines. Though animistic imagery recurs, "Trucks" appears darker in tone than "The Mangler" since even the demonic rationale for machine behavior has been dropped. Moreover, "Trucks" is abrupt: when the story begins, machines are already out of control. "Trucks" illustrates the humanist premise that machines will lead to the "control of human life" (Hillegas 89). The narrator and his fellow captives are forced to refill the gas tanks of a seemingly endless line of trucks, worked until they collapse. Worse, they get a glimpse of what the future holds, if they survive at all—they must be the servants of machines. Though the Mangler was horrific, it acted quickly. Now, machines and people have entered into a long-term relationship which thoroughly degrades humans. The narrator articulates still another humanist fear, that of human obsolescence, when he speculates about the extent of the rebellion, about the probability that machines will eventually dominate all life forms on the planet. Machines, he surmises, can find ways to replenish and repair themselves. People will become obsolete because a superior "species" has supplanted them.

In "The Word Processor of the Gods" (1983) Jon Hagstrom, a computer whiz who dies in an automobile accident, gives his Uncle Richard a word processor for a birthday present. Though the machine may be jerry-built of miscellaneous spare parts, thereby recalling the Frankenstein motif of much anti-technological science fiction, we are not dealing with a fire-breathing colossus. The word processor can, however, "process" far more than words—by means of its Delete button, it can radically rearrange reality, making objects or individuals disappear without a hint that they had ever existed. King removes animism and the demonic from the story, replacing them with involved psychological and moral questions which grow out of the machine-human relationship. Richard Hagstrom does eventually delete his disappointing son and wife, so that a machine can be said to have mastered humans once again. However, the word processor cannot press its own Delete button. A complex, ominous relationship has developed, involving the machine's maker, the machine itself, and Hagstrom. In "The Mangler" and "Trucks" humans were portrayed as the victims of machines; here a person cooperates with a machine to victimize other people. Yet the word processor cannot be called autonomous and that fact triggers substantive questions about evil and responsibility. Is the machine the primary villain, or should its human partners be faulted? True, the word processor permits Hagstrom's dubious, self-gratifying wishes to materialize, but those wishes existed before the machine did. Moreover, he could have used his birthday present for higher purposes. Ultimately, "The Word Processor of the Gods" poses intricate problems of moral legitimacy and limitation.

   Christine (1983) represents King's most detailed treatment of the machine-human relationship. Arnie Cunningham, a lonely high school senior, becomes obsessed with a 1958 Plymouth in terrible condition, which he purchases from an eccentric, foreboding old man, Roland LeBay. On the surface Arnie's association with Christine looks normal enough: he is a passable mechanic and Christine is his first car, one he has paid for by himself. Yet as the novel progresses Christine proves to be a most unusual vehicle. The car's odometer runs backwards, and when it does so Christine repairs or renews herself, seeming to grow new parts the way an exotic species of animal grows new limbs. Christine also appears to have an uncanny connection with Roland LeBay. Dennis Guilder, the story's narrator, Arnie, and Leigh Cabot, Arnie's girlfriend, all see the rotting corpse of LeBay in the car at one time or another. LeBay was an evil character in life and his evil has not only survived him, but has allied itself with Christine, who appears to do LeBay's bidding in his vendetta against society—Christine acts as a focusing device for transcendent evil. Thus, the animistic and demonic images of the short stories reappear in *Christine*.

   Arnie's liaison with Christine appears more complex still, for King develops in greater detail the man-machine interaction he had touched on in "The Word Processor of the Gods". Christine it seems, has feminine qualities, and she appears distinctly jealous of Arnie's contacts with human females. For his part, Arnie treats Christine as if she were a lover. He spends a great amount of time with the car, allegedly restoring her; but often he loses track of the time he devotes to Christine, occasionally discovering that hours have passed which he cannot account for. After several toughs who have vandalized Christine die mysteriously, Arnie steadfastly defends his car from a prying detective, though he knows that she has the power of restoring herself and therefore erasing the clues to her crimes. He and Christine share the car's black-magical powers as though they were a lover's secret. When Leigh Cabot, Arnie's human girlfriend, demands that he get rid of Christine, he refuses to cooperate; it seems that a lovers' triangle has emerged. As Christine's list of victims grows and the police pressure Arnie, his union with Christine becomes more intimate, more overtly sexual. He feels comforted when he is "inside" Christine and draws strength simply from touching her. She develops into his closest companion and a strong ally when Leigh falls for Dennis Guilder.

King has written a parable rich in implications for the man-machine alliance. Christine and Arnie have undergone the familiar role reversal: he serves the car's needs instead of the opposite. Arnie devolves into a technology addict who cultivates a sexually symbolic liaison with a machine. King's metaphoric suggestion of sexual bondage seems less familiar and more intricate than the standard machine-seizes-power motif. In short, *Christine* depicts a perverse form of animism. The car serves as Arnie's means of striking out against the annoyances and misfortunes life has dealt him, destroying his enemies and acting as a surrogate for human companionship. Christine brings to life nineteenth- and twentieth-century humanistic fears about machines (Hillegas 90). The car obviously exceeds "the intentions of those who created it" (Fogg 64). Christine is "indifferent to [human] values," even to Arnie's, though he refuses to acknowledge the fact (Fogg 64). She clearly destroys the "sense of community" in Arnie's life and alienates Arnie from everyone around him (Fogg 64). Christine becomes all things to Arnie; his relationship with her makes human relationships obsolete. Arnie has gone so far as to make an idol of Christine, and thus he has symbolically lost his soul because he worships a metal demon. Of course, Christine does not work alone. Unless there were latent evil qualities and lingering frustrations in Arnie, her attraction would not have been so strong. Christine, a haunted technological derelict, animates Arnie's darkest dreams and the most ominous aspects of his personality. That Christine has given form and power to Arnie's potential for evil seems as disturbing a fact as autonomous machinery itself.

The Stand (1978) and *The Mist* (1980) offer extensive treatments of another anti-technological, dystopian motif—the "destruction and transmutation of nature." Both illustrate the far-reaching effects of technological irresponsibility and support the notion that "the new [scientific] knowledge and the power it brings represent an act of rebellion that goes beyond the order of things" (Fogg 67–68). Complex systems rather than specific machines are the culprits in each case. King dramatizes overt and easily recognized technological damage brought about by the systems themselves and the people who operate them.

The matter of wholesale destruction of nature and human society in King's fiction has been discussed elsewhere in some detail. so that only a few points remain to be made. In *The Stand* military technology releases an apocalyptic plague of deadly germs, but technology cannot control what it has created and the plague virtually destroys the human race, turning civilization into a ruins of deserted streets, burning buildings, and rotted corpses. *The Mist* again singles out reckless technological tampering in the form of the mysterious Project Arrowhead, which has drastically altered the conditions of life on earth by apparently tearing a hole into another dimension and releasing an army of carnivorous creatures.

Mutations of human and animal life are widespread in both novels. Moreover, King implies that a vague but definite, and potentially more disruptive, mutation has occurred as well. In *The Stand* nearly all of the surviving population experiences a marked increase in psychological sensitivity, dreaming, for example, the same recurring dream of a faceless man, Randall Flagg, their demonic antagonist. The narrator of *The Mist*, David Drayton, observes that "new doors of perception were opening up inside" (93) for him and for several of the others trapped inside the Federal Foods supermarket. King uses this heightened perception as a metaphor of the mutation of the human subconscious whose powers have been altered and magnified by technological "fallout." The mutated psyches of characters in each novel have complex, powerful, and unpredictable qualities, lending credence to the idea that "when man is radically reshaped it is at a price" (Walsh 166). The process of mutation has, figuratively, transformed human nature itself and now a great ambivalence prevails, in which primordial forces hold sway, the by-product of meddling with human nature, but what those forces may lead to remains an open question. Could runaway mutation occur? Has the human psyche been so radically reshaped that the species must grope around in a mystical shadowland like a primitive tribe? Technology has been responsible for plunging human nature at quantum speed into the unknown, and the newly mutated psychological environment appears appropriately "mist"-shrouded. Potentially at least, despite the seeming post-apocalyptic utopia hinted at in *The Stand*, new types of monsters have been created, monsters who will be shaped by the as yet undetermined impulses and needs of their mutated psyches. The vast, ambiguous powers such monsters possess may be viewed, animistically, as yet another version of nature's revenge because previously untapped or repressed instinctive drives have forced humanity to reckon with them, with its own "wild talent." Put another way, the "return to the primitive" in both novels is "characterized by the lapse of science into magic and religion" (Fredericks 152); the amorphous "primitive" could well be as dangerous as the rationalistic excesses it replaced.

Technocracy, a more remote, ambivalent and elusive species of technology than those discussed earlier, receives attention in *The Stand* and *Firestarter* (1980). Roger Williams defines technocracy as a "mutation of bureaucracy" which "refers to the actual and potential political power of technical administrators, economists, engineers and related groups," and Bernard Gendron argues that technocracies employ not only overt coercion of many types to achieve their ends, but also more devious, "nonpunitive techniques of control," which include reward giving or genetic engineering (Williams 24; Gendron 99). A subplot of *The Stand* and the main plot of *Firestarter* detail the struggles of an individual or a small group against a technocracy. While the superflu decimates civilization in *The Stand*, the government tries desperately to control the plague, and at this point Stu Redman, one of the novel's protagonists, falls into the grasp of technocracy. Immune to the plague, Redman is given over to technicians who study his metabolism in order to isolate the source of his immunity. However, the so-called medical authorities who look after him soon prove to be an arm of the collapsing police state whose scientists are in collusion with the military. Though Redman undergoes tests constantly, test results are not provided and human amenities are not an issue. He has been turned into a guinea pig, but "that wasn't even the worst. The worst was the guns. The nurses who came in to take blood or spit or urine were now always accompanied by a soldier in a white-suit, and the soldier had a gun in a plastic baggie. . . . If they were just going through the motions now, then he had become expendable. He was under detention" (114–15). Redman eventually breaks out of the plague-control center, but he cannot fully comprehend the fact that he had been dealing with a subtle, insidious technocratic enemy which had seized him before he was sufficiently aware to defend himself (Nelson 178).

Firestarter takes it name from Charlie McGee, a young girl with mental abilities so advanced that she can start fires at will. Charlie's pyrokinesis results from technological carelessness: a small group of scientists, with government cooperation, abuses science by conducting experiments on unsuspecting humans with Lot Six, a drug of unknown properties. Both of Charlie's parents had had their psyches altered by Lot Six, and they passed their "gift" on to her. A monolithic, technocratic "government" lurks in the novel's background, and this aspect of technology preoccupies King in *Firestarter*, for scientific abuse dovetails with political repression and manipulation. A shadowy domestic espionage operation called The Shop kills Charlie's mother and captures her and her father in order to examine and exploit their powers. In police-state fashion, The Shop keeps a thick dossier on the McGees and watches them in much the same way that Big Brother watched Winston Smith in Orwell's *1984*. Agents of The Shop are seemingly everywhere, and those agents include assassins in addition to surveillance operatives of all types. The Shop also has a paramilitary headquarters and intricate technological and computer assistance. As the experience of Andy and Charlie McGee shows, The Shop specializes in two of the forms of tyranny favored by technocracies, mind-invasion and spying (Berger 101). To say the least, ambiguity characterizes The Shop's chain of command. Despite the disaster of the Lot Six experiments, The Shop was not held accountable. Despite the fact that the McGees are imprisoned, deprived of their civil rights, and constantly in danger of death, no one intervenes on their behalf. Metaphorically, The Shop has become the government—remote, machine-like, sending out human robots with computerized instructions, the possessor of virtually all political power. The Shop does not answer to a President, or a Congress, or to the people at large, but only to itself. In theory, of course, The Shop operates on orders from those higher up in the government, but higher-ups are only faceless shadows lost in the complexity of a structure that combines technology with anonymity, massive size, and strength. Day-to-day control of The Shop rests with an elite of spies, technocrats, and elusive political manipulators.

Though technocracy preserves a semblance of order, in *Firestarter* the question of final political responsibility for the uses of technology remains open. Individuals ultimately count for less than systems. Technology has helped to create a vicious cycle, becoming a primary part of an immensely intricate governmental structure, so intricate that only technology can supervise it. *Firestarter*, then, evokes several anti-technological fears, the primary one being that it is virtually impossible to differentiate a "real" government from The Shop. Moreover, The Shop has apparently decided that "social stability and freedom cannot be combined, and has opted for stability," a decision reminiscent of those made by the rulers of Huxley's *Brave New World* (Walsh 112). An overriding anxiety remains, that in the future and perhaps in the present as well, "direct control" of society will be in "the hands of an elite of scientist technicians who will rule by their own norms . . ." (Fogg 69). Though Charlie eventually escapes, *Firestarter* suggests that the evil monolith of technocracy has entrenched itself.

Carrie (1974) and *'Salem's Lot* (1975) both illustrate the most subtle, pervasive, and, potentially, the most dangerous aspect of technology: the technoscientific world view. Walter L. Fogg has described that world view as follows:

> . . . a set of values and a way of thinking which has its roots in the very beginnings of western civilization. . . . The technoscientific world view has eroded other modes of thinking and lifestyles and has demythologized man's world in order to make it technologically manageable. Technology is mistrusted because the values which both created technology and are fostered by it are exclusive of all other values. (70)

Jacques Ellul, Herbert Marcuse, and others, whose arguments Fogg summarizes, maintain that the "technical order" can be thought of as a "*way of life*." If, as Langdon Winner argues, humans have indeed become "thoroughly technomorphic" and have "invested [their lives] in a mass of methods, techniques, machines, rational-productive organizations. and networks," then civilization has been trapped by the "givers" of the technological order. The two novels in questions play off the "charismatic, nonrational elements of history" against the "static designs of intellect" (Winner 201, 42, 200, 180).

Carrie points up the failures of systems, and of the technoscientific world views of which they are a major element, when systems confront the unknown. Technology cannot control Carrie White as she destroys the town of Chamberlain with her telekinetic powers, nor can science, theorizing after the fact, explain her behavior. Technology and the scientific method, King implies, have an arrogance about the unknown, a presumptiveness which causes the several types of researchers who study the White phenomenon to assume that their methods can explain all riddles, that a complex system of inquiry can surely solve one "simple" problem. Those who direct the White Commission investigation are overconfident about their procedures. They cannot imagine that they have failed to find the truth, and their naivete proves dangerous. In Herbert Marcuse's words, the researchers have overemphasized the "*therapeutic* function of . . . analysis" and have worked to eradicate "obscurities, illusions, and oddities" (Marcuse 170). The Commission perpetuates the delusion that a parapsychological power such as Carrie's cannot exist, and in so doing denies the mystical and transcendent. In effect, the technoscientific world view has dismissed metaphysical moral realities in order to make life more "manageable." At the least, King implies, such a perspective leads to narcissism and myopia in those guided by its assumptions.

The Commission's lengthy investigation results in the glorification of false mythologies about the unknown.

'Salem's Lot dramatizes how unaware people are of the long-term consequences of what Jacques Ellul has described as "Technique" (see Ellul 3–23). King pits the archetypal American small town, 'Salem's Lot, against the vampire Barlow, and unifies the novel by means of death metaphors. Predictably, the technoscientific world view has prepared the way for Barlow's reign of terror. Because reductive empirical science has denied the very concept of vampires, it cannot cope with Barlow. Ironically, in fact, science and technology are two of the vampire's strongest allies—while doctors and medical labs waste time performing useless autopsies and studying blood samples from the undead, the number of vampires grows epidemically. Since a vampire comes from the shadowland of myth and legend, he stands beyond technology's reach; technology, by definition, deals best with the "death" of machines and systems. King shows how dangerously vulnerable the desacralizing premises of science leave those who have, by choice or forfeit, internalized them: there is no defense against the darkness in the world. *'Salem's Lot* measures rationalism. scientism, and technology against myth and the supernatural, "superstition and ignorance." The novel's protagonists, Ben Mears and Mark Petrie, can defeat Barlow only by adopting a mythical and "superstitious" attitude, by resurrecting a world view which presumably had been discredited, one which antedates computers, medical advances, and high-powered weapons. Basic human emotional resources (particularly faith), along with simple ingenuity, arc all that will work.

If the technoscientific world view holds no answers, its unwitting disciples in the Lot must be powerless. True, Ben and Mark finally destroy him, yet Barlow achieves considerable success: virtually the entire population falls victim to him and his presence remains in the form of the undead who still haunt the vicinity. Barlow succeeded because the Lot was an ideal target for him, a town whose inhabitants recognized "themselves in their commodities," who "found their soul in their [automobiles] and . . . kitchen equipment." People in the Lot had long been hypnotized by the false mystique of science, gadgetry, and materialism, so that Barlow's victims were, metaphorically, dead before he found them, zombie-like and reconciled to the status quo. Barlow was an ironic liberator who "rewarded" his followers with an alluring escape from a one-dimensional, desacralized world where dreams and anxieties could be "resolved and fixed " by psychiatry and where the population could indulge its materialistic impulses to the fullest extent (Marcuse 9, 70–71). That Barlow, who offered only a demonic half-life, could make such headway in *'Salem's Lot* stands as an indictment of the failures of rationalism. scientism, materialism—the corrosive technoscientific world view, in short.

King's technohorror motif links his fiction with some of the major dystopian themes of twentieth-century literature. Clearly, King denies "the utopian possibilities that modern technology offers mankind" because he can discover no apparent "link between technological development and human progress" (Winner 18–19). Rather, he mocks the notion of technological "progress"—progress devolves into horror. Walter L. Fogg identifies the "destruction and transmutation of nature," "manipulated man," and "manipulated society" as recurring dystopian concerns of the twentieth century (Fogg 67–69). King's handling of these issues in *The Stand*, *The Mist*, *Firestarter*, and *'Salem's Lot* focuses on the variety of crises created by technological tampering and by the technoscientific world view itself. Instead of an impressive era of human happiness, technology ushers in a new dark age of runaway machines, a vengeful nature, and apocalyptic destruction. Demonic allusions and imagery underscore King's attack on technology: typically in his work characters fight losing battles with the "demonic machine, its demonic inventor, or technology itself" (Nelson 174). Such losing battles point to a major argument of contemporary dystopian fiction, that if man is "unfit to be the custodian of his technology . . . he will be victimized by a destructive one . . . or he must submit to the dictatorship of a protective technology" (Berger 34–35). Technology, King implies, reckons inadequately with the Dark Fantastic in human nature and in the vast reaches of uncharted reality outside of the human mind. Since the technoscientific world view relentlessly desacralizes, it produces a psychological rigidity which makes civilization and its sytems vulnerable to the unknown. Technology remains naive about the moral reality of evil, and consequently technological operations of all types, from the mechanical to the political, repeatedly suffer the consequences of naiveté. King's emphasis upon the power and extent of evil indicates that he holds a dystopian world view, that his cosmology is "retrogressive," that he considers civilization and its accomplishments precarious at best and dangerously delusive at worst (Fredericks 151). *Carrie*, *Christine*, and *'Salem's Lot*, in particular, stress that "man is only intermittently and partially rational" (Walsh 168). King shares with other dystopians a fundamental doubt that "man is basically good" and that man and his culture are "perfectible" (Walsh 166; Stupple 26). King's skepticism provides a final thematic link with the dystopian tradition, for he repeatedly voices a dystopian recognition "that there are built-in limits to how much we can change the physical universe, the moral order, and our nature . . ." (Walsh 163). Trespassing beyond those limits invokes horror.

TONY MAGISTRALE

Inherited Haunts: Stephen King's Terrible Children

At the closing address of the 1984 International Conference on the Fantastic in Arts, someone in the audience asked Stephen King the question, "What terrifies you the most?" King's reply was emphatic and immediate: "Opening the door of my children's bedroom and finding one of them dead."

King's dread that his own offspring can be harmed has not inhibited his use of infantile and adolescent characters who more often than not find themselves in precarious situations. His youthful protagonists are besieged by a variety of demons and ghosts, religious extremists and officials representing an assortment of institutions and bureaucracies. Against these oppressive legions, King's children are often endowed with uncommon powers and traits, and these special attributes, combined with a native shrewdness and acute perceptivity, help distinguish them from the adult world while aiding in their survival.

King's most memorable and important characters, and the ones to whom we, as readers, grow increasingly attached, are his children. Most of his fictional adolescents find themselves enmeshed in the dark complexities of an adult world; they are not responsible for either their parents' divorces or governmental errors in judgment, but they are nonetheless forced into coping with the consequences of such events. The writer chooses to place them at the locus of so many of his books because their physical size and worldly unsophistication make them exceptionally vulnerable. King's children, like the female protagonist in one of Mrs. Ann Radcliff's eighteenth-century gothic novels, are perfect victims—their confrontations with evil

From *Landscape of Fear: Stephen King's American Gothic.* © 1988 Bowling Green State University Popular Press.

initially appear overwhelming—and their plights elicit intensely sympathetic responses from the reader. Moreover, the child's heightened sensitivities and imagination put him in a position where fear consists of definite textures and smells untempered by the mechanisms of denial and rationality.

The long-term influence of childhood guilt and anxiety is a fundamental component of the psychological horror story. But this emphasis is not restricted to the horror genre. One thinks immediately of Pip in Dickens' *Great Expectations*, whose adult life is irrevocably shaped by the terrifying events of his childhood. Many of King's tales probe the relationship between childhood fears and adult neuroses. In the short story "The Monkey," a wind-up toy monkey is associated with the violent events and subsequent guilt of Hal Shelburn's adolescence. Nearly half the story is narrated in flashback sequences to various moments of Hal's childhood, and these scenes are unified by the monkey's clanging cymbals as a prologue to someone's death. Since the toy is discovered by Hal and his brother "all the way down at the far end of the back closet" in his parents' bedroom (151), the monkey becomes a metaphor for Hal's most vivid childhood recollections; it represents that part of his subconscious mind which is unable to overcome the events of his tragic youth: a father who abandons him at an early age, his mother's sudden brain embolism, and pets and childhood friends who abruptly die. As Hal, now an adult with sons of his own, discovers one morning in his hotel room when he awakens to find the monkey mysteriously nestling against his face, the creature is an undeniable aspect of Hal himself, symbolizing the dark window of anxiousness that looks back on his past: "There was the guilt; the certain, deadly knowledge that he had killed his mother by winding the monkey up on that sunny after-school afternoon" (158–59).

It is significant that the toy's re-emergence from the deep well in which Hal entombed it twenty years earlier coincides with another series of personal traumas: the death of Hal's Aunt Ida, the loss of a prestigious job, his wife's serious addiction to valium, and his son's growing disaffection. The tragic events occurring to Hal as an adult cannot be separated from his adolescent memories. As a child Hal sought to bury his guilt and neuroses by twice returning the monkey to its box back in the closet and eventually by dropping it to the bottom of an abandoned well. Each time he rids himself of the monkey, his dark recollections are correspondingly silenced. But in order to accomplish this, on each separate occasion he must bury the monkey in a deeper place, an indication of the increasing psychological assault taking place against his consciousness. In finally sinking the monkey in "the deepest part of Crystal Lake" (167), Hal reasserts control over his anxieties by symbolically resubmerging them into the unfathomable recesses of his psyche. Surmounting the life-threatening storm that almost kills him on the lake, his triumphant reunion with his son on the placid shore is an indication that Hal has broken from the childhood pattern of guilt and anxiety now threatening his adulthood.

I

In King's fiction, children embody the full spectrum of human experience; they are identified with the extremes of good and evil. Many of his youthful protagonists come to represent the moral centers of his books and from them all other actions seem to radiate. Some represent the nucleus for familial love. They are often healing forces, as in the first halves of *The Shining*, *Pet Sematary*, and *Cujo*, enabling parents in unstable marriages to forgive one another's human failings. Moreover, King is inordinately fond of testing the moral capacities of his adolescent protagonists. Mark Petrie (*'Salem's Lot*) and Jack Sawyer (*The Talisman*) encounter tremendous adversities and defeats, yet each boy refuses to capitulate to powers vastly superior to his own. As a result of their endurance they not only manage to survive, but also to prevail. Many of King's children represent the principle of good in a corrupt world; they seem both divinely inspired and painfully cursed with prophetic knowledge. Danny Torrance, Carrie White, and Charlie McGee possess superhuman abilities that trigger death and destruction, and yet these children elicit a positive response from us because they are so thoroughly manipulated and abused. It is not really the children who are responsible for their various acts of destruction, but the adults who mislead and torment them.

At the other moral pole are the adolescent hunters—the denim fascists in "Sometimes They Come Back," *Christine*, and *Carrie*—who portray ambassadors from an immoral world, their sole purpose being to wreak destruction on anyone or anything weaker than or different from themselves. One of King's greatest fortes remains his ability to render the most perverse and grotesque aspects of the American high school experience with unflinching accuracy. King's descriptions of the public school system are so concrete and identifiable that they must have been shaped by his own brief exposure to the teaching profession as a high school English instructor. The majority of students and teachers who appear in his books care little about education or the transference of knowledge; his teachers are shell-shocked veterans on the verge of surrendering to a student body that lacks both personal and academic discipline. His modern public schools are sterile environments,

without spirit or mystery, devoid of transcendence. As King points out in
Danse Macabre in the context of a discussion about *Carrie*:

> . . . the book tries to deal with the loneliness of one girl, her des-
> perate effort to become a part of the peer society in which she
> must exist, and how her effort fails. If it had any thesis to offer,
> this deliberate updating of *High School Confidential*, it was that
> high school is a place of almost bottomless conservatism and big-
> otry, a place where the adolescents who attend are no more
> allowed to rise "above their station" than a Hindu would be
> allowed to rise above his or her caste. (169)

In *Carrie*, King works from a bifurcated perspective in analyzing this
setting for adolescent violence. On one hand, he understands that Carrie
White's night of revenge is motivated by the brutality of her classmates. On
the other hand, his exoneration of Carrie is equalled in his contempt for the
boy-men, girl-women who torment her. King's truest sympathies are always
with the high school rejects; they are not only victimized by the cruelty of
the majority, but because of their status as pariahs they often possess a level
of intelligence and sensitivity sadly missing in their more popular peers. As
King continues in *Danse Macabre*, "Against such a backdrop, Carrie becomes
doubly pitiful, because . . . she can only wait to be saved or damned by the
actions of others. Her only power is her telekinetic ability, and both book and
movie eventually arrive at the same point: Carrie uses her 'wild talent' to pull
down the whole rotten society" (172).

King seems most unfavorably inclined toward the superficially well-
adjusted, popular student with an overly active libido and a underdeveloped
value system. His class presidents, football quarterbacks, and prom queens
bear an unmistakable resemblance to the street punks who attend the same
school system as a stopover on their way to jail: both groups of adolescents
have completely severed their bonds with childhood innocence. In their
vicious lust to exploit sex, alcohol, and violence (for they inhabit an exclusively physical plane of existence), their behavior is modeled on an extreme
conception of adulthood. They want all the pleasure of worldly experience,
with none of the responsibilities. Thus, they are simply young versions of the
corruption which animates King's adult society. If they manage to live long
enough, they will become the Jack Torrances, Morgan Sloats, John
Rainbirds, and Greg Stillsons of the next generation.

II

The adults in King's fiction act frequently like the worst of his children; they explore places where they have no business going, their behavior is often immature and without conscience, and, as we have seen elsewhere in this book, their institutions—the church, the state's massive bureaucratic system of control, the nuclear family itself—barely mask an undercurrent of violence that is capable of manifesting itself at any given moment. The daily interactions in their marriages and neighborhoods bring out the evil in King's adult characters; they revert to the meanness of adolescence, acknowledging their selfish urges only after they have set in motion a series of events which lead to catastrophe. In order to circumvent such disasters, King's children must cling to their youthful idealism and romantic innocence, both of which come under fierce attack in his fiction from the oppressive forces of societal institutions and/or the supernatural monsters who emerge as a consequence of adult moral lapses. In *Danse Macabre*, King maintains a sharp distinction, as he does throughout his fictional canon, between the worlds of the child and the adult:

> The drinking age in Maine was then eighteen (booze-related accidents on the highways have since caused the lawmakers to move the age up to twenty), and all of those people [in a bar] had looked about eighteen to me. So I got up and asked the bouncer how he knew that last guy was underage. He shrugged. "You just know," he said. "It's mostly in their eyes."
>
> For weeks after, my hobby was looking at the faces of adults and trying to decide exactly what it was that made them "adult faces." The face of a thirty-year-old is healthy, unwrinkled, and no bigger than the face of a seventeen-year-old. Yet you know that's no kid; you know. There seems to be some hidden yet overriding characteristic that makes what we all agree is the Adult Face. It isn't just the clothes or the stance, it isn't the fact that the thirty-year-old is toting a briefcase and the seventeen-year-old is toting a knapsack; if you put the head of each in one of those carnival cut-outs which show the body of a capering sailor or a prizefighter, you could still pick out the adult ten tries out of ten.
>
> I came to believe that the bouncer was right. It's in the eyes.
>
> Not something that's there; something, rather, that has left. . . . The imagination is an eye, a marvelous eye that floats free. As children, that eye sees with 20/20 clarity. As we grow older, its vision begins to dim. . . . (378)

While it may be difficult to explain the exact "something that has left" in the adult consciousness, King seems to share a strong sympathy with William Wordsworth's emphasis on the differences separating child from adult. In *The Prelude* and throughout most of his major poems, Wordsworth argues that the secrets of existence are hidden from the adult, but the child, because she has lived for so short a time, is still close to the state of pre-existence. As the child grows into the adult, innocence and purity are tempered by a sense of loss, and her perception is no longer unified, but dualized. The child responds to the world with an instinctive joy and with the innocence of a pure soul. Wordsworth further believed that the child could serve as a guide for the adult, teaching the mature man or woman to use his or her own memory of youth to uncover the continuity of existence. As he remarked in "My Heart Leaps Up,"

The Child is the father of the Man;
And I could wish my days to be
Bound each to each by natural piety.

While King adheres closely to Wordsworth's conception of the differences between child and adult, he seldom shares the romantic poet's confidence in the ability of the adult to recapture the "natural piety" of the child. In fact, in spite of their good will and special gifts, King's children are shaped and motivated by the adults who are deeply absorbed in a personal struggle with evil. There are notable exceptions, of course, and we will consider them in the next chapter, but most often King's young people—Gage Creed, Danny Torrance, Carrie White, and Charlie McGee—exercise very little influence over the adults who continue on a self-directed course of destruction. These children are instead forced to pay for their parents' sins of curiosity and selfishness; their innocence becomes the price for an intimate examination of evil.

The short story "Children of the Corn" is a case in point. A young couple, their marriage in disarray, stumble upon Gatlin, Nebraska, a town where time has apparently stopped. Instead of August 1976, Burt and Vicky discover calendars and municipal records that go no further than 1964: "Something had happened in 1964. Something to do with religion, and corn . . . and children" (268). Moreover, there are no adults in this town, only children under the age of nineteen.

The time period is certainly of crucial significance to the story's meaning. But King never completely explains its mystery. Nor is it clear immediately why all the adults have been killed and why no child is permitted to survive past the age of nineteen. Like Vicky and Burt, the reader is supplied only with information about an Old Testament Jehovah whom the children worship in the corn fields. In return for their human sacrifices, he invests the crop with a special purity: "In the last of the daylight [Burt] swept his eyes closely over the row of corn to his left. And he saw that every leaf and stalk was perfect, which was just not possible. No yellow blight. No tattered leaves, no caterpillar eggs, no burrows" (275).

Reading King's best fiction is often like visiting a unfamiliar city with innumerable corners of intriguing complexity and atmospheres that reward prolonged observation. "Children of the Corn" encourages the reader to linger over multiple interpretations. On the most obvious level, it is a story of religious fanaticism dedicated to a malevolent deity. But such a reading does not account for the importance of the 1964 time setting— the initial period of active involvement by American forces in Vietnam—and its relationship to the fertility of the Nebraska corn. They appear irrevocably linked. Listening to the radio outside of town, Vicky and Burt hear a child's voice: "'There's some that think it's okay to get out in the world, as if you could work and walk in the world without being smirched by the world'" (256). And later in the story, after he has learned the awful secret of the town, Burt wonders if human sacrifices were ordained because the corn was dying as a result of too much sinning (268).

Although King is cautious to avoid so overt a nexus, the reader with any sense of history will recall the violation of the land in Vietnam by such toxic chemicals as Agent Orange. Man's technology carried the poisoning of the soil, not to mention the levels of death and carnage, to the point at which the land itself (symbolized in the presence of the corn god) demanded repentance. If we place the events of this story in such a context, it becomes possible to understand why all the adults past the (draft) age of nineteen are sacrificed. These are the individuals who were most responsible for the war, for the "adult sins" that defiled and destroyed acres of Vietnamese landscape, thousands of American and Vietnamese lives, and, finally, what was left of America's innocence. For Vietnam was, among other things, America's collective cultural emergence into the "adult world" of sin and error. Our loss of innocence and our recognition of self-corruption is what gave impetus to the antiwar movement. In trying to decide whose side God favored in this war, we were shown with painful certitude that life is a more complicated mixture of good and evil than we earlier had assumed. King's own view on the immorality of the Vietnam experience, as expressed in *Danse Macabre*, corresponds precisely with such an interpretation:

I was in college at the time, attending the University of
Maine, and while I began college with political leanings too far
to the right to actually become radicalized, by 1968 my mind had
been changed forever about a number of fundamental questions.

Now, I did not and do not believe that the hands of the
Rockerfellers were utterly clean during that period, nor those of
AT&T; I did and do believe that companies like Sikorsky and
Douglas Aircraft and Dow Chemical and even the Bank of
America subscribed more or less to the idea that war is good
business. . . . In various ways throughout this book I've tried to
suggest that the horror story is in many ways an optimistic,
upbeat experience; that it is often the tough mind's way of coping with terrible problems which may not be supernatural at all
but perfectly real. (296–98)

Burt and Vicky are therefore sacrificed because they are adult repre-
sentatives of fallen, post-Vietnam America. Both have strayed from any sense
of a belief in God, their marriage is in disharmony; both appear as selfish,
stubborn, and unforgiving individuals; they are anxious to pass through
Nebraska and travel on to "sunny, sinful California" (258); and Burt is a
Vietnam veteran. References to this last point are made on three separate
occasions, but the most significant citation occurs immediately after Burt
becomes aware of the 1964 time setting. While standing on a sidewalk in
the town, ironically expecting to discover "a school named after JFK" (260),
the president who initiated American involvement in Vietnam, Burt smells
fertilizer. The odor had always reminded him of his childhood in rural
upstate New York, "but somehow this smell was different from the one he
had grown up with. . . . There was a sickish sweet undertone. Almost a death
smell. As a medical orderly in Vietnam, he had become well versed in that
smell" (263). The association between Vietnam and Nebraska and its corn
fields, and the disenchantment inherent in adult experience, is maintained
on similar symbolic levels throughout the story. Nebraska and its corn are
located in the "heartland" of America, its moral epicenter, and out of an
effort to reestablish the purity and innocence of an earlier era, both the
corn and the land itself seem to be demanding adult penance for a sin that
originated in 1964.

King's corn god is furious with the adult world, demanding blood in
exchange for reclaiming the land from its state of spiritual and physical barrenness. Burt discovers the god's maxim written on the cover of the town's
registry: "Thus let the inquitous be cut down so that the ground may be

fertile again saith the Lord God of Hosts" (267). The very fact that the ground needs to be made "fertile again" suggests that it has suffered from some kind of pestilence. And the "disease of the corn" in this tale, while ambiguous throughout, can be interpreted in terms of American defoliation of the Vietnamese landscape, as well as the more symbolic cultural "illness" or moral guilt and spiritual taint that accompanied American involvement in the conflict.

King's use of the corn deity undoubtedly owes its origins to anthropological studies of primitive cultures, where some variation of a corn god is often associated with the fertility of the land. To maintain the fecundity of the soil and to produce a bountiful harvest, these communities made frequent sacrifice in the spirit's honor. James Frazer dedicates an entire volume of the monumental work *The Golden Bough* to documenting these rituals. Various primitive societies conducted elaborate human sacrifices (and several of those still in existence continue the practice), usually to a corn-mother or a corn-maiden, in order to bless the forthcoming harvest. Among the plethora of illustrations Frazer cites, is this particularly relevant example from Mexico:

> We have seen that the ancient Mexicans also sacrificed human beings at all the various stages in the growth of the maize, the age of the victims corresponding to the age of the corn; for they sacrificed new-born babes at sowing, older children when the grain had sprouted, and so on till it was fully ripe, when they sacrificed old men. No doubt the correspondence between the ages of the victims and the state of the corn was supposed to enhance the efficacy of the sacrifice. (Vol. 7, 237–38)

Jessie Weston's *From Ritual to Romance* further considers primitive man's sense of a connection between the status of his land and a deific presence. The legend of the Fisher King, a Christian precursor, emerged as an explanation for crop failure; the Fisher King's personal illness was reflected in the state of the country, which had become a wasteland. According to Weston, the Fisher King, who is a composite figure derived from a variety of fertility images including the more ancient corn god, "is not merely a deeply symbolic figure, but the essential centre . . . a being semi-divine, semi-human, standing between his people and the land, and the unseen forces which control their destiny" (90). Only through the great sacrifice of the Fisher King was it thought possible to construct the basis for a future generation which would make the wasteland fertile again.

The continuing series of human sacrifices commanded by the corn god in "Children of the Corn" have been successful; vitality has been restored to the American soil. The moral wasteland that was the consequence of involvement in Vietnam has been transformed into Nebraska corn growing in flawless rows. Moreover, as Burt discovers while running wounded through the open fields, the soil even contains a mysterious recuperative power: "The ache in his arm had settled into a dull throb that was nearly pleasant, and the good feeling was still with him" (274). The corn diety has made the land, and all that comes in contact with it, into a agrarian Arcadia, a neo-Eden of pristine perfection and harmony. But to maintain this environment, the corn deity exacts from this symbolic American community in Nebraska a never-ending cycle of adult penance and revenge. In fact, at the conclusion of the story the corn god lowers the age of sacrifice from nineteen to eighteen, suggesting that the inherited guilt and shame of Vietnam will never be completely exorcised.

In *Danse Macabre*, King states that he has "purposely avoided writing a novel with a 1960s time setting. . . . But those things did happen: the hate, paranoia, and fear on both sides were all too real" (158–59). King may not have directed his energies into a full-length novel, but in "Children of the Corn" he has provided us with a brief but frightening little allegory of the decade's major historical event. Moreover, King makes his point by setting many of his other stories and novels *just before* the eventful decade of the Sixties. *The Body* is set in 1959; a portion of *It* shares a 1958 reference frame; even Christine was a 1958 Plymouth. Like George Eliot in *Adam Bede*, King often employs historical backgrounds that are *on the eve of* some great upheaval in culture and/or mores.

Perhaps just as significant as the historical setting for "Children of the Corn," especially in light of its emphasis throughout King's canon, is that the "adult world" represented in this story is interpreted as sinful and in need of punishment. In reaction to parental values deemed empty and materialistic, the youth generation of the sixties celebrated its agelessness. "We ain't never, never, gonna grow up," promised Yippie Jerry Rubin in his pre-corporate finance days. "We're gonna be adolescents forever!" American youth were in the streets directing a cultural critique of their country's morality. Those who governed the nation—the adults—became the enemy; they had perpetuated the war in Vietnam and had sent America's children to perform the killing and the dying. Above all else, Vietnam was the sacrifice of the children, just as the trench warfare of World War I was; a needless sacrifice certainly—and even worse, an aimless one.

III

The theme of innocence betrayed is at the heart of "Children of the Corn." Indeed, this concept unifies the major work of King's canon: throughout his fiction, the power of evil to malign and pervert innocence is omnipresent. We have traced this tendency through a number of illustrations: Louis Creed and Jack Torrance sacrifice their families and sanities when they pursue the opposite extreme of innocence—represented by a working knowledge of the world's darkest mysteries and experiences. Most of the examples we have considered so far, however, have focused on adult misadventures—in government, societal institutions, personal morality. In "The Raft," King's retelling of the fall from grace is, in Michael Collings' words, a "rite of passage symbolizing loss of innocence" (146), and it is rendered from the child's point of view.

"The Raft" is narrowly centered around a late afternoon in the lives of four college students—two females and two males—poised on the very edge of adulthood. The significance of this transitional state to the story's meaning cannot be overemphasized. It is not only apparent in their ages and student status, but is likewise mirrored in the setting itself: "the end of the long Indian summer they had been enjoying. . . . Rachel said that summers had seemed to last forever when she was a girl, but now that she was an adult ('a doddering senile nineteen,' Deke joked, and she kicked his ankle), they get shorter every year" (246). Intoxicated on beer, determined to savor the last days of summer and their youth, all four swim out to a raft in the middle of a deserted Pennsylvania lake. Once on the raft, Randy, the story's principal character, notices an iridescent, circular object resembling an oil slick moving toward them. The object turns out to be alive—a gelatinous creature that eventually devours each of the students, one by one.

The monster is never clearly apprehended by any of the teenagers. Its vibrant array of incandescent colors works as a dangerous hallucinogen, entrapping the will of anyone who stares at it for too long. "It floated on the water, round and regular, like the top of a large steel drum, but the limber way it rode the swells made it clear that it was not the surface of a solid object" (249). In its ambiguity and destructive hunger, the dark circle (reminiscent of the spiral imagery in *Pet Sematary*) becomes a symbol of the mystery of adulthood—capable of mesmerizing at the same time as it plunders—and Randy in particular gains acute insight into this realm before he perishes.

Just before the deaths of Rachel and Deke, the first two to die, Randy becomes aware of the change taking place in them as a result of the terror they are encountering. Their apprehension is described in terms that suggest both a loss of innocence and a growing connection to adulthood. In watching Rachel standing on the edge of the raft moments before she is pulled into the water by the creature, Randy observes that beneath her "Sandy Duncan innocence," lurks a "neurotic prettiness" and a look in her eyes that could be interpreted as "free-floating anxiety" (252). Deke, the football star whose body "was as hard as Carrara marble" (259), likewise reveals his vulnerability when confronted with circumstances beyond his control: "Deke was sounding a little pissed off now, a little offbalance. A little scared? For the first time tonight, for the first time this month, this year, maybe for the first time in his whole life? Now there was an awesome thought—Deke loses his fear cherry" (257).

After Deke and Rachel are consumed in particularly graphic and grotesque fashions, La Verne and Randy make love; the act is not motivated by passion so much as stimulated by the need for human contact in the face of nature's cruelty. "The tactile sensations were incredible, fantastic. He was not experienced, but neither was he a virgin; he had made love with three girls and it had never been like this" (266). While engaged in intercourse, Randy's mind spirals back to a series of kaleidoscopic memories from adolescent summers—"the feel of summer, the texture; I can root for the Yankees from the bleachers, girls in bikinis on the beach . . . the Beach Boys oldies . . . firm breasts fragrant with Coppertone oil" (267)—until these memories are abruptly interrupted as La Verne is pulled from beneath him and into the water by a "twisting gruesome membrane" (267). The symbolism of this scene is apparent: Randy's first "real" sexual experience represents the bridge, as it is for most of us, between child and adult. The hydromonster, however, hideously severs Randy's ties to adolescence and thrusts him, naked and alone, into the adult world of pain and loss.

The creature's physical ambiguity helps to support its symbolic function as a living manifestation of the worst anxieties associated with adulthood. One by one his college friends, like his connections to adolescence, are stripped from Randy as he is forced into encountering the realities of adult life. Unlike the hopeful conclusion of "The Monkey," Randy's initiation into adulthood never invests him with any degree of control; the brutality merely intensifies and grows—like the monster itself after it consumes Rachel—until it literally overwhelms him. Stranded on the raft, surrounded by death and the encroaching cold of the autumn night, Randy discovers that his best friend and girl friend are lovers and have betrayed him; he realizes that the bliss of sexuality is only a momentary reprieve from the terrors of the dark; and most of all, in his last hours of life, bereft of human comfort and anticipating his own demise, Randy learns what we all must in the face of adult perimeters—that the cocoon of adolescence, symbolized appropriately in the warm recollections of summers past, is no longer retrievable once we have emerged from it.

IV

In Stephen King's landscape, the failure of love and understanding triggers disaster. Evil is perpetuated through legacies of sin, based in social, cultural, mythical, and historical contexts, and handed down from one generation to the next. Adulthood, because of its litany of selfish mistakes, broken promises, cruel machinations, and drunken excesses, fully embodies this legacy of human corruption; adults show themselves capable of betrayal at any point. The inevitable violence and cruelty which are the usual end results of adult values and behavior force many of King's adolescent protagonists to relinquish their tentative hold on innocence and sensitivity.

In the short story "Last Rung on the Ladder," an attorney becomes so involved with his career and his reputation in the world that he fails to heed his misdirected younger sister's plea for help. As a child, he was always there to protect her and lend his support, but as an adult he is too preoccupied. When she finally commits suicide, in large measure because of his failure to become involved, he is left with an enormous burden of guilt.

The novella *Apt Pupil*, from the collection *Different Seasons*, works from a similar set of suppositions. Todd Bowden, a precocious adolescent fascinated with the grisly details of Nazi Germany, discovers an aging war criminal, Dussander, hiding in his suburban American neighborhood. Todd's attraction to the atrocities that occurred under Dussander's command are initially based on an innocent curiosity: the urge to discover, "with a mixture of revulsion and excitement" (115), what took place inside the concentration camps. In fact, Dussander is absolutely perplexed when he learns that the child has no intention of extorting money from him: "He stared at Dussander with an open and appealing frankness. 'Why . . . I want to hear about it. That's all. That's all I want. Really'" (124).

As Todd practices more devious and intricate methods of extracting a personal history from the former Nazi officer, their interaction brings Dussander back into intimate contact with his past. "He had been forced to give up a part of himself. Now he had reclaimed it" (155). Reliving his moral misconduct during the war affects his new life in California, as he is compelled to commit a series of murders in his kitchen. Moreover, through his daily contacts with the boy, Dussander "tends a small but perfect flame of hatred deep in [Todd's] heart" (245). Over a period of years, this flame enlarges into a conflagration. As a direct consequence of his involvement with the Nazi, Todd's interest in sports and schoolwork is abandoned in favor of stalking and butchering helpless drunks and street people; his emerging sexuality is stimulated only by perverse fantasies of women in bondage, forced to suffer sadistic violations; his sense of personal morality is sacrificed as he doctors his failing report card grades; and his relationship with his parents, formerly characterized by a playful intimacy, is now clouded by Todd's need to sustain elaborate barriers between the vicious self he is becoming and their image of the innocent child he had been.

Some of King's best creative fiction can be found in the first two-thirds of this novella (the last third introduces too many new characters and coincidences so that the book's intensity of focus is severely weakened), as he methodically takes us through a study of negative adult influence and the corrupting fusion of evil. These elements are most effectively handled, especially in the descriptions of the slow metamorphosis taking place in Todd. Early in the book, Todd has several dreams about the world Dussander has been describing, "but it was nothing he couldn't handle" (131). As his obsession with the Nazi deepens, however, Todd's dreams become more vivid, less malleable. His dreams are like the successive stages of embryonic development in a chrysalis, signalling Todd's transformation—from the dissolution of the all-conference, all-American child, to the emergence of the corrupt adult who has lost sight of all moral principles. As Dussander informs him, "Seven hundred thousand died at Patin. To the world at large I am a criminal, a monster, even the butcher your scandal-rags would have me. You are an accessory to all that, my boy" (161).

Following several months of exposure to Dussander, Todd has another dream, as well as his first nocturnal emission, and this dream sequence, like the short story "The Raft," employs sexual initiation as a symbol of the child's emergence into the brutality characteristic of King's adult world. Todd finds himself in front of a half-naked Dussander and a young Jewish girl, the latter bound to the four corners of an examination table. Dussander directs him to secure a hollow dildo over his small, erect penis, which he then uses to penetrate the young woman. In this sadomasochistic fantasy, Todd becomes a literal "appendage" of the Nazi, discovering pleasure in another person's pain. And as Todd rapes this defenseless woman, Dussander is symbolically raping Todd, recording "pulse, blood pressure, respiration, alpha waves, beta waves, stroke count" (189). The dream fully illustrates the price Todd pays for the betrayal of his innocence; he chooses to become a living extension of history, violating the secrets of the past so thoroughly that they erupt into the present. Indeed, near the conclusion of the book, Dussander asks Todd to drink with him in celebration of the student's improved grades. The scene is easily overlooked, but its significance is greater than the Nazi's ostensible toast. The bourbon Todd consumes is symbolic of the corruption inherent in King's adult world, a realm in which Dussander serves as high priest. The jelly-glass Todd uses to drink the whiskey, of course, represents the childhood from which he has forever broken:

> Dussander got up. He went to one of the kitchen cabinets and took down a small glass. This glass had once held jelly. Cartoon characters danced around the rim. Todd recognized them all—Fred and Wilma Flintstone, Barney and Betty Rubble, Pebbles and Bamm-Bamm. He had grown up with them. He watched as Dussander wiped this jellyglass almost ceremonially with a dishtowel. He watched as Dussander set it in front of him. He watched as Dussander poured a finger of bourbon into it.
> "What's that for?" Todd muttered. "I don't drink. Drinking's for cheap stewbums like you."
> "Lift your glass, boy. It is a special occasion. Today you drink."
> Todd looked at him for a long moment, then picked up the glass. Dussander clicked his cheap ceramic cup smartly against it. (196)

As the novella progresses, Todd comes to identify fully with Nazi dogma. He begins to categorize and manipulate people to his own advantage. Paralleling his affiliation with a Nazi worldview, the boy's increasing need to commission his own acts of brutality appears further justifiable when he interprets them in light of his own culture's adult values and rationalizations:

> He supposed he might have to kill again, and maybe more than once. It was too bad, but of course their time of usefulness as human creatures was over. Except their usefulness to Todd, of course. And Todd, like everyone else he knew, was only tailoring his lifestyle to fit his own particular needs as he grew older. Really, he was no different than anybody. You had to make your own way in the world; if you were going to get along, you had to do it by yourself. (213)

Todd Bowden may never have been a paragon of moral purity or innocence; in fact, his psychological torment of the Nazi from the very beginning
suggests quite the opposite. But steady contact with Dussander pushes him
into a deeper, more serious, and personal participation in evil. As psychological studies of exposure to aggressive acts indicate, the more an individual is
exposed to violence, the greater his response to it. Todd's prurient interest in
the adult knowledge Dussander possesses becomes addictive; the simple
curiosity that initiated their relationship—"all the gooshy stuff" (124)—
evolves into an active presence neither man can finally control. *Apt Pupil*
once again suggests the depravity King sees as indicative of adult experience.
The novella more than illustrates the danger inherent in Richard Bowden's
naive assumption that "'for a kid the whole world's a laboratory . . . and he'll
be all the stronger for having knocked around a few corners'" (132). His son,
Todd Bowden, enters the "world's laboratory" as an apt pupil; the monster
that emerges two years later owes its creation to the particular course of
study it discovers there.

V

King's children, like those found in Dickens' novels, illustrate the failings and
abuses of adult society. The destruction of their innocence accomplishes
more than a simple restating of the universal theme of the fall from grace; it
enlarges to include a specific critique of respective societies and cultures as
well. As I have argued elsewhere in this text, King's fiction works from the
premise of a fallen, corrupted mortal world. This tragic vision is provided its
clearest dramatization when King probes the dark realities of adult life as
they are perceived by children. Many of his adolescents—like Todd Bowden
and the children of the corn—are victimized by the influence of adult culpa-
bility and sin. These young people are made to sacrifice their innocence
when they inherit the moral mistakes of an older generation. In making the
transition into adulthood, their knowledge of the world is shaped by painful
tragedy, and often culminates in their own deaths. As Todd Bowden realizes
shortly before commencing his own personal holocaust, the American adult
landscape is composed of treacherous terrain, where even the most intense
light cannot penetrate all the shadows: "It was as if, in the bright and careful
arrangement he had made, in that a-place-for-everything-and-everything-
in-its-place kitchen of his mind, a dark and bloody intruder now lurched and
shambled, looking for a place to die" (215).

In *Danse Macabre*, King asserts that "if the horror story is our rehearsal
for death, then its strict moralities make it also a reaffirmation of life and

good will and simple imagination—just one more pipeline to the infinite" (380). Although to this point this study has provided confirmation of the "strict moralities" operating in King's fictional microcosm more than those elements of reaffirmation, I do not mean to suggest that King writes only about themes of annihilation and spiritual futility. There are, in fact, several major protagonists whose "reaffirmation of life and good will" enables them to triumph over the particular horrors they encounter. The final two chapters of this book focus on the conflict between symbols of human corruption (represented in King's portrayal of social and cultural institutions) and the individual's struggle to avoid its entrapments. Those characters who manage to circumvent such enslavement—several of his adolescent protagonists and a handful of adults who maintain child-like loyalties and a romantic faith in life—are the only true survivors in King's canon. Emerging from their moral voyage into worldly evil with their independence intact, they summon an inner strength that is greater than the forces of destruction, both human and supernatural, that surround them.

ANTHONY MAGISTRALE

The Shape Evil Takes:
Hawthorne's Woods Revisited

"Is not this better," murmured he, "than what we dreamed of in the forest?"
"I know not! I know not!" she hurriedly replied.
—*The Scarlet Letter*, 236

Stephen King's fictional allegories owe much of their formulation to, and are reminiscent of, the romance tradition in nineteenth- and twentieth-century American literature. There are at least two occasions in *Danse Macabre* where King acknowledges his debt to Hawthorne's tales. In his discussion on the origins of *'Salem's Lot*, for example, King tells us that he "wanted to try to use the book partially as a form of literary homage . . . working in the tradition of such 'classical' ghost story writers as Henry James, M. R. James, and Nathaniel Hawthorne" (37–38).

Like Poe, Melville, Hawthorne, and Flannery O'Connor, King often places his protagonists in situations where they encounter the reality of evil, and from this encounter they must make choices which will influence the remainder of their lives. How his characters react to the loss of innocence is a central theme in King's work; their ability to survive is dependent upon what they learn from the fall from grace.

As is so often the case in Hawthorne's canon, the awareness of sin forces King's characters to proceed in one of two possible directions. The first is toward moral regeneration, a spirit of renewed commitment to other human beings that is born from an acceptance of the devil's thesis as

From *Starmont Studies in Literary Criticism 25: The Moral Voyages of Stephen King.* © 1989 Starmont House, Inc.

postulated in "Young Goodman Brown," that "Evil is the nature of mankind" (98), and that the failure to acknowledge either the existence of evil or its nexus to mankind results in spiritual death. On the other hand, the discovery of sin can frequently be overwhelming; it does not always lead to a higher state of moral consciousness. In Hawthorne and King, the encounter with evil is often portrayed as an experience that leads to isolation and self-destruction. Characters in their fictions commit their worst transgressions in refusing to recognize the evil in themselves, and in failing to exert a greater measure of self-discipline.

Dr. Louis Creed, the protagonist in Stephen King's 1983 novel *Pet Sematary*, shares much in common with the darkest characters in Hawthorne. Creed is similar to the impassioned, but misguided idealists who populate Hawthorne's stories; he resembles Aylmer, Rappaccini, Chillingworth, Goodman Brown and Hollingsworth who also fail to recognize the inviolable distinction separating human idealism from the limitations of reality. Like these characters in Hawthorne, Creed violates standards for personal moral conduct and brings about his own destruction.

Early in the novel we learn of Doctor Creed's perspective on death. In response to his daughter's anger over the prospect of someday losing her cat to the mysterious force that has populated the Pet Sematary, Creed responds that "'Clocks run down—that's all I know. There are no guarantees, babe'" (36). Creed's controlled attitude toward death infuriates both his daughter and wife. They see nothing "natural" in the abrupt negation of life. But more important, the novel will also reveal that Creed himself does not believe that death "'is the most natural thing in the w[orld]'" (41). His disciplined attitude is merely a veneer that is shattered when his own child is killed. When confronted with the reality of his child's death, Creed displays his inherent inability to maintain a rational perspective towards immortality. After Louis loses his only son, he seeks to repudiate death's dominion over the human world by availing himself of the resuscitative energies residing within an Indian burial ground located in the woods several miles behind his home.

In the nineteenth century, Emerson and the transcendentalists assured their audience that nature represented a vehicle to true self-knowledge. King and Hawthorne certainly concur with this premise, although the self disclosed by Thoreau in the pines at Walden pond is vastly different than what Louis Creed and Goodman Brown uncover in the wilderness behind their respective communities. Instead of a mirror to the self's purity and limitless potentiality that the transcendentalists associated with New England nature, the woods of Hawthorne and King are a reflection of the self's essential darkness and the human affinity to sin.

The journey into the wilderness in Hawthorne's fiction is always fraught with danger. Within the New England pines of Hawthorne's symbolic landscapes we find the powerful rhythms of primordial and uncontrollable forces. Hawthorne's Puritan ancestors fully comprehended that within the uncut trees surrounding their early enclaves lurked elements that were seldom benevolently disposed toward human welfare. In the woods, one could easily lose direction, encounter hostile Indians and animals, or worse yet, be forced into an immediate struggle with Satan's legions. As Heinrich Zimmer explains in *The King and the Corpse*,

> The forest has always been a place of initiation for there the demonic presences, the ancestral spirits, and the forces of nature reveal themselves. The forest is the antithesis of house and heart, village and field boundary, where the household gods hold sway and where human laws and customs prevail. It holds the dark forbidden things—secrets, terrors, which threaten the protected life of the ordered world of common day. (69)

The Scarlet Letter, "Roger Malvin's Burial," "Young Goodman Brown" and "Ethan Brand" all mirror the Puritan influence on Hawthorne's work. When the protagonist in each of these tales ventures forth into the forest, he returns to his respective village and family in a transformed state. Within the New World forest, Hawthorne imagined a bifurcated vision: the danger of Faustian temptation as well as the possibility for rebirth and transcendence.

Dimmesdale and Reuben Bourne are made to face the realities of their own self-deceptions in the woods; the journey into the dark pines becomes a metaphor for a journey into the self. Separated from the hypocritical pressures of civilized life, Dimmesdale and Bourne acknowledge the true depravity of their natures; from this profound recognition of the evil within themselves, each man emerges from the woods chastened, his life dramatically altered.

Like Dimmesdale, Reuben Bourne is living a lie; his failure to provide Roger Malvin with a Christian burial coupled with his unwillingness to tell Dorcas the truth about her father's abandonment in the woods, create "a moody and misanthropic man . . . feeling few regrets and disdaining to acknowledge any" (19). In order to confront his sins and gain forgiveness for them, Bourne must re-enter the woods and acknowledge his repressed guilt: " . . . in the calmest and clearest moods of his mind, he was conscious that he had a deep vow unredeemed, and that an unburied corpse was calling to him out of the wilderness" (17). The wilderness serves Bourne in a psychoanalytic capacity; by forcing him into contact with that part of himself that he has willfully denied, Reuben's journey takes him deeper into the woods—and by symbolic extension, deeper into himself: "[he] strayed onward rather like a sleepwalker than a hunter" (22). Hawthorne's use of a somnambulistic analogy is important here, as it highlights the function of the woods as a representational arena for the unconscious self, the place where Bourne confronts his darkest impulses, and where civilized hypocrisies are finally stripped clean. As Reginald Cook argues in "The Forest of Goodman Brown's Night: A Reading of Hawthorne's 'Young Goodman Brown,'" Hawthorne's symbolic forests reveal the very turbulence of the human mind, "the form its guilt takes, the contributions of grace and election, the sense of justice, the invocation of mercy" (478).

Over the years, Bourne's sins have corroded his soul: "[his] insulated emotions had gradually made a selfish man, and he could no longer love deeply except where he saw or imagined some reflection or likeness of his own mind" (19). Since Bourne recognizes in his young son Cyrus, "what he himself had been in other days" (19), his child's murder serves as a symbolic death of Bourne himself—the destruction of that part of his psyche, long sustained by a posture of deceptive innocence, which has produced his guilt and anxiety. Bourne's purification is achieved at the expense of his son's life in order to appease "a voice audible only to himself, commanding him to go forth and redeem his vow" (18). In satisfying this primitive "voice" that Reuben hears deep in the woods, his son's blood opens the way to the civilized virtues of exculpation, reconciliation, and a renewal of his Christian faith.

Young Goodman Brown and Ethan Brand are also profoundly changed by their experience in the woods, but for these characters the struggle against the evil they discover there is not positively resolved. Neither Brown nor Brand is spiritually transformed by the insights they gain in the forest; in fact, unlike Dimmesdale or Bourne, Brown and Brand forfeit the opportunity for personal salvation when they reject their bond with the community of sin openly acknowledged in the woods.

Louis Creed's journey into the trees behind his house shares more in common with the negative voyages in "Young Goodman Brown" and "Ethan Brand" than with the redemptive encounters portrayed in "Roger Malvin's Burial" and *The Scarlet Letter*. King's Wendigo, the wrathful Indian spirit that animates the unholy Micmac burial ground beyond the Pet Sematary and footfall, exploits human weakness and vulnerability; it thrives on the doctor's inability to discipline his curiosity and to recognize the distinction between saving lives and playing god. As is the situation in Hawthorne's tales, the woods in King's novel reveal man's penchant for evil, his innate depravity; but unlike the forests of "Young Goodman Brown" or *The Scarlet Letter*, which offer at least the possibility for spiritual advancement concurrent with an acceptance of personal sin, the wild god of King's wilderness makes no such compromises with Louis Creed. Hawthorne's natural landscapes appear to be animated by subtle forces that ultimately invite his protagonists into a confrontation with ethical codes and principles. As "Roger Malvin's Burial" illustrates, the trek into the woods often serves as an unsentimental journey toward moral instruction. In contrast, King's Wendigo is thoroughly amoral: it manipulates human trust through the promised miracle of resurrection— only to deliver a grotesque version of itself.

Goodman Brown and Ethan Brand discover that the forest is much darker and more ominous than they originally anticipated, and Louis Creed eventually gains a similar insight. Each time the doctor ventures into the Indian cemetery, he, like Brown and Brand, experiences a greater level of human estrangement. The encounter with evil narrows each of these men into a position where they become less sensitive to the "magnetic chain of humanity" (285) and more involved with themselves and their own personal quests. Brown's wandering into the woods reveals a progressively deepening awareness of the pervasiveness of evil. The revelation that his perspective on the nature of his community, elegy, ancestors, and even his wife has been naive and inaccurate, pushes Brown from a state of innocence to one of cynical despair. Unable to accept the reality of evil in either humankind or himself, Brown "shrank from the bosom of Faith; and at morning or eventide, when the family knelt down at prayer, he scowled and muttered to himself, and gazed sternly at his wife, and turned away" (100).

As Brown's encounter with evil produces a retreat into himself, Louis Creed's deepening involvement with the dark powers of the Wendigo likewise alienates the doctor from his own family and community. Indeed, Creed's obsession with bringing his son back to life is indulged at the expense of his other, nearly catatonic child and desolate wife: "There had been times in the dark watches of the night when she [his wife] had longed to hate Louis for the grief he had fathered inside her, and for not giving her the comfort she needed . . ." (324). Contemplating a second trip to the burial ground to bring about his son's resurrection, Louis Creed's isolation finds a parallel in Goodman Brown's "dying hour [of] gloom" (100) and Ethan Brand's break from "the universal throb . . . of brother man" (285):

> That feeling of coldness still held; he felt totally unplugged from
> his people, the places that had become so familiar to him, even

his work. . . . Madness was all around him, softly fluttering as the
wings of night-hunting owls with great golden eyes: he was heading into madness. (278)

In the fictions of Hawthorne and King there are definite realms of
experience that highlight man's limitations, his inability to grasp, much less
to manipulate, the mysteries found in nature and deep within the human
heart. Hawthorne's idealists engage actions that violate moral barriers—
whether in the form of perverse scientific quests (as in "The Birthmark" and
"Rappaccini's Daughter") or through personal intrusions into the secrets of
another human being (as in the actions of Chillingworth and Ethan Brand).
Terence Martin observes in "The Method of Hawthorne's Tales, " that "the
cancer of obsession threatens any Hawthorne character—scientist, man of
religion, artist—who prefers an idea to a human being" (17). Louis Creed's
self-corruption occurs as a result of a similar transgression: he consciously
chooses to liberate the malevolent energies residing in the Micmac burial
ground because he wishes control over nature's greatest secrets—the ability
to regulate life and sustain existence.

Like Hawthorne's doctors, Aylmer and Rappaccini, Creed sacrifices the
people who are dearest to him because of his obsession with an idea: the challenge of altering the immutable laws of nature. While it is possible to argue
persuasively that Creed is initially drawn to the Micmac burial site because
of an altruistic love for his daughter and the desire to spare her the pain of
grief over a lost cat, by the conclusion of the novel altruism is no longer the
doctor's primary motivation. Creed's compulsion to deliver the bodies of his
son and wife to the cemetery is not adequately explained as a consequence of
his guilt and grief. Rather, he is more interested in continuing his misguided
experiment under the irrational premise that eventually he will discover a
way to dominate death. At various points throughout the book Creed
appears to be keeping an unconscious personal record against death. Each
time his medical skills aid in saving a human life, Creed whispers to himself,
"'won one today, Louis'" (161). Creed's game against the reaper continues
even as the stakes grow ever larger. Although he has listened to repeated
warnings about the treacherous nature of the place and has even witnessed
first hand the monstrous consequences of his son's resurrection, the doctor
remains convinced of his ability to manipulate the powers residing in the burial ground. As a result of his refusal to accept the workings of Fate, he is transformed into an extension of the amoral Wendigo. Like the insistent Aylmer
in Hawthorne's tale "The Birthmark," who willingly squanders his beautiful
wife for the sake of testing a scientific theory, Creed sacrifices himself and

those around him in his obsession to unlock the mystery that will yield the secret of immortality: "'I waited too long with Gage,' Louis said. 'Something got into him because I waited too long. But it will be different with Rachel, Steve. I know it will'" (370).

In spite of the mechanistic world-view maintained in most gothic fiction, the characters in King and Hawthorne still possess a persuasive element of free will. The majority of their protagonists are like Louis Creed: they choose their own course of action. It is an act of Ethan Brand's own volition that leads him to pursue the Unpardonable Sin, just as Goodman Brown's gloom is a result of his choice to emphasize only the "despair" and none of the "triumph" voiced by Satan's congregation in their communal awareness of evil (98). As Robert Deamer points out in "Hawthorne's Dream in the Forest," "[Brown] did not *have* to journey into the forest and to indulge in doubts of Faith or in visions of orgiastic evil. Faced with the choice of loving his wife or believing in his religion, he chose, disastrously for him, to do the latter" (334).

While it may be true that the Micmac burial ground possesses, as Jud Crandall asserts, "'a power . . . and it's coming around to full again'" (246), Creed freely elects to avail himself of its insidious magic. He essentially acknowledges his terrible freedom moments before he begins his son's disinterment: "his heart told him quietly and absolutely that he couldn't come back tomorrow. If he didn't do it tonight, he could never do it. He would never be able to screw himself up to this crazy pitch again. . . . This was the moment, the only time for it he was ever going to have" (297). Moreover, Creed makes his decision to re-enter the enchanted woods in a flagrant rejection of Victor Pascow's prophetic warning. Pascow's recent death provides immediate insight into the malevolence which resides in the Indian burial ground, and he tries in vain to share this vision with Creed: "'The door must not be opened. . . . The barrier was not meant to be broken. Remember this: there is more power here than you know. It is old and always restless. . . . Your destruction and the destruction of all you love is very near, Doctor'" (70).

In light of Creed's election to disregard Pascow's message, it is interesting that Jud Crandall, who is responsible for introducing the doctor to the transformational properties inherent in the Micmac soil, is soon placed in a position to employ its life-giving powers. After learning that Norma, Jud's beloved wife, has died suddenly, Creed's first thought is of "Jud pulling Norma's corpse on a pagan litter through the woods. Toward the Micmac burial ground beyond the Pet Sematary" (173). But unlike Creed, Jud is capable of exercising a greater measure of self-control; he rejects the temptation to resurrect Norma. His memory of Timmy Baterman remains a vivid illustration of the Wendigo's devastating influence over human interments, and this recollection serves as a sufficient deterrent to keep Jud from further experimentation. Not only is Crandall capable of restraining the selfish impulse to play God by summoning Norma back to life, but he also supplies Creed, after the latter loses his son, with advice that echoes Pascow's warning: "'You know why I'm here,' Jud said. 'You're thinking about things that are not to be thought of, Louis. Worse still, I fear you're considering them'" (230).

Throughout Hawthorne's fiction, his protagonists are offered sage counsel and guidance during the course of their moral struggles. In "My Kinsman, Major Molineux" a friendly stranger encourages Robin to seek alternatives to the patronage of his kinsman or a return ticket home. Mary Goffe reminds Richard Digby of his relationship to other human beings and tries to lure him away from his isolation in "The Man of Adamant." Similarly, Hester Prynne is Dimmesdale's model of endurance and courage in *The Scarlet Letter*. And in "The Birthmark" Aminadab, Aylmer's laboratory assistant, immediately identifies the danger inherent in his employer's quest to remove Georgiana's facial flaw, muttering to himself, "'If she were my wife, I'd never part with that birthmark'" (209). Each of these characters parallels Jud Crandall's role in *Pet Sematary*: they are presented as sensible counterpoints to the encroaching madness of the central protagonists. Like Jud, they embody the human requisite to recognize and exercise a measure of control over the self's most debased and indulgent urges. Moreover, they offer unsentimental alternatives to the main character's choice of action, reminding him of obligations that challenge the limitations of egotism. If their examples and/or advice is emulated, the protagonist usually endures; if rebuffed, self-destruction is the inevitable consequence.

In *Pet Sematary* Stephen King captures the native speech patterns, the elements of life in a cold climate, and the specificity of place that set his readers firmly in a rural Maine world. King is a regionialist for many of the same reasons that Hawthorne chose to write about Massachusetts: each author understands that the universal themes of great literature—human sin, fear, and endurance—can only be rendered truthfully within settings and by personalities an artist has come to know on a first-hand basis. Much as Hawthorne relied on Puritan New England as a setting to describe the foibles and sins that are the inheritance of humanity, King views Maine as a deliberate backdrop for his own allegories, enabling him to utilize specific elements from that culture in his portrayal of the moral conflicts common to us all.

The events which transpire in the woods behind the Pet Sematary are reminiscent of the narrative pattern which occurs in Hawthorne's fiction. An individual loses his innocence in the encounter with tragic circumstances and is faced with the struggle to redefine himself morally. In portraying the negative results of this struggle, both writers suggest that there are certain mysteries man must simply learn to accept, certain secrets he has no business attempting to discover, and certain ethical barriers that he only transcends at the expense of his soul. Hawthorne's tales and King's novel achieve their power in demonstrating that one's humanity is dreadfully easy to lose, and what we abandon ourselves to possess, we necessarily become. The romantic poet William Blake may have felt perfect harmony residing in "the lineaments of gratified desire," but for King and Hawthorne the inevitable end of such self-absorption is the madness of Louis Creed circling back through the woods for another trip to the Micmac burial grounds or the devastation of Ethan Brand's marbled heart.

CLARE HANSON

Stephen King: Powers of Horror

PREFATORY MATTERS

In order to approach the power of horror in Stephen King's work we must
move circuitously, towards the glimpsed abyss via accounts of the origins of
personality offered by psychoanalytic theory, specifically by Freud, Lacan
and Julia Kristeva. King's fiction is concerned above all with origins, with the
grounds of being. His work betrays a fascination with those primary/primal
movements and experiences which impel or force the construction of the self
as a gendered social being. I shall argue that his work itself displays or follows an exemplarily "masculine" trajectory, moving as it were from "mother" to "text": in order to show this I must reverse this experiental order to
follow the epistemological order of psychoanalytic theory, which developed
from a concentration on "text" to a concentration on "mother" in its movement from Freud to Kristeva.

I begin with Freud, and his account of the development of the self.
According to Freud, one of the most striking and distinguishing features of
the human animal is its extreme and extended dependence on its parents
after birth. The human being is born, so to speak, prematurely, and requires
unceasing vigilance and care before it is able to function independently of
its parents. The "family situation" is thus more or less "given" in the construction of human personality, although the nature of the family will vary
from society to society. Freud also suggests that, while we are born with
certain fixed biological needs, such as our need for food, these needs soon

From *American Horror Fiction: From Brockden Brown to Stephen King.* © 1990 Editorial Board,
Lumiere (Co-operative) Press Ltd.

become "perverted" as they become associated/confused with sensations of pleasure (for instance, the pleasure which the infant derives from sucking at the breast). A drive to pleasure is thus established existing independently of need: the object of desire in this sense is by no means fixed (unlike the object of biological need—the breast, for instance). Displacement is thus an inherent part of desire from its inception as part of human experience.

The child in this early stage of development is asocial. She or he cannot be a social animal without a preliminary sense of the self as distinct from others. The movement into social life occurs, according to Freud, via the Oedipus complex, or Oedipal moment. In the early months of life the child exists in a dyadic relationship with the mother, unable to distinguish between self and (m)other. The child is forced out of this blissful state through the "intervention" of the father. The shadow of the father falls between the child and the mother as the father acts to prohibit the child's incestuous desire for its mother. At this point, the child is initiated into selfhood, perceiving itself for the first time as a being separate from the mother, who is now consciously desired because absent, forbidden. The origin of self thus lies for Freud in this absence and sense of loss. It is too at the point of repression of desire for the mother that the unconscious is formed, as a place to receive that lost desire, and it is at this point of repression that the child's early *transgressive* drives become organised and forced towards genital (and gendered) sexuality.

It is now generally agreed that Freud's account of the little boy's passage through the Oedipus is much more satisfactory than his account of the little girl's: it is hard to escape the conclusion that this was because the theory was originally *founded* on the case of the boy, the theory for the girl being something of a lame extrapolation from an already gendered theory. Yet we must look briefly at Freud's account of both the male and female passage through the Oedipus, as it provides the basis for almost all subsequent theories of the origins of sexual identity. For the male child at the Oedipal moment, it is the father's threat of castration which forces him to abandon his incestuous desire for the mother. As the desire is repressed the child has to move away from the mother, but, in giving up the hope of possessing the mother now, the male child does not give up the hope of *at some time* occupying the place of the father. He is able from this moment to aspire to fatherhood himself, to train himself to occupy the position of father/patriarch. For the little girl the case is far different. The first effect of the intervention of the father is that she will perceive herself as different/castrated, and will thus turn from her mother, perceived as similarly castrated and inadequate, to her father. When she finds that her attempts to "seduce" her father are unsuccessful, the girl will turn back to the mother, to identify, albeit unhappily, with the mother's feminine role. In place of the penis which she can never possess, suggests Freud, she then posits as an object of desire a baby which will, she hopes, come from the father. Freud does not explain how the girl will ever progress from this incestuous position: the implication is that female sexual desire remains "blocked," compromised by an ineradicable desire for a father-figure.

The importance of the work of Jacques Lacan lies for us in the further connections which he establishes between the Oedipal moment and the child's entry into language, which he terms the "symbolic order." For Lacan, the moment in which the unconscious is created, via the repression of desire for the mother, is one and the same as the moment in which language is acquired, for it is only on perceiving the mother as absent/different from her- or himself that the child will need to name her. Language, like the unconscious, is thus founded upon loss and absence, upon a lack for which it will try endlessly to compensate. This brings us to a further important insight. Lacan sees a fundamental opposition between the languageless pre-Oedipal state which he terms the "imaginary," and the post-Oedipal world constituted by the entry into a network of social relations and into language. This opposition will be central to our understanding of Stephen King's fiction.

The symbolic is that whole network of family and social relations which the child must "master" in order to be adequately socialised, and it is a network which leads the child away from the mother to the father. The father represents for the child the "first term" in the social network, for it is his prohibition of desire for the mother which is the first social force or coercion which the child experiences. The father's role is also crucial in the child's entry into language, which Lacan sees as particularly important in facilitating the child's passage through the Oedipus complex. Lacan suggests that the phallus, the emblem of male sexuality and power, constitutes the "transcendental signifier." While the child may already have experienced lack and absence before her/his first perception of sexual difference, sexual difference "takes up" all previous differences. The primary marker of difference becomes sexual difference, perceived in terms of fullness in the father (possession of the phallus) and lack in the mother (absence of the phallus).

Lacan stresses the importance of language as a means of controlling and marking one's social and sexual identity: in his view, in order successfully to negotiate the Oedipus complex the child must not only order and repress libidinal drives, but also, as it were, fasten onto language as the only means by which we humans may console ourselves for the absence of "the real." Language offers our only source of power over all that (such as the mother) which we cannot have, all that which must be consigned in its "real" excess and radical energy to the unconscious.

This swift summary of the work of Freud and Lacan will serve to highlight the importance of certain fundamenal elements in the construction of the social being: the parents, the unconscious, the symbolic order. The "narrative" of Freudian and Lacanian theory is of a journey from the chaotic "other" of the unconscious to the symbolic *order* of language, which is clearly characterized as male-dominated. The work of Julia Kristeva leads us back, however, from a male-dominated symbolic to the mother, and to areas of her dominion and influence which have, Kristeva argues, been underestimated in (male) accounts of the construction and maintenance of human personality. Kristeva is best known for her concept of the semiotic, which she mobilises as a means of locating and inserting "the feminine" back into the exclusively masculine post-Oedipal world described by Lacan. Kristeva fully accepts Lacan's account of the symbolic order by means of which social, sexual and linguistic relations are regulated by/in the name of the father. She suggests, however, that the symbolic is oppressive *because* it is exclusively masculine— that is, because it is limited, not just because it is limiting (in terms of the actual social and sexual practices which the symbolic order licences). Against the symbolic Kristeva thus sets the semiotic, a play of rhythmic patterns and "pulsions" which are pre-linguistic. In the pre-Oedipal phase the child babbles, rhythmically: the sounds are representative (though not by the rules of language) of some of the experiences which the child is undergoing in a period when she or he is still dominated by the mother. This semiotic "babble" thus represents/is connected with "feminised" experience, which is of course available at this stage to both male and female children. Kristeva argues that this feminised experience is not completely repressed either by male or by female children, but that it resurfaces in adult life as a kind of disruptive influence moving over ordered language/texts. It is in the breaks and "pulsions" of language and text that we can identify the "feminine" in all of us breaking up and challenging the symbolic order.

But it is Kristeva's concept of "abjection" which will be of greatest concern to us in our consideration of horror in Stephen King: indeed, the concept was first formulated in the book called *Pouvoirs de l'horreur* (*Powers of Horror*). Here Kristeva reaches "back" before the Oedipus complex and the constitution of the self as a subject defined by an object, the (m)other. She posits an earlier "splitting-off" from the mother which takes place in early infancy: this splitting-off may be defined as the merest preliminary turning-away from the mother. The child is not yet a subject nor the mother an object, but the moment of abjection is that in which a space first appears between the two, a space created, necessarily, by a slight movement of rejection or withdrawal. The abject is described in this way by Kristeva:

> The abject is not an ob-ject in front of me that I name or imagine. Neither is it this *"ob-jeu," petit "a"* indefinitely fleeing in the systematic quest of desire. The abject is not my correlate which, by offering me a support on someone or something other, would allow me to be more or less detached and autonomous. The abject shares only one quality with the object—that of being opposed to *I*. But if, in being opposed, the object offers me equilibrium within the fragile web of a desire for meaning which in fact makes me indefinitely and infinitely homologous to it, the abject, on the contrary, as fallen object, is what is radically excluded, drawing me towards the point where meaning collapses.

She speaks of

> This massive and abrupt irruption of a strangeness which, if it was familiar to me in an opaque and forgotten life, now importunes me as radically separated and repugnant. Not me. Not that. But not nothing either. A "something" that I do not recognise as a thing. A whole lot of nonsense which has nothing insignificant and which crushes me. At the border of inexistence and hallucination, of a reality which, if I recognise it, annihilates me.

Here Kristeva is suggesting that the abject, representing the primary "turning-away," can return and rise up through the surface of adult life, welling up to announce its own meaning—which is meaninglessness or fear. Because it is outside (or before) the symbolic order, the abject has no apprehensible meaning, and leads us "towards the point where meaning collapses." It is relatively easy to relate this "whole lot of nonsense which has nothing insignificant and which crushes me" to horror as we associate it with the traditional iconography of horror fiction or horror films. As Kristeva explains, the abject in this sense can be represented by any kind of transgressive state, or any condition which challenges the limits and boundaries of being. She focuses on filth, refuse, cloaca: these "entities" challenge the limits of being because they are ever on the border of living existence, verging on death or decay. The corpse is the ultimate example of refuse which works in this way to destroy limits; as Kristeva writes,

> The corpse—seen without God and outside science—is the
> height of abjection. It is death infesting life. Abject. It is some-
> thing rejected from which one is not separated, from which one
> is not protected as is the case with an object. An imaginary
> strangeness and a menace that is real, it calls to us and finishes by
> devouring us.

However, it is important to note that Kristeva's theory of abjection is
founded on a specific turning-away, *from the mother*. The images of abjection which she mentions (blood, faeces, and so on) suggest a preoccupation
with the body splitting from itself, but this is a later "version" or image of
the original source of anxiety, the split with the mother, which inspires,
both fascination and horror' for the abjected mother both is, and is not,
"me." In the moment of abjection, "I expel *myself*, I spit *myself* out, I abject
myself in the same movement by which 'I' claims to be me." "I" oscillates
between a "pole of attraction and repulsion." Hence the compulsive *fascination* of horror: what I am concerned particularly to explore in this essay
is the corresponding sense of *repulsion* or distaste for the mother and the
maternal body, as this is expressed in a variety of texts.

CARRIE: ABJECTION

Carrie is concerned with an apparently trivial incident—the onset of menstruation in a sixteen-year-old girl–and with its monstrous, far-reaching consequences. The onset of menstruation in Carrie White is traumatic: this
trauma releases her latent "telekinetic" powers and results in the virtual
destruction of the small town in Maine where she has lived all her life. After
the disaster we are told that the town is "waiting to die." Why should such a
trivial-seeming incident have such consequences? And why should Carrie
White be endowed by her creator with "telekinetic" powers? To answer such
questions we have only to turn to Kristeva's developing account of the abject
in *Powers of Horror*. As we have seen, Kristeva associates images of *waste* with
abjection. She suggests further than this waste falls into two categories: the
excremental, which threatens identity from the outside, and the menstrual,
which threatens from within. Menstrual waste is for obvious reasons also
connected particularly closely with the body of the mother and with "memories" of the primary abjection of that body.

In *Carrie* we as readers are placed as voyeurs, forced(?) to witness an
extreme distaste/horror inspired by the menstrual blood of others. The novel

thus functions for its readers as what Kristeva would call a "defilement ritual," but on a massive scale. The whole novel acts as a purifying rite of passage, exorcising the power of the abject and of the loved/hated maternal body. In *Carrie* the exorcism sets a whole town ablaze, with a fire the fierceness of which mirrors the force of feeling stirred by the menstrual/maternal.

Revulsion from the menstrual "fires" two of the strongest scenes in the novel. The first is a scene among schoolgirls showering after volleyball. Carrie, showering with the others, sees blood trickling down her leg: she does not yet know what menstruation is and screams, significantly, "I'm bleeding to death." The other girls crowd round her with a true herd instinct, chanting "period, period," "you're bleeding, you're bleeding":

> Then the laughter, disgusted, contemptuous, horrified, seemed
> to rise and bloom into something jagged and ugly, and the girls
> were bombarding her with tampons and sanitary napkins. . . .
> They flew like snow and the chant became; "Plug it *up*, plug it *up*,
> plug it—

We are told that the girls felt first a "mixture of hate, revulsion, exasperation and pity," then "welling disgust": the meaning and force of the group reaction is deepened when this scene is linked metaphorically with a second "shower" scene. We see this second scene from various points of view, but the full force of the horror is this time felt by Carrie alone as she is once again horribly exposed in front of her peers. As they sit (incongruously) on the "thrones" set up for the "King and Queen" of the May Ball, Carrie and her escort Tommy are suddenly drenched in pig's blood. We are shown the childish vindictiveness of the teenage conspirators who have set this ritual scene of defilement up, but there is something deeper than childishness in the boy Billy's chant "Pig's blood for a pig," and, especially, in Carrie's apprehension of the horror of the scene:

> Someone began to laugh, a solitary, affrighted hyena sound, and
> she *did* open her eyes, opened them to see who it was and it was
> true, the final nightmare, she was red and dripping with it, they
> had drenched her in the very secretness of blood, in front of all
> of them and her thought
>   (oh . . . i . . . COVERED . . . with it)
> was covered a ghastly purple with her revulsion and her shame.
> She could smell herself and it was the *stink* of blood, the awful
> wet, coppery smell . . . she . . . felt the soft pattern of tampons

and napkins against her skin as voices exhorted her to plug it UP,
tasted the plump, fulsome bitterness of horror. They had finally
given her the shower they wanted. (167)

The surface of life is peeled back in such a scene to show the abject which
lies "behind" it, that which is "secret" (blood should remain *within*). Carrie
feels "revulsion" and "shame," but more significant is the phrase "the plump,
fulsome bitterness of horror." King suggests through this the primary and
affective nature of abjection through its connection with primary sense
impressions (here taste) and suggests too the mingled fascination and horror
with which we view the abject which is so nearly a part of ourselves. So his
almost oxymoronic phrase "fulsome bitterness" gives us the particular feeling of this kind of horror, the abject as a source of horror. This quality makes
us experience an almost vertiginous sense of existing on a borderline between
sense and non-sense, meaning and non-meaning.

Carrie thus pivots on the reader's horror of the abject as it resurfaces
in adult life, but also exploits the reader's potential pleasure in contempla-
tion of the abject. As one is drawn back to a point before entry into the
symbolic order, one may experience pleasure on two grounds. First, one
may experience pleasure in breaking the taboos which surround and constitute the symbolic; one may experience the pleasure of transgression as
one reaches back to experience and to a mode of being which is forbidden.
Secondly, one may be placed back in touch with the pleasure which one
originally felt in the presymbolic state, pleasure derived from unmediated
experience of the maternal body and of one's own bodily functions.

If *Carrie* as text puts us back in touch with the pre-symbolic it does so
despite (or because of?) the fact that for the character Carrie herself there can
be no *proper* connection either with the maternal semiotic or with the pater-
nal symbolic. Carrie, like her mother, is doomed to exist as what Kristeva
would call a "borderline case," tied to the ambiguity of abjection, blocked or
thwarted in her development. It is significant that both Carrie *and her mother* have an absent father. Mrs White's father was killed in a "barroom shooting incident" and immediately after this she began to attend "fundamentalist
prayer meetings": the connection between the loss of the father and the turn
to extreme religious fundamentalism is made clear. Mrs White's marriage
was brief, for Carrie's father was killed, in another accident, before she was
born. Mrs White, unstable herself, takes over the role of the father in
Carrie's upbringing, acting as a kind of crazed, overstated representative
of the symbolic. Uncertain of her own identity, she finds relief in a "false"
identification with the masculine role, and this has the effect—vital of course

to the power of the novel—of intensifying Carrie's feelings of disgust and shame towards the feminine and the maternal. Carrie is brought up to fear and distrust the generative sexual powers of the female body: it is impressed on her not only that sex is sinful, but that sex has its origins in the sinfulness of the mother, in her lust and desire. Her mother tells of her own pleasure in the sexual act in a kind of retrospective frenzy of repudiation, and then moves into a ritualistic chant, the main theme of which is again the sinfulness of Eve, who "loosed the raven on the world" and who was visited by "the Curse of Blood."

In the absence of a real father, the image of a "kind, vengeful" God, to use her mother's happy phrase, takes the place of the father in Carrie's childhood. Godfather, God-the-father instils revulsion from the feminine semiotic but offers no way into the masculine symbolic. Carrie is haunted through childhood by dreams in which she is pursued by a "mutilated Christ," "holding a mallet and nails, begging her to take up her cross and follow Him." Towards the end of the novel, having destroyed an entire town through the force of her telekinetic powers, Carrie makes a last, desperate appeal to God/the masculine/the symbolic, confronting what she sees as "the abyss." Her appeal falls into nothingness and she takes the only option left to her if she is going to come to terms with the abjected mother-figure. Carrie and her mother must destroy each other in order to put an end to an intolerable relationship in which each perceives the other as an aspect of herself. Carrie and Margaret White perceive each other as aspects of the self which they reject but from which they can never be freed. Margaret casts her daughter as her own mother, projecting onto the child Carrie the disgust/need which she felt for her own mother, and Carrie returns these ambiguous feelings with interest. Margaret White has, however, moved beyond both a sense of need and the possibility of help by the time we reach the climactic scene of the novel, in which she murders Carrie with the same knife with which she had cut the umbilical cord at the time of Carrie's birth. The weakening Carrie has time only to "will" the death of her mother before she drags herself off to die in an anonymous parking-lot. Carrie's is a death in which we participate, via the consciousness of a witness, Sue Snell, who finds herself being drawn unwillingly into Carrie's mind at the point of death. What is most striking about this "horrid" death scene, with its "orthodox," so to speak, vision of the abject corpse, is the way in which the mother, not the father, is presented as the ground of all meaning and being. Sue Snell is overcome by her sense of Carrie's need for her mother, and feels a terror *which she cannot name* as she feels that without the mother she/Carrie cannot *complete her thought*. The mother seems to be at least as important as the father in the mastery of the symbolic as well as immersion in the semiotic:

> (momma would be alive i killed my momma i want her o it
> hurts my chest my shoulder o o o i want my momma)
> (carrie i)
> And there was no way to finish that thought, nothing there
> to complete it with. Sue was suddenly ovewhelmed with terror,
> the worse because she could put no name to it. The bleeding
> freak on this oil-stained asphalt suddenly seemed meaningless
> and awful in its pain and dying.
> (o momma i'm scared momma MOMMA)
> Sue tried to pull away. . . . (211)

THE SHINING: THE OEDIPAL

The Shining is one of King's most powerful and haunting novels, bearing comparison with Poe's "The Masque of the Red Death," the story which provides an epigraph and a central image for King's text. In *The Shining* King is concerned again with the origins of being, with the construction of the subject in the unconscious and conscious mind, with the interplay between what Lacan would call the symbolic, the imaginary and the real in the construction of that subject. The text plays with images of disintegration and doubling, images of the dissolution and dispersal of the individual subject, but what is striking about the text overall is its strong recuperative thrust. The story is concerned with the entry into the symbolic of the young boy Danny, and with the difficulties he experiences because of a disruption of the symbolic caused by his father. The whole project of the novel is to place Danny securely in the symbolic order and to insert him equally securely into the social world. The power of the text stems from the tension between Danny and his father, the tension between the nightmare images produced by the (joint) unconscious and the everyday world of narrative and action. Jack, the father, has been disturbed by dreadful images coming from the shadow world of the unconscious: these images must be "mastered"; and Danny must take a different path from his father if he is, literally, to survive the story. The novel is concerned very obviously with an opposition between image and text: text, or language, must be preferred over the fatal image. In this preoccupation with language (which offers a direct road, so to speak, to the symbolic and the social order), in its concern to establish Danny in a particular (white, American, male) social and symbolic order, *The Shining* might be considered a "conservative," regressive text. Yet, paradoxically, the strong drive to the symbolic in *The Shining* is of course founded precisely on the overwhelming power of those oppositional images which haunt reader, writer and protagonist.

The Shining follows a male journey through the Oedipus complex, the journey of Danny, who is endowed with supersensory powers of second sight and telepathy. These powers are, as it were, symbolic, and, rather like Carrie White's telekinetic powers, suggest the power of the collective unconscious. (One of the themes of *The Shining* is the way in which our lives, conscious and unconscious, interrelate and intersect with others; also the way in which we are doomed to double and repeat the lives of others. Here Danny's relationship to his father is particularly important.) Danny is locked in the Oedipal moment, unable to progress through it, and his situation is explicitly related back to the Oedipal position of his parents. We are told of his mother's inability to move beyond the "blocked" Oedipal relation to her father which Freud described: we are told that she had been her father's from the beginning and that she, as the father's primary love object, was responsible for her parents' divorce. Jack at one point asks her whom she wants to marry, her father or him. Wendy is particularly sensitive to the threat of repetition patterning, and to the life-or-death dangers which surround children as they struggle to establish a free, stable self. She knows that "to children adult motives and actions must seem as bulking and ominous as dangerous animals seen in the shadows of a dark forest. They were jerked about like puppets, having only the vaguest notions why"—which makes them of course like us, an emblem of the vulnerability of humanity. Endlessly, restlessly, Wendy links her own past and Danny's past and future—"Oh we are wrecking this boy. It's not just Jack, it's me too, and maybe it's not even just us, Jack's father, my mother, are they here too?"

It is, however, Jack's inability to free himself from his father which poses the greatest threat to Danny. Jack's early closeness to his father ended when his father (associated repeatedly with phallic emblems: a gold-headed cane, an elevator) "suddenly" and for "no good reason" beat his mother, his cane whistling through the air. From that point on Jack exists in an ambivalent relation to his father, who still has power over him despite (or perhaps because of) his alcoholism: after his father's death he is haunted by him, as an "irrational white ghost-god." Through all this we can detect a repeating pattern going back from Jack to his father and so on, in which feelings of social insecurity combine with or give rise to irrational behaviour and drunkenness. The father, in other words, seems to be insecure in his place in the symbolic/social order, and this seems to be obscurely linked with a revulsion from the feminine or more specifically from the wife as *mother*. So Jack thinks of the relations between his mother and father with a kind of savage black humour:

> The thing he'd never asked himself, Jack realised now, was exactly what had driven his daddy to drink in the first place. And really . . . when you came right down to what his old students had been pleased to call the nitty-gritty . . . hadn't it been the woman he was married to? A milksop sponge of a woman, always dragging silently around the house with an expression of doomed martyrdom on her face? A ball and chain around Daddy's ankle? . . . Mentally and spiritually dead, his mother had been handcuffed to his father by matrimony. Still, Daddy had tried to do right as he dragged her rotting corpse through life. (355)

What threatens Danny is *Jack's* insecure hold on the symbolic: this insecurity is expressed through his rejection of his wife, Wendy, and his failure to hold down his job as a teacher, to fill his appointed social role. Jack resists what Sartre would call the "thetic," the "real" world of propositions and action. Almost consciously he embraces the unreal, the irrational, the "sleep of reason" which, as Goya says, "breeds monsters."

Significantly, Jack has been a writer, but as *The Shining* progresses he literally begins to lose his hold on language. He finds it increasingly difficult to write, daydreams, becomes overinvolved with a kind of degraded text, a scrapbook full of old newspaper cuttings through which he searches for some kind of lost meaning. As he declines in this way, be begins to act the part of the father in an overstated way rather reminiscent of Carrie's mother: this hollow acting is reflected in Danny's nightmare dream-visions, in which he is pursued by a mysterious "shape" or "monster," wielding a mallet which echoes with a "great hollow boom." Meanwhile Danny works, patiently to master the symbolic: he is desperate to learn to read in order to decipher the riddling words which have flashed before him in his dreams:

> He hunched over the innocuous little books, his crystal radio and balsa glider on the shelf above him, *as though his life depended on learning to read*. His small face was more tense and paler than she liked. . . . He was taking it very seriously, both the reading and the workbook pages his father had made up for him every afternoon. Picture of an apple and a peach, the word *apple* written

beneath in Jack's large, neatly made printing. . . . And their son would stare from the word to the picture, his lips moving, sounding out, actually *sweating* it out. (117)

As his hold on language becomes stronger, Danny becomes better and better able to confront the nightmares which pursue him. At first he represses the meaning of his dreams—"It's like I can't remember because it's so bad I don't want to remember"—but gradually he is able to confront the dreams and relate them to through the symbolic. At the crisis of the book it is through language that he overcomes his father. As the father, transformed into a maniac figure with a swinging (phallic) mallet, looms above him, Danny has only words with which to oppose him—but words are finally enough and everything as Danny brings to the surface and into speech that which his father had forgotten:

> (you will remember what your father forgot)
> . . . Sudden triumph filled his face; the thing saw it and hesitated, puzzled
> "The boiler!" Danny screamed. "It hasn't been dumped since this morning! It's going up! It's going to explode!" (400)

Danny is now through, so to speak, his unbearably fraught passage through the Oedipus: he has, unlike his father, established a proper relationship between the pre-symbolic (imaged in the typography of the novel through everything in "the basement" including the boiler), and the symbolic. He achieves his place in the symbolic at great cost because his father has offered no stable or proper model for him. As a result, he has to split his own image of his father, blending all the beneficent aspects of his father into an image of the good father which can be split off from the crazed maniac who faces him in the final scene. The split father guarantees the healing of the split(s) in Danny, guarantees the establishment of a stable and unified self.

The Shining has a complex and shifting meaning which "is" more than the sum of its parts. Much of the power of the text derives from the fact that the images of death in it—images which form the stock-in-trade of most horror fiction—function precisely *as images*. King sees that their power lies in their ability to evoke our most secret and fundamental terrors, terrors which are *not* of death itself, but of the extinction of personality, of which death itself is an image. We may never overcome these terrors; we may remain always "overlooked" ("The Overlook" is the name of the vast hotel in which the main action of the novel takes place) by forces beyond our control, which continue to threaten our fragile, vulnerable constructions of self.

MISERY: TEXT

Misery is a highly sophisticated and self-conscious text. It constitutes an exploration of itself and an exploration of the genesis of all King's fiction, of the origins of what he calls his "Gothic" horror. The novel's protagonist is a writer (compare Jack, in *The Shining*). Paul Sheldon has written a string of best-selling detective novels featuring an aristocratic nineteenth-century Englishwoman, Misery Chastain (the name itself is a little image complex, combining the words "misery," "chastise," "chain," "stain," etc.). After a bad car accident in which he is nearly killed, Paul finds himself, by a series of bizarre coincidences, not in hospital, but locked up in the isolated house of his "number one fan," an ex-nurse, Annie Wilkes. Annie holds him as a prisoner, "caring" for him by splinting his legs in an amateurish fashion and dosing him up with illegally obtained pain-killing drugs. She then strikes a strange bargain with him. In his last "Misery" novel Paul has finally, and to his great relief, killed Misery off—he wants to get on with more "serious" writing. Annie has been waiting to read this particular "Misery" novel, and does so just after Paul has come into her power. Finding that Misery has been killed, she accuses Paul of "murder," and dictates that he shall write another novel, immediately, bringing Misery back to life. Paul is in no position to argue: he senses that the underlying threat is that of a different murder, of himself by Annie, if he does not "restore" Misery to her. Paul is thus placed in the position of literally writing for his life, a latter-day Scheherazade; all the time he is needed to write this text and tell this story, he will live–but he understands that he will die when "his tale is told" (the closing lines of King's "real" novel).

The text thus explores the relation between "misery" as a common noun (defined by King as "pain, usually lengthy and often pointless") and the generation of texts, stories. The access to misery must be there, King seems to suggest, in order for the text to be: indeed, it is indicated in the second half of the novel that Paul actually needs (and perhaps courts) the hellish circumstances in which he finds himself in order to write well, convincingly. The worse his situation becomes, the better he writes, and so, ironically, he colludes with Annie in his captivity. The writer too is a "borderline" case in the Kristevian sense, not so fixed in the symbolic as would appear—he has to have or to generate access to the pre-symbolic too, to forms of feeling which in this case are acutely painful. King's writing would seem to suggest that the production of a Gothic/horror text is connected with an ability to reach down to experience before the symbolic, "stirring up," so to speak, some of the horrors which (can) attend the birth of the self: the text works in this way as an exorcism.

The central opposition in *Misery* is between Paul and Annie: an opposition between masculine and feminine, between writer and muse. Annie is the mother; she is the monstrous feminine, the castrating female. At the very beginning of the novel we are told of her "maternal" feelings for Paul: we hear of her "maternal love and tenderness"; she is "Annie the mom." She is presented as monstrous from the opening of the novel too. She is described as an idol, and this image is developed through the novel, her implacability being stressed. She has a curious sexual quality: she is at once very feminine in the obvious physical sense, having large breasts, for example, and yet she is at the same time "defeminised" in the social-sexual sense, unsubdued and unsubduable to the feminine as it is viewed/constructed by man: "Her body was big but not generous. There was a feeling about her of clots and roadblocks rather than welcoming orifices or even open spaces, areas of hiatus." She operates as the castrating female in the most horrifying scene in the text, when she amputates Paul's foot, wielding an axe and a blow-torch. The castration image is underscored: we are told that Paul is sure, in this scene, that Annie will castrate him, and later Annie coyly confesses that she had thought of cutting off Paul's "man-gland."

There could hardly be a clearer image, then, of the feminine as monstrous. Annie is to Paul an image prompting only one response, "a feeling of unease deepening steadily toward terror." Yet Annie, like the mother, *must* exist in order for the self/the text to begin to be born, in the primary movement of abjection. Like the mother she must be there in order that she may be abjected: in *Misery* that is the role of woman; she has no other function. There are *no* positive images of the feminine in this misogynistic text. Annie is particularly closely associated with the pre-symbolic and the movement of abjection because she is herself a "borderline" case, one whose problems are situated on the borderline between neurosis and psychosis. Paul describes her in this way:

> Because of his researches for *Misery*, he had rather more than a layman's understanding of neurosis and psychosis, and he knew that although a borderline psychotic might have alternating periods of deep depression and almost aggressive cheerfulness and hilarity, the puffed and infected ego underlay all, positive that all eyes were upon him or her.

Her psychosis leads her towards self-mutilation, i.e. to a breaking-down of
the divisions between self and world, and her hold on language is also weakened; she speaks a kind of nursery English which is frighteningly at odds with
the realities of her situation and actions.

Annie and Paul have in common a skewed relation to language. Overall
they exist in a close, symbiotic relationship in which Annie acts, as we have
seen, as Paul's hellish muse, leading him back into the past and his personal
prehistory *in order that he should write*. For, although Paul has fantasies about
a miraculous escape from Annie, he knows that the only way out of the situation he is locked in is through writing: he must, as it were, write himself into
the symbolic. In this way he will gain control not only over language, but also
over plot. For "writing," in the widest sense, does not just give us control
over language as *understanding*—the kind of control Jack is seeking in *The
Shining*. "Writing" also gives us control over plot, action, endows us with the
power to intervene in the life and destiny not just of ourselves but of others
too. Paul, in bringing Misery back to life, has to find a parallel way of writ-
ing/plotting himself back to life, away from Annie. The connection between
the plotting he undertakes for *Misery's Return* and the plotting of his own
escape is underscored in the text; also, when Paul first realises that *Misery's
Return* is turning into a better novel than any of his others, a "Gothic" novel,
he notes that the book was "thus more dependent on plot than on situation.
The challenges were constant."

Paul's successful completion of the new novel occurs immediately
before the successful completion of the plot to murder Annie, the "Dragon-
lady." We may thus read our text *Misery* as signifying this: Paul, a writer, has
tried to kill "Misery," to banish misery in the sense of "lengthy pain" from
his life. He had thought that this would lead to better writing. Yet Annie's
intervention, her insistence that he should bring "Misery" back to life, and
her production of "lengthy pain" lead Paul to write a book which is better
than any of his other "Misery" novels. Paul begins to wonder whether Annie
may not have done him a favour in insisting on the resurrection of Misery,
and he reflects on his astonishing productiveness as a writer under the strin-
gent, painful conditions she has imposed. It is thus as though Paul is driven
to master the symbolic when he is impelled by fear, when he is in flight from
images and situations which recall painful experiences (usually repressed)
from the pre-symbolic, semiotic world. The text *Misery*, opening with Paul's
"second birth" after the car accident, thus has a double dimension. On one
level is the apparent text, telling of Paul's incarceration with Annie and his
eventual escape. On a second level the text constantly comments on itself,
drawing attention to the processes of its own production as a horror text as

Paul moves from the darkness of his first awakening after the accident (analogous to the "darkness" of early infancy) to the daylight clarity of his final vision and production of text and situation at the close of the book. Annie, the monstrous feminine, has acted as the necessary catalyst to bring him from the darkness of infancy (Latin *infans*, "unable to speak") to the wielding of textual power.

FEMINIST AFTERWORD: GENDER AND GENRE

Horror fiction is, primarily, produced and consumed by men. Why should this be? It would seem that the experience derived from horror fiction (as opposed to the experience of horror in "real life") is peculiarly fascinating to men, or rather to the masculine subject, i.e. the subject constituted as masculine through the particular nature of his/her experience, particularly in early childhood. For the masculine child, the movement away from the mother, expressed as it is through abjection and the passage through the Oedipus complex, seems to be more traumatic than for the feminine child. For the feminine child there remains at least a possibility of reunion with the mother through *identification*; also, the feminine subject is actively encouraged to retain links with the maternal semiotic through the cultivation of such qualities as "intuition." The masculine subject by contrast depends for his very identity on the effectiveness of his repression of the maternal semiotic and of desire for the mother.

Horror fiction is constituted of images designed precisely to stir "memories" of the early abjection of the mother and of the later traumatic passage through the Oedipus to the symbolic. As we have seen in the work of Stephen King, images of the monstrous feminine are common in horror fiction, as are images of castration, and fearful phallic power. The "horror of horror" overall, however, seems to lie in the (r)evocation of the experience of abjection. Horror fiction is dominated by those images of waste, putrefaction and decay which Kristeva associates with abjection: these are, so to speak, the staple of horror. When we think of "the horrid" we picture blood, corpses, the violation of bodily limits. Via these images horror fiction returns us to the scene of primary horror in the abjection of the mother, a scene which, however, *particularly for the masculine subject*, possesses fascination, the power of the taboo. Images of abjection lead the *masculine* subject back not only to the movement away from the mother but also to the original repressed desire for the mother, which returns with all the force of the repressed, of that which can be allowed no place in adult life.

Horror fiction thus seems to be designed to work for the masculine subject as an exorcism: it offers a way of repassing through abjection and of distancing oneself once again from the power of the mother. Horror fiction works in this sense as a kind of obverse of romance. For the feminine subject, the most painful aspect of early development is not the abjection of the mother but the movement into the masculine symbolic. It can and has been argued that romantic fiction exists precisely in order to "cover up" the painful nature of the female insertion into the symbolic/patriarchal order. Romantic fiction offers a way of "repassing" that insertion, "tricking it out" with compensatory fantasies which are gratifying to the (feminine) ego. Horror fiction, we might argue, has a similar compensatory function, giving the *masculine* subject the opportunity to revisit and to "repass" the crisis points of his early development. The masculine subject is thus allowed, via horror, to revisit forbidden realms in recompense for the day-to-day repression of certain desires. Horror fiction is, no less than romance, a genre which is tied to gender: awareness of its gender bias and of the role which it plays in social-textual terms as what Kristeva would call a "rite of defilement" is long overdue.

JEANNE CAMPBELL REESMAN

Stephen King and the Tradition of American *Naturalism* in The Shining

The Shining is no ordinary ghost story, for Stephen King is no ordinary ghost story writer. Having sold close to 100 million copies of his books, King is one of the most popular and prolific writers in the history of American fiction. Yet despite the label "popular," he is also writing in a long-standing American literary tradition that opposes a humanist world-view to a naturalist one. This conflict occupied Hawthorne, Melville, James, London, Faulkner, and Hemingway, to name a few, before King. Perhaps more than any other of King's books, *The Shining* portrays a complex psychological dilemma that, like Ahab's or Quentin Compson's, comments morally on all of our lives. King makes the vicious struggle for survival in the snowy mountains of western Colorado enacted by the Torrance family an ontological statement about our modern world. King shocks us into recognition by deftly joining our very real natural weaknesses to the supernatural devils they create—or allow to exist—and he manages to make our daily moral dilemmas reflect the large cultural questions of our contemporary world. This tendency to join the everyday to the cosmic, conscious to unconscious, light to dark, might be called (with a nod to M. H. Abrams) a "supernatural" sort of naturalism. One may clarify King's position among other American writers and describe a bit further his extraordinary contribution to American literature by reading *The Shining* as a "supernatural natural" tale of moral as well as physical survival.

As early as 1979, *Carrie*, King's first book, was said to contain "universal

From *Starmont Studies in Literary Criticism #30: The Shining Reader.* © 1990 Starmont House, Inc.

fairytale features" that indicate its debt to mainstream American folklore. It "responds to deeply rooted sexual and social anxieties" of its age; it is a "sophisticated" work that "feeds on universal myths" (Alexander 287). To an even greater degree than *Carrie, The Shining*, King's first hard-cover best-seller, combines our modern-day angst with buried archetypal fears. Through its "supernatural naturalism," it opposes these realms—and connects them at the same time. It is a novel as much concerned with social questions as it is with psychological ones, for its ghosts and ghouls symbolize the materials of the unconscious coming into conflict with the materials of a present-day personal and social reality. In *The Shining*, our civilization's agreed-upon pieties of hard work, success, and stable relationships are challenged, and, in Jack Torrance's case, self-destruct, when confronted with truths of the unconscious. On one level, *The Shining* is a naturalistic pathology of mental illness; on another, it could be seen as a battle between two opposed spirits in humankind. It is a "Young Goodman Brown" of our day, in which the naturalist hero is destroyed by his refusal, or inability, to admit the awful power of that "other" world of the unconscious.

Authors who focus on King's chosen opposition of values, Hawthorne, Poe, Norris, Dreiser, and London, are most frequently mentioned by himself and by his critics. The settings in his novels clearly reflect particular American traditions, such as the Hawthornian device of using the woods as a place of moral choice. Indeed, King heavily favors the New England setting. In *The Shining*, one also recognizes the importance of the characteristic American westward movement on Jack's part to try a new beginning. The pastoral setting at the novel's conclusion certainly suggests the old American tradition of the pastoral ideal, as in Thoreau, Hawthorne, and Twain. King shares the American writer's suspicion of machines in the pastoral landscape; in *Pet Sematary*, an oil company truck smashes Gage Creed on the new highway, and in the wonderfully odd little story, a very early one, "The Mangler," a laundry machine becomes possessed by a murderous demon.

King has modernized the genre of horror fiction as he has Americanized it. Languishing since the days of H. P. Lovecraft and other late nineteenth-century ghost story writers, supernatural fiction was revived by King—and revitalized through his portraits of contemporary life: his vampires and ghosts intrude on a world of school lunches to he packed, beds to be made, love affairs to be pursued, professions to be attended to. King works with the "real stuff" of the world, as Peter Straub notes; his characters are never stereotypes, and King is fond of all of them (Underwood 9). Don Herron agrees: "Horror springs in King's stories from contemporary social reality, and I'd say it is this quality more than any other which has made King a bestseller" (Underwood 92). And King brings the supernatural into our everyday world without detracting from its eeriness. His vampires are vampires and will not be explained away. King's supernaturalism critiques our naturalism by challenging all of our usual assumptions, even about ghost stories.

In asking the questions he does, King is pursuing the American tradition of a hermeneutics of doubt. What is the modern, declassed, autonomous American to do? this tradition seems to ask. King portrays his characters' moral decisions within an American conflict of choices that largely involves our contemporary success, for we have managed today more than ever to translate survival into material—i.e., monetary—success. The Russian serf or French peasant of the past was not so concerned with such a "success"— America invented that for the common man. King connects our naturalistic drive for "success" with our deepest doubts about such designs of power and wealth; he proposes a competing reality with his phantoms and demons. They challenge our naturalism, yes, but of course our naturalism has given them credence. King's work exists at what he repeatedly calls "the place where the horror story so often hits home," our ". . . central switching point somewhere inside, a transformer, maybe, where the wires leading from . . . [our] two masks connect" ("Foreword," *Night Shift* xviii).

In *The Shining*, writer Jack Torrance admires the naturalist writers, as King himself does (albeit with a more critical eye): he calls Frank Norris's *McTeague* a great novel, even comparing his father to *McTeague*'s dentist, "handcuffed to a dead man in the wasteland" (379). In an essay titled "On Becoming a Brand Name" King also compares himself to Norris; he says that like Norris, he has always wanted to "respond to critics, in my own mind if nowhere else, by saying: "What do I care for your opinion? I never buckled. I told the truth'" (Underwood 16). But even more than the connection to Norris, it seems to me, King evokes Jack London's naturalism because he invokes London's accompanying attack on it. London's work both exemplifies and questions naturalism as a philosophy of life, for London experienced a shift similar to King's: in his career he moves toward a call for integration of opposite values, and his skepticism about any "ism" in itself is one of his most distinguishing American characteristics. Interestingly, for a comparison with King, the so-called naturalist London's last and greatest works, his South Seas stories, are overtly indebted to Jung's ideas about the human psyche, particularly the necessity of recognizing the power of the unconscious.

In a 1980 interview, King confesses that "'I lean towards all those naturalistic books . . . where everything just goes to hell.'" When he taught creative writing, he had his students read naturalist fiction, particularly James M. Cain's *Double Indemnity* and David Morrell's *First Blood*. He explains that young writers need to know the importance of realism, and this he defines in terms of character, which he calls the most important ingredient of a story: "'I think the characters should be real, and they shouldn't do anything in the course of the story that is false. . . . Characters should be able to move on their own.'" He likes *The Shining* best of all his works, he says, precisely because "'all the characters seem to do that.'" In horror fiction, King says, "'you don't get scared of monsters; you get scared for people'" (Janeczko 9-10). Such a realistic emphasis upon the characters actually works to *replace* naturalism with humanistic values because of the focus on the mystery of individual human identity. King sounds like the great humanist writer Faulkner as he describes the individuality and autonomy of his characters, and his moral messages over and over again seem to echo Faulkner's insistence on portraying in his work "love, honor, pity, pride, compassion, and sacrifice" as the great truths of the heart. Thus naturalism in King, as in the work of London and others, is actually a vehicle for humanism—it is offered only to be replaced, as it is for the protagonist on London's "The Water Baby" or for the correspondent in Stephen Crane's "The Open Boat." To this list of American writers whose naturalism is "compromised" by humanism, I would also add Kate Chopin and Ernest Hemingway. In *The Awakening*, Chopin purports to write a realistic novel about the position of women in late nineteenth-century America, but compromises her naturalism, best expressed through Dr. Mandelet, with a disturbing romanticism. And Hemingway causes us in *The Sun Also Rises* to question his main character's naturalism with a subtle pattern of undercutting that philosophy in his portrait of the barrenness of the post-World-War-I world-view.

In response to an interviewer's question, "What makes a good horror story?", King states:

> I think it's important that the reader knows that the writer is not playing. There isn't going to be a Hardy Boys story where everybody survives at the end and there never was any real danger. I think that you know you've grown up when you say to yourself, "I don't want to read any more Supermans because he is the man of steel and he's always going to get out of this jam, whatever it is, and nothing serious is really going to happen to him.

To the next question, "How does Stephen King see the world?", King responds:

> I'm not very optimistic about the world. I think that shows in the

books. The books that influenced me the most when I was growing up were by people like Thomas Hardy, Frank Norris, and Theodore Dreiser. All those people of the naturalistic school believed once you pull out one rock, it's sort of a relentless slide into the pit. I don't think that any thinking person can look at the world in our society and see anything very secure. The whole situation is bad. I try to do as well by my family as I can. I try to raise my kids to be good people. You know. The good guys. That sort of thing. But I don't think the future looks very bright. (Janeczko 10)

I take these observations of King's as a justification for his "supernatural naturalism." The profound dualism in his attitude toward naturalism is what allows him to examine its attractions and failures. In much of his work he seems to be suggesting that one must first realize one exists in a naturalistic universe, and then give up that realization in favor of a more expanded sense of reality that includes the supernatural as well. Although that supernatural is usually presented in a horrifying, even inhuman manner, it paradoxically points towards more traditional value systems. When the characters of *It*, for example, reassemble in their hometown of Derry to fight the evil that has revealed itself there, they are acting morally—and some of them quite unconsciously—to face evil. Their behavior is an illustration on a larger scale of Wendy and Danny Torrance's family dilemma in *The Shining*.

King's characters get into trouble when they will not open up their minds to extra-normal phenomena that call for moral choices. Indeed, his suspense is largely due to the characters' reluctance to face up to such possibilities. The old horror movie trick of a disbelieving hero's sudden and long-delayed confrontation with complete evil is employed by King to create, I think, a greater effect than just suspense. He is using the supernatural to intrude on our everyday awareness of ourselves in order to shock us into awareness of a deeper moral reality than that to which we are accustomed. It is often observed that King appeals to children's sense of reality (much like Stephen Spielberg) rather than to adults'; like Flannery O'Connor, he recaptures this crazy world in his fiction in order to break down our adult complacencies and our resistance to unconscious feelings and fears, as well as to invoke our collective sense of right and wrong. King's characters, when they succeed in being aware of the evil around them, echo Henry James's advice: "be one of those people on whom nothing is lost." In King's work, then, the reader finds an ironic set of oppositions: supernaturalism (horror) vs. naturalism (reality), and good (unconscious knowledge) vs. evil (conscious knowledge). The first opposition causes the second to occur as a moral choice for a character, and only very morally astute characters can perceive the truth phrased as a reversal of everyday suppositions about the primacy of consciousness and rationality. When the supernatural upsets "reality," the characters' naturalism, sometimes translated into survivalism, is usually not enough to sustain them or their families. What is called for is a Jungian integration, a rebalancing of "natural" and "supernatural" elements of reality. King's characters' confrontations with evil suggest those in James's "The Turn of the Screw" in that what is symbolized is the Shadow, the unfamiliar and hence frightening part of the psyche. The unconscious must be confronted, Jung suggests, for it is only frightening when it is unaddressed, as becomes clear with Jack and Danny Torrance's opposite reactions to the evil of the Overlook Hotel and in their own family.

King's dualism also means that evil can prevail, that victories over evil are fragile. Yet one really cannot stop trying to be one of the "good guys," and most of King's characters keep trying to do just that until the last extremity, behaving much better than we might expect. Many of them succeed in defeating the forces of evil precisely because of their determination to be "good guys." Deborah Notkin feels that the overwhelming impression to be gained from reading King's books is that "the kinks and the sadists are the exception, not the rule." In King's novels, "the average person is reasonably honest, caring and upright, and can be relied upon in most circumstances—not a fashionable concept, these days, but one which has obvious attractions for contemporary audiences" (Underwood 152). In a hermeneutic circle, so very like other major American writers, King moves from tentative statement to tentative statement, asking us to believe that evil exists, is a threat, and calls for moral action without the assurance even of survival, let alone victory. In comparison, James's compromised conclusions and negative silences, like Faulkner's suspense by omission and disunified structures, insist, with many others, on a hermeneutic view of "truth." Like them, King gives us no neat answers in the end, no gathered suspects or lucid detective to explain things to everyone.

Douglas E. Winter characterizes King's dualism by stressing that "the tale of terror is an inextricable element of the human condition—a guilty fascination with darkness and irrationality, with the potential for expanding human consciousness and perception, and with the understanding of our mortality and our universe." Winter quotes D. H. Lawrence on Poe's fiction: "'it is lurid and melodramatic, but it is true.'" Like Poe, King suggests "a dark truth that we all suspect: that rationality and order are facades, mere illusions of control imposed upon a reality of chaos." Winter refers to "The

Boogeyman" as a story that most clearly defines the shattering of boundaries between the supernatural and the empirical, "offering the chilling possibility that there is no difference" (Underwood 209, 211). Another illustration comes from *'Salem's Lot*: Ben Mears, kneeling for the first time in the confessional just before going out to do real battle with real vampires, notices "something in the corner of the confessional," an empty Junior Mints box "fallen from the pocket of some little boy, perhaps." Its reality is "undeniable": "the cardboard was real and tangible under his fingers. This nightmare was real" (325). And earlier in the book, King makes it clear in Chapter 10 that "the town knew about darkness" before the advent of the vampires. In a set-piece of several pages, King's narrator details the inner desires and secrets—many very ugly ones—of the townspeople of 'Salem's Lot. He concludes the chapter: "These are the town's secrets, and some will later be known and some will never be known. The town keeps them all with the ultimate poker face. The town cares for devil's work no more than it cares for God's or man's. It knew darkness. And darkness was enough" (208–12).

Americans found darkness too in their search for light; as they conquered a continent they created the very type of imperialism they had sought to escape. Winter comments: "We see ourselves as independent and democratic, even though two political machines control the electoral process, many of us never vote, and the spirit of independence is likeliest to be shown by dissent." According to him,

> our heroes typically have been cowboys and rugged individualists—only recently have we embraced our martyrs. We think of ourselves as non-violent and peace-loving, but we cannot successfully regulate, let alone ban, the sale of handguns. We have conquered ruthlessly when our destiny has been challenged, and we have found war to be a cleansing experience. Our science created the atomic bomb to end a great war, and we must live in its shadow evermore.

Because of all this, "we pursue happiness, believe in progress, materialism and the infallibility of science, but we doubt our success, our power, ourselves. As we watch the evening news, we begin to question the validity of the engine of progress." Our society is in a precarious position "principally because of our misguided belief in the divinity of civilization and technology." And, Winter concludes, as King's works make very clear, our doubts are intensifying (Underwood 215–16). But this doubt is healthy: George A. Romero, director of *Creepshow*, claims that King's work shows how those conflicting emotions we all seek to repress eventually catch up with us, "and a good thing, too, because if we try to survive an emotional bankruptcy we'll go insane, like sleepers deprived of dreams." We must surrender every now and then, and "that surrender makes us feel good. It confirms our humanity" (Underwood 254).

The darkness present from the beginning in the Torrance family is enough to destroy all of them, just as Wendy's and Danny's hidden moral strength proves to be enough to save some of them. It is an obvious response to *The Shining* to point out that Jack Torrance hardly needs ghosts and evil topiary animals to complete his breakdown—he will, it seems clear early on, accomplish that on his own. His family history, his alcoholism, his attitude towards Wendy and Danny are all in place before he ever encounters super-natural agents of evil, but their presence presents an opportunity for moral choice which Jack tries very hard, until it is too late, to avoid. *The Shining* starkly outlines the evil and danger in our daily lives. But to stop here would he to miss the more subtle point the book makes: So what? What will a given person do when confronted with evil? Jack may be truly helpless in the face of Lloyd the bartender and Grady the waiter, but the reader quickly finds in another character a strong contrast to Jack's pattern of choices: Wendy. In her agonizing moral decisions about what to do with Jack after he has gone berserk, Wendy demonstrates to the reader that his succumbing to evil is not necessarily the only possible response to evil. Wendy responds to the call for survival, it is true, and yet she does more than that. She thinks for herself, but she bases her decisions on what she believes to be the right thing to do, not the selfish thing. In a sense, like Marlow's watching Mr. Kurtz's slide into "the horror," *The Shining* is Wendy's and Danny's story of self-discovery fol-lowing upon the disintegration of Jack. In the end, they will be all right, but that is no accident. They fought for what was right, against horrible odds. Jack fought for himself, in the face of all that is right, and his tragedy, if there can he said to be one, is that he knew it.

The Shining contains some of King's darkest personal introspections: speaking of his stay in Colorado in 1974, during the writing of *The Shining*, King comments that the "countryside" of that novel was "dim and drear." It "seemed to be primarily a story about a miserable, damned man who is very slowly losing his grip on life, a man who is being driven to destroy all the things he loves." He connects Jack to his own earlier experiences as a writer struggling to provide for his family: "I seemed to be back in that trailer in Hermon, Maine, with no company but the buzzing sound of the snowmo-biles and my own fears—fears that my chance to be a writer had come and gone, fears that I had gotten into a teaching job that was completely wrong for me, fears most of all that my marriage was edging onto marshy ground and that there might be quicksand anyplace ahead" (Underwood 35–36).

The plot of *The Shining* moves along because of naturalistic motivations: Jack's anxieties about his job, a very mundane concern, is a very real one to everybody in the story. Jack makes his choices based solely on his hopes to succeed in his career. He feels as though he "'can't win,'" but he is willing to keep struggling. When his wife questions his repairing the elevator, he replies: "'It . . .Wendy, it's my job'" (299). And later, he thinks madly to himself, blood and destruction all around him, "He would show them that . . . that he . . . that he was of managerial timber!" (415). Jack's first thought in the book, indeed, the first line in the book, conveys his attitude toward his potential employer: "Officious little prick."

Naturalism thus immediately suggests itself as a world-view when the reader is confronted with Jack's anger, violence, alcoholism, and failure—in addition to Wendy's initial weakness. This combination of character attributes, all in place by the end of Chapter 2, seems inexorably dire. For the Torrances, the facts of their lives fly in the face of their hopes—horror inevitably results when their fears about their problems are confirmed in reality. The Torrances live "in grief and loss for the past, and terror of the future" (15); for them, the Overlook is "an inhuman place that makes human monsters" (143). Jack's answer to this is naturalism, but he dies by that code. Ironically, it allows him to avoid facing the reality of the problems he has. For Jack physical realities, boilers, wasps' nests, keeping the hotel properly maintained are the most important concerns, and the boiler is no ghost. It is an old boiler, and it will blow up if it is not tended. But in *The Shining*, it becomes the role of readers, aided by Wendy and Danny, to admit the actuality and the danger of the "other" reality Jack tries so hard to ignore: the boiler inside of him.

Despite bloated ladies in bathtubs and murderous gangsters, Wendy fears Jack more than anything else, specifically that part of Jack that does, as Danny calls it, "the bad thing": "A distant part of her thought that the worst thing was that it had all come back to this, she and her drunken husband" (367). Jack describes his illness this way: "There was a broken switch somewhere inside, or a circuit breaker that didn't work, and he had been propelled down the chute willy-nilly, slowly at first, then accelerating . . ." (109). But his descent into madness is more mystifying to him than to readers, who are aware that his naturalism does not provide him with any way of preventing the denigration of his faculties. When he frantically and stupidly calls Ullman, for example, he really can't say why he does it. When he first becomes interested in the scrapbooks in the basement, he replies to Wendy's query about his interest with evasions only because he himself is out of control.

For much of the story dazed by the presence of evil, Danny engages in a constant struggle with a choice to believe or not believe in ghosts: he keeps telling himself it's nothing, it's his imagination, just as Jack does with the topiary animals. But Danny and Wendy soon take seriously the threat of the hotel, while Jack succumbs to it. Danny's childhood fears become more real than his adult father's notions of the world. The clock Danny fears is a naturalistic symbol whose horror he recognizes: it embodies an inexorable quality of doom that refers as much to Jack's progressive alienation as it does to the witching hour in the haunted hotel. The motif of "unmasking," connected like the clock to Poe's "The Masque of the Red Death," accompanies the clock as a naturalist symbol. What is *really* real, it suggests, *will* be made known. The greeds, lusts, perversions, and murders of the hotel guests down through the years occurred in this naturalist universe. Other naturalist details in the story include the wind, the snow, the carefully stocked kitchen, the action of defending oneself physically, the isolation of man against nature, and of course the cold.

King often uses juxtaposition to convey naturalism and its limitations: he places side by side personal, inner trauma with a hard fact of nature. For example, Jack, being shown for the first time the "musty-smelling" boiler room by the attendant, Watson, remarks the boiler's pilot light, a "steady blue-white jet hissing steadily upward channeled destructive force." But the "key word," he thinks, is "destructive and not channeled: if you stuck your hand in there, the barbecue would happen in three quick seconds." Aside from the question of why he thinks of sticking his hand into the flame, what follows this observation is telling. Jack recalls the haunting accusation from his past, "Lost your temper." Then, one more line down, "(Danny, are you all right?)." Another such juxtaposition occurs when Jack thinks that he is getting better because he successfully deals with the wasps: "it was possible to graduate from passive to active, to take the thing that had once driven you nearly to madness as a neutral prize of no more than occasional academic interest. And if there was a place where the thing could be done, this was surely it." But the next, and concluding paragraph of the chapter reads: "He went down the ladder to get the bug bomb. They would pay. They would pay for stinging him" (116). His petulance compromises his naturalism. Predictably, Jack later sees, with horror, with "an almost superstitious dread," that the wasps come back. "He had killed the wasps but they had come back" (135).

Naturalistic physical details often stand out amid the building psychic horror of the novel: when Jack checks the snowmobile's battery, the reader is relieved by the sudden sharp sensory detail: "there had been a crackle of electricity and a small odor of ozone . . ." (281). King is in fact a master of naturalistic detail, and that huge wasps' nest is one of the best examples: "You might just charge right off the edge of the roof while you were trying to get away from them," Jack thinks. "All from those little things, the biggest of them only half the length of a pencil stub" (108). We are told that Jack had "unwittingly stuck his hand into The Great Wasps' Nest of Life" (110). Yet this naturalistic fact, like many others in the story, becomes a symbol that works against the naturalism of the novel.

Such symbology occurs in a self-conscious literary context. The way alternating chapters are told from different characters' points of view questions "facts," or absolute truths. This interpretive bent narratively defeats a single-minded naturalistic reading by offering the human imagination as a key element in survival, more powerful, in the end, than cunning, "rational" self-preservation. Even the poetic repetition of certain lines in the story works against naturalism, as it does in Crane's "The Open Boat": "Come out and take your medicine," "You will remember what your father forgot," or "Just close your eyes and it will be gone." The repeated lines suggest an artistic imagination on the part of the author that warns us against characters like Jack. Similarly, literary and Biblical references tend to work against naturalism for the same reasons as repetition. They allude to a world of values where everyday survival is interpreted through art. The Torrances are, like Christ in the wilderness, shown the kingdoms of the earth spread out before them: "The whole valley floor was spread out below them, the slopes that they had climbed in the laboring bug falling away with such dizzying suddenness that she knew to look down there for too long would bring on nausea . . ." (63). The poems and songs used as epigraphs and in text also contribute to the book's poetry of the imagination. Goya's remark, "the sleep of reason breeds monsters," prefaces the novel.

Accordingly, King's naturalistic details do not merely enjoin rotting flesh or heads split in two. He sees things as we really might see them, thinks about them as we really do. For example, he tells us that when Jack sees "the peculiar angle Danny's forearm had to his elbow" he thinks that "no arm was meant to hang quite that way in a world of normal families" (17). As he does here, King almost never fails to accompany a physical descriptive detail with an interpretation of it. Indeed, most of King's naturalistic details, when examined closely, reveal a latent symbology that transcends naturalism. For example, even an overtly naturalistic reference or descriptive detail betrays "supernatural naturalism": Wendy looks at the Colorado mountains early in the novel and thinks, "They were beautiful mountains but they were hard.

She did not think they would forgive many mistakes. An unhappy foreboding rose in her throat. Further west in the Sierra Nevada the Donner Party had become snowbound and had resorted to cannibalism to stay alive. The mountains did not forgive many mistakes" (62). Here the operative word is the repeated "forgive." Even though the idea being expressed is naturalistic, King's constant use of such language when referring to these details makes the point that in spite of all of nature's "hardness," people will go on thinking as people think, that is, they will think of mountains as not "forgiving" them. Such an attitude on Wendy's part concerning the rights and wrongs of earthly relations fits into King's pattern in other novels of making moral choice the center of his stories. For example, the Wendigo in *Pet Sematary* is much less interesting than the main character's struggles with his choices between good and evil. By the time we actually see the Wendigo (the required "BEM"), the story is over.

In certain respects, as I suggested earlier, the story is over in *The Shining* after a few chapters. Jack's prognosis is easy to make; his pathologies have their own logic. What becomes interesting, aside from those awfully scary hedge animals and hotel guests, is the question of what Wendy will do. In spite of Danny's central role, it is Wendy who must make the crucial decisions. What choices will she make? Will she choose to survive, and if she does, what will that mean? The importance of moral choice is driven home once more in the conclusion when Hallorann is nearly tempted in the storage building to lapse into the hotel's evil charms. He makes what can only be described as a moral choice—not to succumb. And the ending leaves Danny's and Wendy's futures open.

Early in *The Shining*, Wendy observes Danny out on the curb waiting for his father to come home, a very natural thing for a small boy to do; she does not observe, of course, the waking nightmare of gore and death going on in Danny's mind. This passage is an excellent example of how King succeeds by incorporating the supernatural into the everyday. But King even more insistently valorizes the supernatural at the expense of the natural in *The Shining*. The supernatural becomes the vehicle for moral choice, neither good nor evil in itself, but generally turned to evil because of people's moral lapses. The vampires of *'Salem's Lot* furnish a strong comparison to Jack in *The Shining*. What do vampires want? Power, eternal life, adulation, just like Jack. And the characters of the stories in *Night Shift* immediately strike one as suffering from very similar drives and desires: money, control, power. Jack Torrance wants one thing that symbolizes all of this: career success. King repudiates such "survivalism" through Wendy and Danny, and through the example of the laid-hack Hallorann, who more than anyone demonstrates that life holds more than just "success." This point King makes not with more traditional dilemmas, such as served Austen or Thackeray, but with horror.

King suggests that the act of *recognizing* "horrors" in everyday life is itself the basis of moral choice. When Jack thinks of his alcoholism, he recognizes it as an "emotional alcoholism" long before a physical one, "but it didn't much matter to him if the root causes were interrelated or separate, sociological or psychological or physiological. He had had to deal with the results . . ." (110). What is going on is real, and that is the point Jack misses. Poor Danny hopes that what he sees are "just like pictures in a book. Some pictures were scary, but they couldn't hurt you. They . . . couldn't . . . hurt you" (94), but he learns differently. Jacks' naturalism is no match for his own or the other reality of the pictures. And Jack fails in all his responses to a complex reality.

The moral questions in *The Shining* are quite explicit, and they are representative of all of our questions: "When you unwitting stuck your hand into the wasps' nest, you hadn't made a covenant with the devil to give up your civilized self with its trappings of love and respect and honor. It just happened to you. Passively, with no say, you ceased to be a creature of the mind and became of creature of the nerve endings; from college-educated man to wailing ape in five easy seconds" (110). But this is followed by: "He thought of George Hatfield" (110), indicating the importance of Jack's own unresolved moral dilemma with this student. To Jack's weakness the reader contrasts Wendy's own speculations on what one must do as she later faces her choices.

Jack is the lone naturalist of the book's main characters, and, alone, he of course loses. Naturalism as a philosophy of life does not get him very far in either his parenting, his marriage, or his career. His later rationalization about why he has to kill Wendy and Danny involve only one thing: his survival. Jack's philosophy is "Living by your wits is always knowing where the wasps are" (378), but of course this fails him. His egoism makes him believe the hotel wants him more than it wants Danny, and through this sin of pride the hotel nearly gets them all: "That was foolish, of course—why would they want the son when they could have the father?—but employers often had foolish ideas; and that was the condition that had been made" (380).

And Jack does have a struggle: after his night thoughts of murdering his wife and child, he sees Danny out playing in the snow and wonders to himself, "(What in the name of God were you thinking of?) The answer came back with no pause. (Me. I was thinking of me.) (278). He thinks of the physical evidence of the hotel's evil: "The puffed circles of bruises around Danny's neck. The twinkling, half-seen bottles in the deserted lounge. The radio. The dreams. The scrapbook he had found in the cellar" (280). But he finds it easier to continue in his denial: "And yet, through it all he hadn't felt like a son of a bitch" (110). Neither emotional nor physical evidence can stop him.

In the pastoral fishing scene at the end there is an idyllic conclusion to the nightmare. Hallorann gives Danny some advice:

> "The world's a hard place, Danny. It don't care. It don't hate you and me, but it don't love us, either. Terrible things can happen in the world, and they're things no one can explain. Good people die in bad, painful ways and leave the folks that love them all alone. Sometimes it seems like it's only the bad people who stay healthy and prosper. The world don't love you but your momma does and so do I. You're a good boy. You grieve for your daddy, and when you feel you have to cry over what happened to him, you go into a closet or under your covers and cry until it's all out of you again. That's what a good son has to do. But see that you get on. That's your job in this hard world, to keep your love alive and see that you get on, no matter what. Pull your act together and just go on." (446).

King's moral position here suggests *Moby Dick*—the whale and its interpreter are still at sea in the end, and there is no final defeat or victory. To a moral pragmatist in the American vein, there are always other voyages, and other moral decisions. But I wish to return, in conclusion, to the comparison with Jack London: London and King were and are incredibly popular, prolific, and talented writers who churned out good and bad work and at the same time have profoundly addressed issues central to American thought. Both are spurned by most critics—and neither needs them to sell books. Both use writers as characters quite frequently. Both have become heroes in their own right, with the concomitant fan clubs and newsletters. Their readers cannot get enough of them: well-thumbed copies of their books are the rule. Their political horror novels, *The Iron Heel* and *The Dead Zone*, are similar, as are their published writings about their roles as writers: although King lacks London's socialist politics, his comments in interviews and fiction powerfully describe the contemporary social and political reality in his novels. Both write influenced by naturalism and set stories in the real world; both write adventure stories, but, using naturalism as a tradition, they critique it to make it more complex and interesting in their "supernatural natural" tales. Both use a sensationalistic genre to make their fame, but chafe at it too. And that they present a naturalism undercut by humanism and moralism, I think, helps to explain their popularity as well as their place in American literature.

Both King's and London's characters undertake Jungian night journeys of self-discovery. That London's White Silence of the Klondike wasteland is replaced by King's Mr. Barlow and Wendigo and It does not alter the similarity of their characters' situations: survival. But neither writer stops there. As Melville uses the whale as an archetypal symbol for the mysteries of the knowledge of the self, London reinterprets his earlier naturalism of the Klondike tales with his late South Seas fiction, redirecting his heroes' struggles from the outer environment to the inner. King's heroes encounter this same struggle through their creator's symbology of Goodness and Evil in the form of supernatural agents.

Surely it is obvious that America is experiencing a resurgence of naturalism today, both in "low" and "high" culture. From *First Blood* to *Full Metal Jacket*, the media is awash in survivalism, chauvinism, brutality. But King's transformation of naturalism into "supernatural naturalism" both feeds on and attacks our "neonaturalism" today, as London's did in his day. King's incredibly popular horror fiction is in certain very important respects a moral fiction that addresses contemporary Americans more seriously than many of his readers perhaps recognize. Our fears about survival have unbalanced us, King suggests, and they come home to haunt us in unexpected ways. Talented suspense artist that he is, King, fittingly, maintains that quality of unexpectedness in his use of traditional American literary naturalism.

I think the important thing to stress about Stephen King, after we have recognized and described the complex use of American naturalism in his works, is that he does not come to his success in a vacuum. He is very talented, he is more complex and interesting than literary critics would like to admit and, at his best, he addresses widely shared fears and desires about the place of modern human beings in their world. That he is part of the American tradition of questioning our "natural" realities and then warning us about our responses is one more reason to read him. The first, of course, is that he is a consummate artist who writes stories about complex, believable people. That really is enough.

KATHERINE K. GOTTSCHALK

Stephen King's Dark and Terrible Mother, Annie Wilkes

What makes Stephen King's novels so engrossing? For many readers (including me) King is enthralling because he terrifies us with our own seemingly normal world—a world in which, just as we suspected all along, horrifying supernatural forces turn out to be at work. With *Misery*, however, King sets aside supernatural forces and terrifies us just as thoroughly with natural ones. This time he embodies our ancient, archetypal fears in a one-time nurse, country neighbor, and Good Samaritan, Annie Wilkes.

King has observed that horror story writers such as himself write about deep fears, the ones people usually don't talk about. "Horror appeals to us because it says, in a symbolic way, things we would be afraid to say right out straight . . . it offers us a chance to exercise . . . emotions which society demands we keep closely in hand. " What is he himself afraid of? More than of death, he says, he is afraid of writer's block; and not surprisingly, King regularly confronts this and other writers' nightmares in his novels. In *Misery* Paul Sheldon, a historical-romance novelist, resolves some traumatizing questions about creativity: Can he keep writing, and what will he write? What kind of writer is he? Is he a serious writer to be taken seriously by serious critics in serious journals? Sheldon is forced to face and resolve these issues by his "number-one fan," Annie Wilkes.

Why does King choose "Annie" as the means for Paul's experience? In King's novels as in many conventional male lives, a nice woman often supports the male writer through dark times. As Adrienne Rich and countless others have observed, women have always served as "the painter's model and

From *The Anna Book: Searching for Anna in Literary History*. © 1992 Mickey Pearlman.

the poet's muse, . . . as comforter, nurse, cook, bearer of his seed, secretarial assistant, and copyist of manuscripts." Male artists have relied on this seemingly benign feminine force. But as a writer of horror stories, King imagines the worst that may be hiding behind the seemingly benign and commonplace, and so in *Misery* King doesn't simply elaborate on what bad luck it is to have overly enthusiastic fans and on how hard it is to be a writer, especially of bestsellers. Rather, he turns into terror some commonplace notions about women and writers—the notion, for instance, that female fans adore you; that mothers and other nice motherly women take care of you and encourage you to write; that women act as muses; that they nurture you physically and emotionally. In *Misery*, then, King embodies a writer's fears about himself as a writer and about the continuation of his creativity in a richly elaborated and horrific "muse," in a psychotic woman, Annie Wilkes. King's Annie resonates with the dark side of the ancient Great Goddess or Earth Mother, the Dark and Terrible Mother, and with the threatening aspects of such descendants as the fearsome Near Eastern goddess, Anath, the Greek Artemis (Goddess Anna), and the Roman Di-ana. The latter two "Anna" goddesses emerge tamed in Christianity as St. Anne, Mother of Mary, with whom Annie Wilkes shows primarily ironic resemblances.

A quick review of *Misery* for the uninitiated (and don't rely on the movie version): Paul Sheldon is a successful writer of eight historical-romance novels featuring his extremely popular heroine Misery Chastain. We learn that he had grown truly tired to death of Misery and finally killed her off in the last of the series, *Misery's Child*. Since publishing *Misery's Child* he has completed the manuscript of a novel with serious literary pretensions, *Fast Cars*. Enter Annie Wilkes, a retired registered nurse who since early adolescence has been successfully murdering people she doesn't like. Annie rescues Paul from a car wreck caused by his drunken driving at the start of a trip out West to make a fresh beginning. As his self-proclaimed number-one (insane) fan she secrets him to her house, where she begins to read his one-and-only manuscript copy of the new novel. She dislikes it and resumes her reading of *Misery's Child*, only to discover that in it Misery dies. She insists that Paul burn the manuscript of *Fast Cars* and return to Misery, to bring her back to life. Under Annie's close supervision, Paul's writing of *Misery's Return* begins. When he finishes the novel, about which he has now grown enthusiastic, he pretends (to Annie's horror) to burn the manuscript in order to attack and kill her. Finally rescued he returns to writing; *Misery's Return* will be a best-seller.

King's full-page epigraph for *Misery* displays just two words: "goddess" and "Africa." In early societies the ultimate female deity always "represented the principle of creativity and of power over both life and death." Erich Neumann has described some of the darker characteristics of the Archetypal Feminine, the Great Mother:

> The dark half of the black-and-white cosmic egg representing the Archetypal Feminine engenders terrible figures that manifest the black, abysmal side of life and the human psyche. Just as world, life, nature, and soul have been experienced as a generative and nourishing, protecting and warming Femininity, so their opposites are also perceived in the image of the Feminine: death and destruction, danger and distress, hunger and nakedness, appear as helplessness in the presence of the Dark and Terrible Mother.
>
> Thus the womb of the earth becomes the deadly devouring maw of the underworld and beside the fecundated womb and the protecting cave of earth and mountain gapes the abyss of hell, the dark hole of the depths, the devouring womb of the grave and of death, of darkness without light, of nothingness. For this woman who generates life and all living things on earth is the same who takes them back into herself, who pursues her victims and captures them with snare and net. Disease, hunger, hardship, war above all, are her helpers, and among all peoples the goddesses of war and the hunt express man's experience of life as a female exacting blood. (*GM* 149)

Characteristics of the dark and terrible goddess reappear in Anath, in Artemis/Diana—and in Annie Wilkes. Near Eastern Anath/Anat, for instance, was "lady of Birth and Death." Each year she killed Mot, who represented death or sterility, in order to save Baal, the god of fertility. Mot did not fare well at the hands of Anath: "Like the harvested grain, he was cut with a sickle, beaten with a flail, ground in a mill, and scattered in pieces over the fields by his Goddess, Anat [Anatha]. . . . After each of his annual ceremonial 'deaths' he was always resurrected by the Goddess" (*EMS* 679). She was "a dread Goddess" (*EMS* 58): "Anath's capacity to curse and kill made even the Heavenly Father [El] afraid of her. When El seemed reluctant to do her bidding, she threatened to smash his head and cover his gray hair and beard with gore. He hastily gave her everything she asked, saying, 'Whoever hinders thee will be crushed'" (*EMS* 31). Greek Artemis or Goddess Anna was a moon goddess, mother of creatures. "Yet she was also the Huntress, killer of the very creatures she brought forth. In Sparta her name was given as Artamis, 'Cutter,' or 'Butcher.' . . . Her Huntress aspect was another form of the destroying Crone or waning moon" (*EMS* 58). Greek Artemis was, of course, Roman Di-ana—"'Queen of Heaven,' Roman name for the Triple Goddess as (1) Lunar Virgin, (2) Mother of Creatures, and (3) the Huntress (Destroyer)" (*EMS* 233).

It doesn't take long to find dark reverberations of the Great Goddess/Anath/Artemis in King's Annie Wilkes. Paul Sheldon notices immediately and repeatedly that he has been imprisoned in the world of a woman who resembles a goddess or some stone idol in a novel. Looking at Annie blush girlishly, he thinks, *"That's what it would look like . . . if you built a furnace inside the mouth of one of those idols in the H. Rider Haggard stories. That is what it would look like at night."* A mouth that swallows men up, a night ride into the underworld—Paul finds himself in threatening feminine spaces: While the vessel and the house are symbols of the positive nourishing side of woman (*GM* 153), the "[g]ate, door, gully, ravine, abyss are the symbols of the feminine earthwomb; they are the numinous places that mark the road into the mythical darkness of the underworld" (*GM* 170). Paul awakens from gray mists of unconsciousness in a small bedroom. He can't get out of this room, and when he finally does manage to maneuver his wheelchair out the bedroom door, he can't get out of the house; to be safe he must return voluntarily to the bedroom and lock himself in. The room into which Annie locks him is a place of both birth and death: In it he nearly dies, and in it the five lives created in *Fast Cars* die when he burns the manuscript. In this room he also writes his ninth (a birth number) and best Misery book ever, *Misery's Return*; in this room he both is "'reborn'" in an infantilized state from his nearly fatal crash and experiences a major rebirth in his understanding of himself as a writer. He realizes that not *Fast Cars* but *Misery's Return* is his best book, the one in which there is creative force; he discovers and accepts his limitations and his strengths as a writer.

Annie is the keeper of this hidden world: She controls the key, a phallic symbol (Paul has to use a hairpin of hers to open the door of his bedroom), and when she isn't at home, she carries Paul down into a deeper underworld (the cellar). When she is in a manic-depressive state, she deliberately leaves home and hides in a place in the hills in order to recover. Paul crashed his car at the bottom of a small slope in the snows of February; when the spring thaw comes, the car is washed down into a gorge, where it is hidden from view. The gorge provides protection for Paul; he knows that when the police find his car, Annie will have to kill him in order to protect herself. The breath with which Annie at one point resuscitates him comes from "dark and sour chambers" within her (*M* 159); it is "a dirty wind from hell"

(*M* 160). Paul looks at Annie and sees in her face an abyss, "the black nothing of a *crevasse*" (*M* 12); Part 1 of *Misery*, entitled "Annie," is prefaced with a quotation from Nietzsche: *"When you look into the abyss, the abyss also looks into you"* (*M* 1). Paul is in a strange land.

Thinking of Annie as an idol/goddess, Paul visualizes himself as a captive in Africa, the Dark Continent; he also visualizes himself as a strange imprisoned African bird (*M* 30). That image emanates from a powerful childhood memory of weeping with grief after seeing an African bird kept prisoner in a zoo—his mother marvels at this sensitive and imaginative child who writes. When we join the images (Paul himself does not do so), he is the strange African bird held captive in Africa by a woman who in her very angriest moments calls him a dirty bird. When Paul writes *Misery's Return*, Misery Chastain's adventures conclude in Africa and in the caves behind the forehead of a stone Bourka Bee-Goddess. The Goddess is modeled on Annie, just as Geoffrey, one of the heroes who defeats her, is Paul. The book ends with a view of "that distant, disappearing cloud on the horizon—that cloud which was the coast of Africa" (*M* 312). As his own adventures with Annie Wilkes draw to a close, as Paul prepares to kill her and somehow to end his captivity, he feels not just fear but something else: " He supposed it was the receding coast of Africa" (*M* 314). But Africa lingers: Looking at Annie in what he believes to be her death throes, "he realized she actually was turning into the Bourkas' idol" (*M* 319), just as earlier when she killed a policeman he visualized her as actually a goddess. The two Africas are intimately linked, for Annie Wilkes is creator of Paul's daily world, which he both escapes from and carries into his fictional world. In *Misery's Return* and in Paul's life, at least some of the gods are insane (*M* 310).

Representing a cruel, dark side of the creative goddess, Annie is a Dark and Terrible Mother, and Paul's life under her is, as Neumann put it, one of "death and destruction, danger and distress, hunger and nakedness" (*GM* 149). With both legs crushed in his automobile accident, Paul is totally at Annie's mercy. Paul lives, but lives in danger that Annie will murder him; she does cut off one foot and his thumb. Custodial care becomes custody. His health deteriorates, and he is under constant duress to placate her, a mother-goddess who is terrible and unpredictable. Annie views Paul in a madly maternal way. Early in her custody of Paul, she brings him pills for his excruciating pain, but he must suck them off her fingers in a grotesque parody of a nursing child and of sexual activity: She is "a pair of fingers poking into his mouth (and soon enough he learned to suck eagerly at those poking fingers)" (*M* 8), those "intimate, dirtily welcome" fingers (*M* 20). Annie ensures his childlike dependence on her with his addiction to the drug. Under Annie's care—and Annie treats him like a child who must be educated—Paul's life is reinvented; he learns the story of what happened in his accident only from her: The story is "created like fiction" (*M* 11). If she leaves him untended too long, he wets the bed, and she must change him; when he is tired or frustrated, he weeps like a small child. When he has been bad, she disciplines him (say, by cutting off his thumb) but in motherly fashion often comforts him while doing so, once her rage is over. And, of course, Annie will prevent Paul from letting Misery Chastain die in childbirth. She must live and a novel must be born, whether Paul likes it or not. Paul must learn to be good so that the female can live and so that Annie will be happy.

Behind Annie's "expression of maternal love" (*M* 159), which Paul comes to loath, he sees only "total solid blackness" (*M* 159). Like many goddesses, Annie does not just sustain life; she takes it away. She is an "Angel of Death" (*M* 175), a murderer who keeps a detailed record book. Among others, she killed her father, and in her years as a nurse, she terminated the lives of both elderly patients and babies. Shortly after she rescues Paul, she almost kills him with a drug overdose. She saves him from his respiratory collapse, however, by literally breathing life back into his lungs. Paul, horrified at the contact with her body, sees her resuscitation of him as rape: Just as "a man might force a part of himself into an unwilling woman. . . . She raped him full of her air again" (*M* 5) and "back into life" (*M* 6). Destruction lies behind Annie's maternalness: Although Annie is keeping Paul alive, both know that she will kill him when he completes *Misery's Return*. The sacrifice must be made to keep the goddess alive. The return of spring and the discovery of his car when it emerges from the melting snow will bring not renewed life but Paul's death.

Escape for the goddess's pet writer seems impossible because Goddess Annie, like Artemis and Anath, is a ferocious hunter. In fact, King links Annie to Artemis, the Amazonian moon goddess. In a constantly repeated image, Annie becomes the moon controlling the tide of drugs to control Paul's pain: "The pills were the tide; Annie Wilkes was the lunar presence which pulled them into his mouth like jetsam on a wave" (*M* 8). Lest we think gently of Annie's domesticity, King also creates an unforgettable scene of lunacy. Angry at Paul's *Fast Cars* manuscript, Annie smashes a bowl of soup in his bedroom. She scrubs up the resulting mess slowly and ever so thoroughly, making Paul wait in agony for his pain-killing pills. When she finally doles them out, he must swallow them down with scrub water drunk from a yellow pail that "filled his field of vision like a falling moon" (*M* 25). The moon controls the tides, the cycles: The moon mother controls Paul.

Like Artemis, Annie is a "cutter" or "butcher" when she hunts down her enemies. Her favorite tools are axes, electric knives, chainsaws. King elaborately describes how she kills a policeman who is looking for Paul because his car has at last been discovered: Annie repeatedly impales the young man with a wooden cross (with which she had previously marked the grave of a cow). Then she decapitates him by running over his head with a Lawnboy: "cut with a sickle, beaten with a flail, ground in a mill, and scattered in pieces over the fields" (*EMS* 31). Annie makes sure that, like Anath, "whoever hinders her will be crushed" (*EMS* 31). As the Heavenly Father El realized of Anath, Paul knows Annie will not be hindered. Nothing will interfere with her safety or the birth of the book she is nurturing. Annie's curse may lack the dignity of Anath's "Anathema Marantha," but her own humble and even ridiculous curse, "you old dirty bird" (*M* 262), with which she accompanies her attack on the policeman (and others on Paul), is no less terrifying.

Like Artemis/Di-ana, Annie (although once married) is virginal; as with them, her virginity can be frightening. Paul sees her body as having the solidity of a stone idol: It is a "solid fibrous unchannelled body . . . like an idol in a perfervid novel" (*M* 8), a body that contains no feminine passages. Annie is also, however, childlike in a way that suggests not Artemis but the maidenly propriety of St. Anne and the Virgin Mary. She uses the language of a child, calling people she doesn't like (and sometimes murders) "cockadoodie brats. "Things that are unpleasant are "oogie." She blushes about Paul's own sexuality and doesn't cut off what she refers to as his man-gland, although, Paul knows, she considers doing so. Virginal and childlike though she may be, nevertheless, Annie is even more the Mother and Huntress: Her lust for each chapter Paul produces of the new *Misery* ("some sort of fuck" [*M* 245]) keeps her from killing him (or herself) during a depressive fit. Annie "raped" Paul back into life, and she will hunt him down if he tries to escape.

Annie makes a poor St. Anne. St. Anne gave birth to Mary, whose birth became immaculate at the moment of conception. Mary, in perfect immaculate conception, gave birth to Jesus. Misery Chastain (note the last name) is also a virgin, a romantic heroine who may have lovers and a baby boy and still remain pure as pure can be in the eyes of adoring readers such as Annie. Like St. Anne, then, Annie acts as a "virginal" and protective mother of this virgin, Misery, and Misery in a strange way is the mother of the writer/god, Paul. For it is through Misery that Paul has been successful; his writing truly is "born of misery," rather than causing misery (*M* 99). But while Annie's concern for Misery is intense Annie herself is a fearsome caretaker of god/Paul, and she is scarcely immaculate—King makes unforgettably clear how masculated her spirit is: The breath with which Annie breathes life into

Paul is so foul that he can barely stand the smell of it, and during her depressive fits, Annie's body and house become disgustingly smeared with food. Further, the ancient archetype behind the tamed St. Anne shows in Annie's negative caretaking. Annie may put up a cross over the grave of a cow, but she killed the cow through neglect, and, as Paul observes, she uses the cross like a goddess come to life in order to murder the policeman, a threat to her world. As a good Christian St. Anne, she should help Paul write, should be a female secretarial assistant for the literary birth. Annie does buy Paul a typewriter, but it gradually loses all the crucial keys. At first she fills in some of the missing letters, but gradually Paul has to take over this laborious work himself. Instead, Annie tends to exercise "editorial authority over [Paul's] body" (*M* 287) trimming it to keep him under control. She remains the goddess, just as St. Anne in some representations recalls her Great Goddess derivations, for she holds Mary in her lap like a child, who in turn holds Christ.

Annie has no conception of herself as a goddess. She sees herself merely as the caretaker for Paul, whom she reveres as a god, a creator who breathes life into his characters. She points out to Paul that he chose to kill Misery Chastain and that he can choose to bring her back to life. Paul insists that this is not so, that his characters dictate the course of their own lives, and we believe him. Nevertheless, he can and does bring Misery Chastain back to life when Annie provides a creative impulse, namely fear of his own death. Furthermore, when Annie makes him sacrifice his *Fast Cars* manuscript, Paul thinks of himself as killing five lives, the five characters he lovingly created for the novel. As a writer, Paul is indeed a god in charge of life and death, but Annie is in charge of his, and she knows it—God has two broken legs and is in her house, as she observes (*M* 36), and she easily imagines how to keep him there. Although she will not often acknowledge her power, she keeps firm and creative control of the story of Paul's life.

As Annie seems to know, Paul Sheldon himself seems to resonate with New Testament symbolism. St. Paul founded orthodox Christianity, replete with its avoidance of women and sexuality, and it has been noted that with St. Paul came "separation of male and female principles in religion. Father Heaven and Mother Earth were no longer wedded. Women were no longer participants in sacred mysteries according to Paul"; Artemis was obviously no longer welcome (*EMS* 775). Annie Wilkes believes she does not partake of the sacred mysteries or in the creating of lives in fiction; these mysteries are in Paul's control. She believes Paul is good, she loves him, and she treats him as if sex were taboo and deeply sinful; she does not, therefore, castrate him because she cannot acknowledge his sexuality. Annie makes Paul

maintain her image of him: He must use clean language; he must also sacri-
ficially burn his *Fast Cars* manuscript (since there are lots of "f" words in it)
of his "own free will" (*M* 45); and he must burn at least a few pages himself
"as a symbol of [his] understanding" (*M* 45). Token nods to Christian free
will and understanding notwithstanding, Paul is allowed neither, and Annie
acts like a vengeful, controlling Artemis/Anath, not a peaceful St. Anne. She
is no more welcome to the modern Paul than to the biblical.

Not surprisingly, the Old Testament image of David and Goliath
comes to Paul's mind when he finally sees rescue in the form of the two
policemen—one huge, one small, both powerful—who ultimately remove
him from Annie's house. One must not forget, however, that this David and
Goliath do not kill Annie; they find her dead in the barn. Paul has become
complicitous in his creative captivity. For Paul as for Annie, finishing *Misery's
Return* has become more important than anything else, including Paul's life.
When the policemen first appear at Annie's house, Paul could probably have
initiated his rescue. He does not. He wants to kill Annie himself—to finish
the story Annie has been controlling—and he wants to finish his book: It isn't
done yet, and so rescue and Annie's death must wait until after it is finished.
Paul finally tries to kill Annie by stuffing his *Misery* manuscript down her
throat: "*I'm gonna rape you, all right, Annie. . . . So suck my book. . . . Suck on it
until you fucking CHOKE*" (*M* 317). Paul tries to kill the goddess on her own
terms, to reclaim control of the creative territory.

Yet Paul does not actually succeed in killing Annie when he tries to
burn her up like a sacrifice with his manuscript, stuff it in her mouth to
"rape" her with it, and break her back with his typewriter. She eventually dies
from the head wound she receives when she trips over the typewriter during
their battle. And even after her death, she is not, as King makes very clear,
really dead. In a dramatic vision, both reader and Paul see Annie alive and
attacking him in his new apartment in a scene that is completely "real."
Annie's creative force cannot be killed; she lives in a creative part of the
writer's mind where she will not die. Her death will never be a reality, any
more than Misery Chastain's death could be a reality—Paul observes that
both Misery and Annie will always be restless in their graves (*M* 336). For
Paul, Annie can never be mentally reduced to just a "crazy lady who had hurt
[him] for reasons of her own" (*M* 335). That final feminine creative space
will always be there waiting for him, the hole in the page that opens up and
into which Paul finds himself falling whenever he writes.

Perhaps it is in the abyss of *Misery's* blackness that Stephen King finds
and resolves his own misery. What does a writer fear? King has shown us that
the Great Goddess of creativity, of birth and death, can be awful. His writer,

Paul, escapes when he sees rescue close at hand in the form of two policemen standing outside the house. He attracts their attention with a figurine on which there is a legend reading "NOW MY TALE IS TOLD!" And Paul thinks. "*Yes! Thank God!*" (*M* 325). He throws the figurine through the window, and his story is over—almost. There is always more to tell. *Misery* ends as, nine months after his rescue, Paul begins a new novel. One imagines King staring at the word processor, watching his own tale of *Misery* unfold, and finally bringing it to a close with these last words: "Lowell, Maine: September 23rd, 1984/Bangor, Maine. October 7th, 1986: *Now my tale is told*" (*M* 338).

In the age of *Misery*'s birth, the world no longer acknowledges a Great Goddess; Artemis and Anath are relics sitting in the half-light of an obscure past. Realizing man's ancient fears of the creative force in a modern and (alas) acceptable way, Stephen King embodies them in a woman who is a psychopathic murderer. But the Dark and Terrible Mother lives, and as both Paul Sheldon and Stephen King know, they will continue to tell her tale. "*You c[a]n't kill the goddess. The goddess is immortal*" (*M* 319).

JONATHAN P. DAVIS

Childhood and Rites of Passage

The child in adult life is defenceless
And if he is grown-up, knows it,
And the grown-up looks at the childish part
And despises it.
    —Stevie Smith, "To Carry the Child"

Anyone who has read Stephen King extensively will find that he spends a large amount of time exploring childhood. Childhood to King is a magical time, a time when the world seems magnificent in its literal beauty, a time when a human being is most splendid because of ignorance of worldly evil. King recollects with fondness an age when imaginative capacities are boundless because they are not yet bogged down by the spirit-corrupting concerns of adulthood. This preoccupation with youth in his fiction becomes both significant and inspirational when seen from the light that King is writing in an America that attempts to desensitize its young by exposing it continuously to violence and sex in both the entertainment and news media, forcing it to mature at too early an age. Children to King are like lumps of clay on a potter's wheel waiting to be sculpted into the individuals they will later become; they are the most impressionable beings in the human chain.

While they begin innocent, not yet concerned with how they look or where they will get money to buy a new car, children still are forced at some point to exit the gates of purity and enter the arena of adulthood, which

From *Stephen King's America*. © 1994 Bowling Green State University Popular Press.

occurs through some initial earth-shattering discovery that causes them to recognize the imperfections of their world. For some children, the initiation may be discovering that their fathers are not the spotless, faultless men they thought they were but rather pathetic alcoholics. Others may find their untainted visions of their world clouded by a first exposure to a pornographic magazine depicting radically different images of sexuality than those which they'd been taught. King revels in both the pre-corrupted and corrupted states of youth. He feels that they are periods that people must return to in later years to complete the wheel of humanity; if people cannot remember both the magic of childhood before its corruption and the lessons reamed during and after its corruption, then they will never be complete but will succumb to the evils of the adult world.

First and foremost of King's fascination with children is the imaginative capacity they have that makes them stronger at heart than the adults who claim superiority over them. While adults claim to be wise, they are ignorant to the fact that the imaginative atrophy often resulting from an inability to adapt to innocence's corruption actually limits them. Adults often can no longer discover the beauty in a sunset; they cannot remember the golden moments of childhood bonding, a period when same-sex friends seemed the most important aspect of being alive, and it is this incapacity to recollect these times that often leads to an increasingly burdensome adult life in King's fiction. Unless the adults in King's world can escape into the realm of imagination first experienced and shared with others in childhood, unless they can approach oncoming evil with a child's mentality, they are doomed to adult reasoning. Because evil in itself is intangible and cannot be reasonably rationalized, it is often both adults' adherence to their belief in reason and their insistency on literalizing reality and unreality that often result in a catastrophe in King's fiction. Only when they open themselves up to combatting evil from a child's perspective, one which believes in monsters and ghosts, can they openly battle adversities.

King's interest in children's imagination could be linked directly to his feelings on moral choice discussed previously. Adults are unable to see their shortcomings because they are too enveloped in a subjectively egocentric universe based on the rules of rationality. A child, who is ever open to the threats of vampires, killer cars, haunted hotels, and killer clowns, is not yet able to reject the thought of entering the world of the irrational. Clive Barker, one of King's leading contemporaries in horror fiction, says of King, "In King's work, it is so often the child who carries that wisdom; the child who synthesizes 'real' and 'imagined' experience without question, who knows instinctively that imagination can tell the truth the way the senses never can" (63). Often in King's books, it takes the imagination of a child to cast away the evil that reduces adults to whimpering fools: It's The Loser's Club, a group of socially outcast children who possess the imaginative capacities to recognize the evil plundering Derry and therefore acquire the power to stop it; 'Salem's Lot's Mark Petrie, whose belief in the world of monsters allows protagonist Ben Mears to return to his own childhood fears which upon retrospection provide him with the power to combat the vampires quenching their thirsts on the small town; The Shining's Danny Torrance, whose childish imagination provides a welcome birthplace for supernatural powers capable of turning back the all-consuming evil of the hotel that has claimed his father; and The Talisman's Jack Sawyer, who because of his youth and separation from the adult world of reasoning becomes his ailing mother's savior while an evil adult society led by his malicious Uncle Morgan tries to destroy them both. The child heroes in King's fiction continue to increase, merely because of King's awareness that their innocence is the only hope for survival in an unimaginative adult world that is swallowing itself.

King often highlights the plight of American children by portraying an adult society that is trying to soil its young by stealing their purity. The sad truth lies in the fact that while children are stronger than their elders in their ability to utilize their imaginations in the face of adversities, they are incapacitated by their dependency on adults. As a result, adults possess the power to make lasting impressions—often negative ones—on their young simply because of both their physical superiority and worldly mentality, something Bernadette Lynn Bosky points out:

> Children do not resist their impressions partly because they have not learned adult standards of sanity and already exist in a shocking and primal world that adults can barely recall or comprehend. It is a sad irony, exampled in books like The Shining, Cujo, and Pet Sematary, that children, who often understand the intrinsics of evil best, have the least power to change it. (216)

While children basically possess the true weapons for survival—a productive imagination, a love for simple things, a gentle nature—they are often made vulnerable by an adult society that teaches them violence, hostility, and greed. In their vulnerability, children become sponges that absorb the impressions their adult society gives them, which King himself explains:

> What is it about kids that they can look at the most outrageous thing and just see it and, unless there's a reaction they can play

off, just deal with it? If a kid sees a guy that's dead in the street, who's been hit by a car, if he's by himself he'll just look at the dead guy and then maybe run off to find somebody—after he'd had a good look to see what it was like. But if a lot of people are standing around crying, then the kid will cry too, because he's got a mirror reaction. Kids by themselves sort of interest me that way; they seem to me to be the place where you should start to explore wherever people come from. (BB 105)

As King suggests, children learn from the adult reactions to which they are exposed. King's fiction which deals with the gap between young and old tends to argue that the negative responses children register from adults are those that are most often recollected later in adult life, serving as a basis for chronic human flaws. In *The Library Policeman*, a novella in *Four Past Midnight*, King speaks this observation through Dirty Dave Duncan's mouth:

I don't think kids know monsters so well at first glance. It's their folks that tell em how to recognize the monsters. . . . And when they went home [from Ardelia Lortz's terrifying renditions of fairy tales], they didn't remember, in the top part of their minds, anyways, about the stories or the posters. Down underneath, I think they remembered plenty, just like down underneath Sam knows who his Library Policeman is. I think they still remember today—the bankers and lawyers and bigtime farmers who were once Ardelia's Good Babies. I can still see em, wearin pinafores and short pants, sittin in those little chairs, lookin at Ardelia in the middle of the circle, their eyes so big and round they looked like pie-plates. And I think that when it gets dark and the storms come, or when they are sleepin and the nightmares come, they go back to bein kids. I think the doors open and they see the Three Bears—Ardelia's Three Bears—eatin' the brains out of Goldilock's head with their wooden porridge-spoons, and Baby Bear wearin' Goldilock's scalp on his head like a long golden wig. I think they wake up sweaty, feelin sick and afraid. I think that's what she left this town. I think she left a legacy of secret nightmares. (527)

The Ardelia Lortz that Dirty Dave speaks of is a stain on his memories. She is the embodiment of the adult world that strives to swallow its young. In the past, she had run the public library in town where children's readings took place. Once the doors were shut and the parents had gone, Ardelia perverted all of the children's favorite fairy tales into her own gory versions where the protagonists are killed and maimed because they are naughty little children. When the listeners showed fear, she took them into another room and fumed into a monster with a funnel-shaped mouth that sucked the tears of fear right from their eyes; she sucked them dry of all the imaginative capabilities that kept them young, staining their youth with her corrupted adult vision.

Ardelia is central to the story because it is she who comes back as a ghost to feed on protagonist Sam Peebles' fear, one which was never resolved as a child. Sam's fear is of libraries; what once were places of limitless possiblities, places of magical learning, are now to Sam the manifestations of a dark memory from past years—the memory of being raped by a homosexual child molester when Sam was returning an overdue book to the public library. The child molester had claimed that he was punishing Sam for being a naughty boy who did not return his book on time. The young Sam, who, like children everywhere, was impressionable in his youth, took the molester's accusation to heart, and from that point on, had his childish fascination with libraries reduced to repulsion. Dirty Dave, who had followed Ardelia's persecution of the young when she was living primarily because of an adult lust for her, also admits that corrupting children was appealing to his adult mind:

> There's a part of me, even now, that wants to sugarcoat it, make my part in it better than it was. I'd like to tell you that I fought with her, argued, told her I didn't want nothin to do with scarin a bunch of kids . . . but it wouldn't be true. I went right along with what she wanted me to do. God help me, I did. Partly it was because I was scared of her by then. But mostly it was because I was still besotted with her. And there was something else, too. There was a mean, nasty part of me—I don't think it's in everyone, but I think it's in a lot of us—that liked what she was up to. Liked it. (520)

The combination of supplicating himself for Ardelia's body and secretly enjoying the corruption of youth alienates Dirty Dave from the children whom he had respected and admired prior to meeting Ardelia. His feelings about the role he played in Ardelia's perversion of Junction City's children is significant when put together with the other adults in the story who thrive on eradicating the magic of youth, a tendency in adults that Sam has difficulty understanding, keeping him from being whole. Because Sam Peebles had never been able to come to terms with the reality of his perversion, he cannot defeat Ardelia and the Library Policeman of his past until he can return to his childhood and retrieve the golden moments that were stolen from him.

Prior to being raped, Sam had purchased a pack of red licorice. The red licorice, like the library, had become a negative memory, one that prior to his manipulation by the molester had been a meaningful token of his youth. Sam defeats Ardelia and the Library Policeman by buying several packs of the same red licorice and jamming them into the mouth of the monster—which ultimately becomes a union of Ardelia, his molester, and all the negative memories those adults represent—that is trying to swallow him the same way it did his innocence. Because he is finally able to return to the magic of his childhood, using those memories to oppose his enemies, the adult Sam is able to reclaim a portion of the innocence that the adult world had taken from him.

King's stories that depict a conflict between children and adults may be seen as having their foundations built in the portrayal of the age gap as presented by the American media. Television and movies often portray the young as threatening to the adult world, something easily identified in films such as *The Exorcist*, a story about a young girl who, after being possessed by the devil, strikes out at the adults surrounding her; *The Omen*, which uses a child as the vehicle through which the coming of the Beast as promised in the book of Revelations is realized; *The Class of 1984*, a film that tells the story of a man's battle against a group of delinquent high school students who represent all of the destructive impulses in humankind; and the number of movies that portray youths and adolescents as wanting nothing but a good time void of responsibility—drinking, getting high, playing rock music, wanting constant sex (*Porky's, Friday the 13th, Fast Times at Ridgemont High*). The media has indeed tended to condition society into believing that the young are a threat to the adult world's standards of living. By presenting youths in such a fashion, the media has succeeded in stereotyping them. While these presentations may be seen on one side as reactions by youths who are fighting against their elders who are suppressing them, most often they are viewed as the mirror opposite: the young lack respect for the old and therefore suffer in failing to adhere to adult precepts. The sad truth lies in the fact that the media, which is run by adults, often does not look back on adolescence as a meaningful time but rather focuses on the tragedies that occur during youth: a painful loss of virginity, illicit experimentation with controlled substancies resulting in negative consequences, painful pranks on vulnerable peers. Instead of portraying children and adolescents as having the strength and imaginative capacities to combat their adversities, American media has often presented them as weak, disturbed individuals with ambiguous identities who perish because of their helplessness and lack of moral direction.

King seems to be aware of the misinterpretation of the young in the media, and he tries to provide an alternative viewpoint by portraying his young people as being stronger than the corrupt adult world. Often in his books, the initial coming of age occurs when children first become wise to the several rites of initiation into adulthood offered by their elders. The optimism King has for American youth shines through in his belief that children have the capacity to achieve mature growth when passing through these rites of passage; more often than not, King's young people are able to leave their states of innocence with their heads held high and are strong enough to recognize the significance of the step in human development they are taking. In *The Sun Dog*, Kevin Delevan, the young owner of the Polaroid Sun 660 that so captivates Pop Merrill's attention, has the strength to determine when he will be ready to cross the line separating purity from experience, an ability to discriminate that shines clear in his recollection of a hunting trip with his father:

> "Bet you wish it'd been your turn in the puckies, don't you, son?" the game-warden had asked, ruffling Kevin's hair. Kevin had nodded, keeping his secret to himself: he was glad it hadn't been his turn in the puckies, his rifle which must be responsible for throwing the slug or not throwing it . . . and, if he had turned out to have the courage to do the shooting, his reward would have been only another troublesome responsibility: to shoot the buck clean. He didn't know if he could have mustered the courage to put another bullet in the thing if the kill wasn't clean, or the strength to chase the trail of its blood and steaming, startled droppings and finish what he started if it ran. He had smiled up at the game-warden and nodded and his dad had snapped a picture of that, and there had never been any need to tell his dad that the thought going on behind that upturned brow and under the game-warden's ruffling hand had been No. I don't wish it. The world is full of tests, but twelve's too young to go hunting them. I'm glad it was Mr. Roberson. I'm not ready yet to try a man's tests." (756)

These reflections take place when Kevin is facing the dog that Pop Merrill had released from the camera because of his greedy adult anxiety. This is a turning point in the story because it is this moment when Kevin must decide whether to turn the camera that will be used to combat the dog over to his father or whether to take on the task himself, a man's task that he had not yet been prepared to face while hunting at the age of twelve. Kevin recognizes that the present moment is the time to make that step, for where before crossing into manhood would have been done in vain (shooting a deer), he is now in a position to save both his and his father's lives:

> The thought of turning the Polaroid over to his father crossed his mind, but only momentarily. Something deep inside himself knew the truth: to pass the camera would be tantamount to murdering his father and committing suicide himself. His father believed something, but that wasn't specific enough. The camera wouldn't work for his father even if his father managed to break out of his current stunned condition and press the shutter. It would only work for him. (757)

After recalling the time when he was tempted to enter the adult world, a transition that could have been accomplished by aiming his rifle at the deer and mortally wounding it, Kevin remembers that he had in his heart resisted the temptation, knowing truly well he was not yet ready. The coming of age into adulthood occurs when he realizes that he is in a position to react like an adult, yet the magic of the transition rests in the fact that Kevin also understands that he is not stained because of this awareness but rather is in close enough contact with his youth to have the imaginative capacity to defeat the inexplicable atrocity bearing down on him and his father. While recognizing that his father is slightly aware of what is going on as the dog prepares to strike, Kevin has the inner strength to speculate that his father is still too out of touch with such phenomena because of the imaginative atrophy of adulthood. The combined abilities to walk through his rite of passage with confidence and utilize his childish capacities result in Kevin's life-saving effort.

The Body, King's tour de force of coming of age stories, also portrays young people as having the inner strength to make the transition from innocence to experience. After hearing of a boy from town who had disappeared after venturing out to pick berries, a group of four young boys embark on a journey through miles of railroad tracks and vegetation to find the boy, who they believe is surely dead. Along the trip, the four begin to realize the significance of their union in their search and are able to grasp the splendor of childhood bonding, which provides the catapult to accomplishing their task. Gordie Lachance, the story's narrator, acts as spokesperson for the group when he explicates his growing realization that both he and his friends are taking a significant step toward maturity in searching a first exposure to death:

> Unspoken—maybe it was too fundamental to be spoken—was the idea that this was a big thing. It wasn't screwing around with firecrackers or trying to look through the knothole in the back of the girls' privy at Harrison State Park. This was something on a par with getting laid for the first time, or going into the Army, or buying your first bottle of legal liquor.
>
> There's a high ritual to ail fundamental events, the rites of passage, the magic corridor where the change happens. Buying the condoms. Standing before the minister. Raising your hand and taking the oath. Or, if you please, walking down the railroad tracks to meet a fellow your own age halfway, the same as I'd walk half-way over to Pine Street to meet Chris if he was coming over to my house, or the way Teddy would walk halfway down Gates Street to meet me if I was going to his. It seemed right to do it this way, because the rite of passage is a magic corridor and so we always provide an aisle—it's what you walk down when you get married, what they carry you down when you get buried. Our corridor was those twin rails, and we walked between them, just bopping along toward whatever this was supposed to mean. (415)

Gordie's passage suggests that he and his friends have reached a point where they are prepared to traverse into the world of experience, leaving their innocence behind. The passage is inspirational in that it does not portray youth teetering on the "unstable legs of adolescence" but rather suggests that the boys are indeed ready to make the transition confidently. In the end, they are able to complete their rite of passage with authority. After they discover the dead body, a group of older boys wanting media exposure burst in to claim the body for themselves. The younger ones, realizing the trials they had to endure in achieving their end goal, use their accumulated strength to turn the interlopers back. Once again, King has presented a vision of youth that has the capacity to grow from change and heed the lessons it provides.

King also attempts to show in his fiction that children and adolescents are not always the blank slates that adults believe them to be. While King's adults boast a knowledge of the world, they are often ignorant of the fact that their intimate relationship with rational explanation gives them less an understanding of the line separating reality from unreality that youths in their imaginative splendor can access. King's young people, while still innocent, are indeed often aware that there are some things that they can comprehend that their elders could not even if they tried. In effect, it is the imaginative capacities that King's children possess that ultimately alienate them from adults. A scene from *'Salem's Lot* that supports this idea: upon arriving home after visiting the Marsten house, where he hears the voice of head-vampire Barlow in the cellar, young Mark Petrie is greeted with dismay by his parents, who have been worried sick over his extended absence:

> "Where have you been?" She caught his shoulders and shook them.
> "Out," he said wanly. "I fell down running home."
> There was nothing else to say. The essential and defining characterstic of childhood is not the effortless merging of dream and reality, but only alienation. There are no words for child-hood's dark turns and exhalations. A wise child recognizes it and submits to the necessary consequences. A child who counts the cost is a child no longer.
> He added: "The time got away from me. It—"
> Then his father, descending upon him. (293)

Mark Petrie comes home looking like he'd just been run over by a car, an appearance caused by his stumbling and falling while running from the Marsten house. But he cannot tell his parents the truth, because in their adult tendency to adhere to reason, they could not possibly understand or believe him. Mark understands and endures the ensuing interrogation.

Other examples of a child's interpretation of the world as opposed to an adult's can be found throughout King's canon. In *The Library Policeman*, Sam Peebles begins to make the distinction after observing a grim poster Ardelia Lortz had put up on the door to the children's reading room in the public library:

> The door was closed. On it was a picture of Little Red Riding Hood, looking down at the wolf in grandma's bed. The wolf was wearing Grandma's nightgown and Grandma's nightcap. It was snarling. Foam dripped from between its bared fangs. An

expression of almost exquisite horror had transfixed Little Red Riding Hood's face, and the poster seemed not just to suggest but to actually proclaim that the happy ending of this story—of all fairy tales—was a convenient lie. Parents might believe such guff, Red Riding Hood's ghastly-sick face said, but the little ones knew better, didn't they? (418)

Peebles recognizes during a retrospect on childhood that there are some things that children can see in their vivid imaginations that adults, members of the "Reasonable tribe" never could. Likewise, in the short story "The Boogeyman" (*Night Shift*), protagonist Lester Billings begins to grasp his own lack of childish imagination that, had it been present, may have saved his children from the monster preying on them from their closets:

I started to think, maybe if you think of a thing long enough, believe in it, it gets real. Maybe all the monsters we were scared of when we were kids, Frankenstein and Wolfman and Mummy, maybe they were real. Real enough to kill the kids they said fell in gravel pits or drowned in lakes or were just never found. Maybe grownups unmake that world because we're so sure of the world's normalcy. ("The Boogeyman," Fogler Special Collections 6)

Up until this point, Billings had reprimanded his children for dreaming up the monster in their closets. Because of the separation between what his children believed and what he was not able to believe, Billing's ignorance ends in their deaths. The children who were able to understand the world of monsters were completely helpless to stop the one living among them; their only savior, their father, did not have the imaginative capacity to heed their call of distress. (Note: "The Boogeyman" is also interesting in its implications of an adult world persecuting its young. Billing's disbelief of the monster in his house also arises from his hostility toward his children, who, rather than being seen as a blessing, are seen as extra baggage. Prior to his children's deaths, Billings had come to think of his children as unwanted responsibilities. In effect, what Billings denies to be the cause of his children's deaths also arises from his subconscious desire to see himself rid of them.)

Although King often attempts to explain the imaginative capacities that separate the young from the old, thereby making children better prepared in the shadow of oncoming danger, he does not make children completely spotless in their understandings of the human condition. On the contrary, while

King writes to show the differences between the imaginations of the young and old, he also explicates that there are certain awarenesses to which adults have access while children do not. From this perspective, while a child is often aware of an adult's misunderstanding of the supernatural and imaginable realm, an adult is cognizant of a child's inability to estimate human nature. This concept would tend to argue that a child, who has not yet been exposed enough to the evil ways in which the world operates, is vulnerable in his or her ignorance of adult human behavior. The following exchange between Andy McGee and his daughter, Charlie, in *Firestarter* suggests this important differential between an adult's understanding of the world as compared to a child's:

> [at a Best Western hotel after Andy has rescued Charlie from The Shop agents who have just executed his wife]
> "I want Mommy," she sobbed.
> He nodded. He wanted her, too. He held Charlie tightly to him and smelled ozone and porcelain and cooked Best Western towels. She had almost flashfried them both.
> "It's gonna be all right," he told her, and rocked her, not really believing it, but it was the litany, the Psalter, the voice of the adult calling down the black well of years into the miserable pit of terrorized childhood; it was what you said when things went wrong; it was the nightlight that could not banish the monster from the closet but perhaps only keep it at bay for a little while; it was the voice without power that must speak nevertheless.
> "It's gonna be all right," he told her, not really believing it, knowing as every adult knows in his secret heart that nothing is really all right, ever. "It's gonna be all right."
> He was crying. He couldn't help it now. His tears came in a flood and he held her to his chest as tightly as he could.
> "Charlie, I swear to you, somehow it's gonna be all right."
> (180)

The difference in worldly knowledge between children and adults is apparent in the novel. Charlie possesses the talent of pyrokinesis, which enables her to set fires at will. Her understanding of her talent is representative of a young child's: she does not yet understand the power she holds within her, and she is often left in a state of disorientation after she uses it. Too young to understand controlling it, Charlie only uses the power, much as any young child would, spontaneously; she only uses it when either she or her father is in danger. The adult world, on the other hand, wants to use her as a secret governmental weapon. Because they recognize the massive destruction Charlie's power can inflict, the adult world (represented as The Shop and the U.S. government) tries to apprehend her and harness her wild talent. In her youth, Charlie is too young to understand that adults wish to manipulate her, much as she is too young to realize that things are not "all right"— a consolation that her father must prevaricate to ease her tension. Only Andy, a grown-up member of the adult society, possesses this understanding that will take years for his daughter to comprehend.

King's analysis of youth does not end with pre-adolescent childhood. On the contrary, he spends an equal amount of text exploring life after the initial coming of age, which takes place after children have lost their innocence through an initiation to worldliness. He is just as concerned with the next stage of human development, adolescence, which actually serves as the void between the extremities of childhood innocence and adult experience. Adolescence to King may be the most turbulent period of people's lives because it is a time when they must develop their personalities without any firm ground to stand on; no longer wearing the pure skin of childhood, yet also not bearing the experienced colors of adulthood, adolescents are often trapped in identity crises. The development that takes place during this period carries tremendous implications concerning what people will become as adults. Susceptible to confusion about themselves, King's adolescents are vulnerable to adversity. Douglas Winter, quoting author Charles L. Grant, indicates King's preoccupation with adolescence by arguing, "In King's view, 'the struggle toward adolescence and adulthood is as fraught with terror as the worst possible nightmare, and as meaningful as anything a grown-up has to contend with'" (SK 32). Critic Tom Newhouse provides what is perhaps the most accurate description of the dilemma facing King's adolescents when he writes that" they are often outsiders who turn to violence as a response to exclusionary social environments which deny them acceptance, or who resort to destructive attitudes that they believe will advance them upward" (49). While a student at the University of Maine at Orono, King wrote a weekly column titled "King's Garbage Truck," which appeared in the campus newspaper, *The Maine Campus*. In his May 21, 1970, column, the last "Garbage Truck" column he wrote, King said this about his own transition into the adult world after completing his required studies:

> This boy has shown evidences of some talent, although at this point it is impossible to tell if he is just a flash in the pan or if he has real possibilities. It seems obvious that he has learned a great

deal at the University of Maine at Orono, although a great deal
has contributed to a lessening of idealistic fervor rather than a
heightening of that characteristic. If a speaker at his birth into
the real world mentions "changing the world with the bright-
eyed vigor of youth" this young man is apt to flip him the bird
and walk out, as he does not feel very bright-eyed by this time; in
fact, he feels about two thousand years old.

It is implicit in this statement that even King, who when he wrote this was
writing non-ficton, was weary of the tasks that lay ahead of him in making
the complete transition to adulthood. Perhaps it is a realization such as this
one that has been the motivating factor behind devoting a large portion of
his literature to the uphill battle young people must endure when struggling
through the crises brought about by fighting to understand who they are.

Finding a meaningful identity is perhaps the most pervasive conflict
facing King's fictitious adolescents. The vulnerability arising from having no
sound identity often opens them up to the constant fire of adversities being
cast at them by adults and peers alike. No better example can be found than
in King's first published novel, *Carrie*. *Carrie* is the story of an ugly-duckling
with an extraordinary gift, telekinesis, which enables her to move stationary
objects by merely using her will. She is simultaneously persecuted by her
peers, who take advantage of her humble docility, and her religious fundamentalist mother, who interprets everything Carrie does as being sinful.
While trying to discover her identity, Carrie's view of herself is continuously distorted by the ways in which her immediate associates react to her.
Winter argues that "she is at the center of an ever-tightening circle of control, of a society laden with traps that demand conformity and the loss of
identity" (35). Her significant others seem intent on dictating to Carrie
exactly how she is to view herself. Yet while she is discouraged from asserting herself as an autonomous individual, she carries on with the human
desire to persevere. She is granted the opportunity to grasp her femininity
when a classmate, Sue Snell, takes pity on her after succumbing to the guilt
from her involvement in taunting Carrie and forfeits her prom date,
Tommy Ross, whom she persuades to escort Carrie to the dance. Carrie
reacts to the invitation by making herself up, allowing her natural beauty
hidden beneath her humble exterior to shine through, which stuns her
adversaries. The peers most preoccupied with making Carrie's life a living
hell respond by dumping pig blood on her when she is mockingly elected
prom queen. When she returns home after wreaking destruction on those
who shamed her, she walks into the second trap, her mother, who, believing

Carrie had been out behaving immorally, rebukes her. Like Carrie's peers, her mother ultimately dies at the hand of Carrie's wrath. The results of prom night are catastrophic, and the tragedy lies in the fact that Carrie had finally summoned the courage to exercise her autonomy only to have her peers and her mother deny her that opportunity.

Carrie is metamorphasized into a monster by the society that tried to repress her. But all the while, the reader never truly views Carrie as an atrocity; on the contrary, she demands the reader's sympathy. She does not willfully conduct evil against others but rather is forced to lash back at those who try consistently to eradicate the one thing that has any significant meaning in Carrie's adolescence: her self-worth. Critic Ben Indick explains King's treatment of Carrie as a victim rather than as an aggressor when he says that "the heroine of *Carrie*, no more mature than most of her fellow teenagers, nevertheless tries to understand herself and particularly her mother. Her destructive acts come only because she has no way to respond emotionally and intellectually" (160).

Another prime example of a King adolescent who is pushed into mayhem is Arnie Cunningham in *Christine*. Arnie is the male counterpart of Carrie. While he does not possess any wild talent, he is similar to Carrie in his awkwardness and forced humility because of his lack of physical prowess. Like Carrie's peers, Arnie's never accept him but insist on keeping him humble. Girls will have nothing to do with him, thinking he is a geek with zits. Boys intimidate him because he is weak. Arnie even feels alienated from his parents, who expect him to follow the blueprint of his life they have drawn for him. When Arnie finds and purchases Christine, a '57 Plymouth Fury in which he takes great pride, his feelings of persecution are reinforced from all sides: his parents reject the car because they think it will keep him from his studies, and his peers react with distaste because they realize his fixation with it has made him bolder in his stand against them. His parents discourage his involvement with the car by prohibiting him from parking it in front of the house, and his teenage adversaries at one point pulverize it. Aside from Dennis Guilder, Arnie's one true friend, Arnie is under constant pressure to refrain from establishing any meaningful identity of his own—an identity he feels the car could provide. Dennis summarizes Arnie's plight and that of any other high school outcast when he says that:

> he was a loser, you know. Every high school has to have at least two, it's like a national law. One male, one female. Everyone's dumping ground. Having a bad day? Flunked a big test? Had an argument with your folks and got grounded for the weekend? No

problem. Just find one of those poor sad sacks that go scurrying around the halls like criminals before the home-room bell and walk it right to him. (1)

In effect, Arnie comes to believe that his only purposes in life are to play both the punching bag on which his peers take out their frustrations and the obedient son who must respect his parents' wishes, even if those wishes conflict with his own.

As Arnie's attachment to Christine grows stronger, so do the lines separating Arnie from his significant others grow clearer. In an exchange with Dennis, Arnie discloses his unhappiness with his parents, a feeling not unfamiliar to many adolescents:

> "Has it ever occurred to you," he said abruptly, "that parents are nothing but overgrown kids until their children drag them into adulthood? Usually kicking and screaming?"
>
> I shook my head.
>
> "Tell you what I think," he said "I think that part of being a parent is trying to kill your kids. I know it sounds a little crazy at first . . . but there are lots of things that sound nuts until you really consider them. Penis envy. Oedpial conflicts. The Shroud of Turin . . . I really believe it, though . . . not that they know what they're doing; I don't believe that at all. And do you know why? . . . Because as soon as you have a kid, you know for sure that you're going to die. When you have a kid, you see your own gravestone." (26–27)

Arnie's feelings of no way out—his despair in establishing a positive meaningful identity while under fire from significant others—combined with his lack of faith in people willing to form substantial relationships with him lead to his fall from humanity and susceptibility to evil. As Bernadette Lynn Bosky brings to light, Arnie's feelings of great potential hidden by ugliness, of being unappreciated and socially excluded, pave the way for his seduction by Christine (227). While Arnie does begin to understand Christine's evil late in the book, he still rejects the option to do the right thing—to destroy her—because he is unwilling to surrender the feelings of self-worth she has given him. Though he makes a severe lapse in moral judgment, it could be argued that he has been conditioned by the society persecuting him to dismiss any notion of brotherhood. In the end, Arnie, like Carrie White, can be observed as a sympathetic character even in the shadow of the mass destruction he causes because his downfall is the result of being denied his autonomy.

While King often expresses his sympathies for children and adolescents who are persecuted by a suppressive society comprised chiefly of adults, readers must not overlook that King is also making a call to adults that they may redeem themselves by thoughtfully looking back on their own youth and remembering the magic of those times and the lessons learned. What King is most concerned with in adults is their ability to complete a wheel: to begin life as innocent beings who are eventually corrupted by worldly evil who may then circle back to the period of innocence so that they may not lose touch with beauty of the human experience. Says King, "I'm interested in the notion of finishing off one's childhood as one completes making a wheel. The idea is to go back and confront your childhood, in a sense relive it if you can, so that you can be whole" (Winter, AOD 185). King fears that too often adults become so enveloped in the trials and tribulations of adult life that they drown themselves in the pools of logic and reason; in doing so, they forget the wonder of viewing the splendor and mysticism of life as seen through a child's eyes, an experience they must return to time and time again if they want to avoid being swallowed by the world:

> Rather than indulge in a spurious attempt to recapture a social milieu, King's fiction often looks to our youth as the earlier way of life whose "swan song" must be sung. His stories are songs of innocence and experience, juxtaposing childhood and adult-hood—effectively completing the wheel whose turn began in childhood by reexperiencing those days from a mature perspective. (Winter, AOD 10)

Often in King's fiction, the dilemma facing the adult characters stems directly from two inabilities. The first is the inability to return to childhood and remember the magic of those moments. The second is the failure to understand the significance of an event that happened during that time period—an event that is repressed rather than resolved as one grows older. King attempts to point out that there must be a synthesis between childhood and adult experiences—that one must be able to interpret life by merging the sensory and emotional input that occurs throughout the cycle of one's life. In *The Library Policeman*, the main conflict arises from Sam Peebles' initial inability to return to his childhood and face the atrocity (a homosexual rape) that was dealt to him then. Until the end of the story, instead of going back and facing what happened to him from a mature perspective, Sam hides the memory far back in his mind. But without the synthesis between childhood and adulthood, he is never really whole. Rather, he finds himself trapped solely in one period or the other, as adults can tend to do:

> [after the Library Policeman has stormed into Sam's house]
>   Sam felt a triple-locked door far back in his mind straining to burst open. He never thought of running. The idea of flight was beyond his capacity to imagine. He was a child again, a child who has been caught red-handed
>   (the book isn't *The Speaker's Companion*) doing some awful bad thing. Instead of running (the book isn't *Best Loved Poems* of *the American People*)
>   he folded slowly over his own wet crotch and collapsed between the two stools which stood at the counter, holding his hands up blindly above his head. (487)

The reason the Library Policeman has come after Sam again is because Sam had recently failed to return two library books. Yet while Sam is cowering in the corner of his kitchen under the shadow of his intruder, the emotional salad being tossed in his brain tries to remind him that it is not only those two books for which his intruder has come back; to Sam, the Library Policeman is also asking once again for the Robert Louis Stevenson book he'd not resumed as a child on the day the man raped him. Sam is bounced back and forth between the two time periods because he has not yet been able to complete the wheel and understand what had happened to him. Only when he is able to accomplish that circling back to his younger days can Sam efficiently battle his adversary. As Naomi Higgins, Sam's girlfriend, acknowledges when observing Sam's revival of spirit in confronting his enemy, "he looks like a man who has been granted the opportunity to return to his worst nightmares . . . with some powerful weapon in his hands" (576).

A similar situation can be found in *'Salem's Lot*, where protagonist Ben Mears has returned to the town of his childhood carrying some heavy emotional baggage. When a youth, Ben had entered the Marsten house on a dare, and, after entering, had found the house's owner hanging by his neck from a support beam in an upstairs bedroom. Mears had fled from the house then and has returned to the present with that trauma still unresolved. This lack of resolve in understanding death is intensified by the recent death of his wife, who was killed in a fatal motorcycle accident in which Ben had been driving. Ben's predicament exists until he benefits from the aid of a child, Mark Petrie, who becomes the connection with childhood Ben needs in returning back to his own youth to understand death and dying. Ben then becomes emotionally equipped to combat the league of vampires presently spreading death throughout 'Salem's Lot once he is able to complete the wheel joining youth and adulthood.

What both Sam and Ben do in the end of their stories—complete the wheel—is elemental to King's understanding of the life cycle:

> None of us adults remember childhood. We think we remember it, which is even more dangerous. Colors are brighter. The sky looks bigger. It's impossible to remember exactly how it was. Kids live in a constant state of shock. The input is so fresh and so strong that it's bound to be frightening. (BB 95)

As King points out, because the input is so powerful when perceived as a child, it becomes all the more difficult to recollect it as years separate adults from that experience. By making a mental effort to return to those days and recognizing the distance from them created by time, adults can capitalize on magical childhood moments by synthesizing the memory with an adult's perspective of life. King revealed this belief years before his first published novel in the March 27, 1969, "King's Garbage Truck," written at age 21: "Somehow everything seems to get just a little dirtier and more selfish as we get older. It's good to remember other times, once in a while. We'll have to do it again some time." Once adults can accomplish the synthesis, they will have taken a giant step toward becoming whole.

The need for adults to access their childhood and adolescent memories and observations resonates throughout King's fiction, published and unpublished. *Blaze*, an unpublished King novel held by the Raymond H. Fogler Library Special Collections Department at UMO, is a fine example. The story is about the life of Claiborne Blaisdell, Jr., an oversized man who has a history of criminal behavior in his adult years. Once a promising student as a youngster, his intellectual capacities were destroyed after a brain injury resulting from being thrown down a flight of stairs by his father. The injury caused Blaze's brain to slow, keeping his mind perpetually adolescent. His actions as an adult are correlative to a young person's for he is not cursed with the adult tendency to cheat and deceive. However, his limited intellect often leads to his manipulation and persecution. In order to console himself about the evil of the adult world, he reflects on memories such as the following, a time when he and a friend from the orphanage where he'd been raised played hookie to travel to Boston:

and they began to laugh with each other, laughing into each
other's faces in a rare moment of triumph that comes only once
or twice in the richest of lifetimes, a time that seems wholly natural and right when it occurs, but is golden and soft in retrospect,
too beautiful to be looked at often. It is a time that is usually
recalled in future circumstances that are bitter, a time that is
wholly childhood, often painful in late-remembered truth. Blaze
never forgot it. (70)

The story creates a valid argument that Blaze's slowed mental growth
is a blessing in disguise. It allows him to see life continuously from a child's
perspective which enables him to view simple things with wonder and imagination. The best example of this can be found in Blaze's attachment to Joe
Gerard III, a baby Blaze kidnaps at the prompting of the voice of his dead
partner in crime, George Rockley. Although Rockley is dead, his spirit is
recreated in Blaze's mind to ease Blaze's utter isolation and feelings of lone-
liness that occur once his only friend is deceased. Blaze kidnaps the baby with
the intent of ransoming it, but soon falls in love with it in a way that no rational adult could:

The dawning of the child's possibilities stole over him anew,
and he shivered with the urge to snatch it up and cradle it to
himself, to see Joe open his eyes and goggle around with his
usual expression of perpetual wonder. With no knowledge of
Wordsworth or Rousseau, he grasped the essential attraction
infants have for adults; their cleanliness, their blankness, their
portentious idiocy. And with Blaze, this feeling existed in a
pureness that is rarely common to parents. He was not bright
enough or motivated enough to have ambitions for the child or
to want to mould its direction. Like a naturalist with a new
species of plant, he wanted only to watch it grow. (141)

The story of Blaze is a prime indication of what King is trying to tell
his readers: that it is important to synthesize child and adult perspectives. For
while Blaze is a lovable character in his grownup state of innocence who can
appreciate life in the way only a child can, it is his ignorance of adult behavior that culminates in his demise. His constant slip-ups, typical of inexperienced individuals, lead the law directly to him, and he is shot down in the
woods where he has taken refuge with the baby. Blaze is merely an example
of one extreme: the individual who can recall and perceive life through a

child's eyes, and the one who avoids taking life too seriously. Yet, as has been explained, because Blaze cannot blend child experiences with adult experiences, he remains a helpless victim of a hostile world.

By thoroughly exploring the significance of youth in the chain of human development, King has succeeded in both continuing the theme as presented by his literary predecessors and commenting on the condition of young people in America. The concern for childhood and rites of passage can be linked directly to those American writers who made it a significant part of their fiction: Mark Twain, William Faulkner, Sherwood Anderson, Willa Cather, Flannery O'Connor, Joyce Carol Oates. The themes that pervade stories such as Twain's *Huckleberry Finn*, Oates' "Where Are You Going? Where Have You Been?," and Faulkner's "Barn Burning" are the same ones that have had a profound influence on King's writing. Twain's Huck Finn embarks on a journey down the Mississippi River where his childhood innocence is constantly threatened by the adult world; likewise, King's Jack Sawyer in *The Talisman* ventures west across the expanse of America, a physical journey that correlates his evolution from innocence to experience. Oates' protagonist, Connie, is escorted away by evil incarnate, Arnold Friend, when she selfishly alienates herself and succumbs to wordly desires; King's Arnie Cunnigham in *Christine* makes a similar departure after isolating himself from society while searching for an identity. Faulkner's Sarty comes of age when he turns in his father for having burned a neighbor's farm after Sarty had repressed the truth of his father's evil acts for many years; in a similar situation, King's Danny Torrance (*The Shining*) confronts his father after deciding he is too enveloped in his own selfishly evil impulses to save himself. While these may be crude synopses, the themes concerning youth that King explores with such careful detail are the same that have helped earn his literary predecessors their greatness.

Because King is able to present an image of youth that is both optimistic and sympathetic, he provides a meaningful counterpoint to the tendencies of the American media to stereotype youth as troublesome. In a modernized America where young people are regularly exposed to input that consistently threatens to corrupt their innocence, King's portrayal of youth should be hailed as nothing less than splendid. By writing about youth as a time to be cherished, King assures his readers that they are not too far away from avoiding the self-destruction that can arise from failing to grasp the memories and lessons of being young. Closer scrutiny of King's fiction should convince readers that youth need not be observed as a strenuous period of development but rather one of significant meaning; by returning to younger days and rejoicing in their wonders and steps toward growth from a mature perspective, Americans can save themselves from being devoured by the moral, social, and economic pressures that so often dilute the magic of the human experience with age.

The material covered thus far does not do King proper justice. If one were to accumulate an adequate amount of critical interpretation on the political, social, and moral subtexts of King's works, one would easily fill up rows of library shelves much like those that are weighted with critical inter-pretations on Faulkner and Shakespeare. The material discussed up to this point is an attempt to provide the reader with the knowledge that King is not just an entertainer—that there is more to acquire from a Stephen King book than just scares and thrills. As the ensuing sections aim to prove, King does not limit himself to any one area but rather attempts to address all spectres of the human condition in his canon, a feat that lesser writers of today's pop-ular culture have been unable to achieve.

KAREN A. HOHNE

Dialects of Power: The Two-Faced Narrative

Bakhtin is plainly useful in working with the novel, but it is perhaps less well known how productive is his theory when applied to shorter prose works. One of the most helpful concepts he developed in this respect was that of double accentuation, which when expanded and modified becomes quite effective in the analysis of writing other than the novel and which provides particularly efficacious tools to deal with power struggles as they appear in verbal texts.

In order to explicate double-accentuation in a way that will be useful for the present, we begin where Bakhtin begins, with double-voicedness—the Russian dialect story (*skaz*). He first develops the category of double-voiced discourse, of which the double-accented is a subcategory, to deal with stylization, parody, dialogue, and the Russian dialect story. Double-voiced discourse is torn in two directions at once toward the object of speech and toward someone else's speech. The dialect story, whose name indicates the language used by the narrator, is based partly on "oral everyday narration," but it is a stylization of that narration (1981, 262). The author of such stories speaks in another person's language, but he does not act simply as a tape recorder (no walking mirror here); the other's speech is refracted through the author. Thus the dialect story contains "two semantic intentions, two voices" in one utterance (1984, 189). Further, the dialect story recognizes someone else's way of speaking as representing a particular point of view. In fact, according to Bakhtin, when such a narrative mode occurs it is generally "introduced precisely for the sake of *someone else's voice*, a voice socially

From *The Text Beyond: Essays in Literary Linguistics*. © 1994 The University of Alabama Press.

distinct, carrying with it precisely those points of view and evaluations necessary to the author" (1984, 192).

Double-voiced discourse in the dialect story is then clearly not merely
a question of rubbing two languages against each other—after all, parody can
do that, and there is nothing truly interactive about parody's two languages,
for there the other's speech is simply forced to bear witness against itself. In
parody, the point is to devoice others through their own words; it is a battle
rigged from the beginning. Bakhtin's definition of parody is almost identical
to his consideration that the monologic author uses other languages in order
to further his own ideology, so that "[a]ny intensification of others' intona-
tions in a certain discourse or certain sections of the work is only a game,
which the author permits so that his own direct or refracted word might ring
out all the more energetically" (1984, 203–4).

What is different about the dialect story is that there the other's speech
acts on and influences the author's intention, a key concept, since in this relationship of author/other, the author is the one with the power. Therefore,
one of the primary differences between language interaction in the dialect
story (and, we will see, in other texts that utilize the self/other dichotomy in
terms of the languages incorporated) and in parody is that in the former the
other's language (which would for instance be the parodied in a parody) does
not function as a helpless victim in the struggle between the two languages;
indeed, the other's speech, although divested of power in society, in the work
is capable of profoundly affecting the language of power, able almost to put
it on the run. The other's speech thus has more vitality in the dialect story
than in other types of double-directed discourse. The other's speech is in the
vernacular and extraliterary, opposed to literary language; when literary and
extraliterary languages interact, they are deformed, and it is then that "discourse loses its composure and confidence, becomes agitated, internally
undecided and two-faced. Such discourse is not only double-voiced but double-accented; it is difficult to speak it aloud, for loud and living intonation
excessively monologizes discourse and cannot do justice to the other person's
voice present in it" (1984, 198). It is thus clear that the dialect story, so other
directed, has more in common with the dialogic novel than with the monologic poetry to which it is usually connected on account of what is called its
language play and the estrangement it generally uses. For Bakhtin, the difference between the dialogic novel and the double-accented dialect story
seems to be that the latter is binary (literary/extraliterary) in terms of the languages at work, whereas the dialogic novel involves multiple language sets
that apparently do not fall into these neat categories.

These two language sets in the dialect story are usually designated as written (literary) and oral (extraliterary), but in actually working with double-accented texts and developing the concepts associated with double accentuation, I found that these language categories were oriented incorrectly, revolving as they do around either literature or the written word. The real pole around which the two languages turn is power, in relationship to which they fall into the categories of languages of social power and disenfranchisement, or, as I called them, official and unofficial. Looking at the two categories from this slant allowed me to take the concept of double-accentuation out of the skaz's narrow sphere and apply it to, for instance, general works of literature and popular culture, which application greatly enriched and developed the idea.

Official language is not singular in any society; it is a set that includes any language (even nonverbal languages) that attains value in that society based on its association with entrenched power—the language of the State (the political rhetoric of an in-power entity), of legal documents, of "distinguished" journalism, of high literature, or in a society with a high illiteracy rate, the written word. Although there is clearly some sort of hierarchy of language in society, these dialects of power may be nearly interchangeable in a given work, for they all buy into the system of power and thus in the final instance serve the same master; one may watch them scramble over each other's backs in an attempt to be first and best at giving voice to those who rule. It is notable that whatever particular language is most the language of power in any society, its energy is not wasted attacking other official languages; for instance, political rhetoric generally coexists peacefully with various literary languages in these texts. Officiality knows that other official languages all recognize authority, even if that authority is other than itself; should those other official languages attempt to garner for themselves monologic power, officiality understands and can even forgive, since monologism and the urge to it is the only value in its world. In these texts, official languages feel relatively free to cadge expressions from each other but do not demystify each other. Indeed, since there is so little difference between them in essence, they would then be in effect demystifying themselves, an impossible situation for ideologies that consider monologic power the only kind worth having. Official languages rarely dip into the murky waters of unofficiality to snatch a word or two. A word torn free of its language/world context must experience a change in meaning, but what is more, since unofficial language is always aimed against monologism, monologic forces cannot co-opt its expressions without disarming them, without replacing their meanings entirely, in other words, without obliterating their worlds.

Official language usually embodies its adherence to the ruling forces by its adherence to the rules for language set up by that power; it is grammatically correct according to the grammars penned by those who (consciously or not) serve entrenched power. In contrast, unofficial language as a category is composed of languages that are not valued (or, further, underground or illegal languages) in a particular society and that usually are furthermore rule-breaking in their form as well as their spirit, being ungrammatical, slangful, bastardized, and generally nonlinear. In the case of the dialect story, unofficiality may appear as the speech of peasants or uneducated urban workers; in other works, it may be the speech of children, criminals, and similarly marginalized people.

Whatever the instantial language, it is clear that what is official and unofficial depends on the society and is subject to historical change. At the same time, the power/not-power dichotomy that gives rise to these two language sets may not exist in all societies; thus this essential organizing force is not ahistorical. However, wherever there is official language, there must be unofficial language. We may refer to Bakhtin—monologism is never complete, for even in silence is response.

In the world, officiality either completely erases otherness or attempts to render it voiceless by reporting its speech incorrectly (lying, with which officiality is preoccupied). It smears unofficiality by attributing to it its own crimes and killing off, either literally or figuratively, its speakers. In texts, official ideology does not simply ignore the other (figuratively killing the other by making the other absent) but aggressively seeks others out, weighs their loyalty, and grants its benediction or places them under its interdict. The greatest sin against officiality is unofficiality (the greatest offense to power is powerlessness). It is not so much an act that offends, but existence itself, although one may say that officiality views existence as action. Any manifestation of unofficiality is a crime against nature—in other words, against officiality's scheme of things—and thus is considered (even if not intended as such) a blow directed against its rule. In texts (and, unfortunately, even in life), unofficial others are first deprived of their own voices as officiality reads their lines for them. Unofficiality in a masquerade version may be made to stream from others' mouths in a sort of divine manifestation as they are forced to accuse and condemn themselves of the great crime of unofficiality. Finally, they may be executed.

Just as it is often necessary to learn the language of a country in order to get along in it, one may find oneself taking on official language as one's own, in a text or otherwise. Officiality's most damaging effect on those who try to learn it as a second language is the loathing and fear towards the unofficial other it produces, be that other another person or within the speaker's own psyche. Within the individual, officiality's general attitude towards the unofficial other in the world is reproduced in miniature. The war between official and unofficial raging in society is duplicated within the individual in some of these texts.

Unofficial ideology, on the other hand, is distinguished not merely by its vocabulary but by how it behaves. It constantly tries to enter into dialogue and is apparently incapable of exiling others to absence or stripping them of their rightful voices. It embraces otherness, with which it must sense the kinship of all outcasts and disenfranchised. It is eclectic, borrowing from various aspects of unofficial culture—slang, obscenities, advertising, popular music, yellow journalism, the speech of children, peasants, workers, the illiterate, etc. When the mongrel of unofficiality meets prim officiality in the contest of literature, the general result is that unofficial language/ideology sticks out its tongue and reveals official language/ideology as a lie. Yet as aggressive as unofficiality is in its demystification of officiality, it does not usually attempt to gain the position of power, to officialize itself by obliterating officiality and clambering onto the vacated throne. It seeks only to unseat, not to be coronated.

The kind of narrative that showcases double-accentuation takes monologism as its topic, revealing its negative effects. But these texts are no one-sided depictions of the horrors of some version of fascism, real as those horrors are. They speak not only monologism's deadly effects, but its slithery attractions. They duplicate the only two categories that monologism allows—self/good/true and other/bad/lie—but turn them on their heads. And if official language is usually the language of the author/reader, then taking monologism as a subject means monologism not just out there somewhere in the world, but in the internal world; in other words, writing (and reading, if one reads dialogically) this kind of text means attempting to demystify not only the world but the self.

I have observed double-accentuation in the short fiction of writers as diverse as Isaak Babel, H. P. Lovecraft, Raymond Chandler, and Stephen King. All have a relationship with the canon that is at least troubled. Babel flickers in and out of the world of officiality; during his lifetime, he was considered literature and thus official by most but was more or less erased from Soviet literature for a good twenty years after his execution. He is still not a dependable soldier in canon's ranks; even in the West he has never enjoyed the popularity he deserves—not monologic enough, perhaps, especially in his relationship to the Soviet State. Lovecraft has endured (totally unmerited) criticism for years, even from his fans, and although he has occasionally been taught in universities, one may rest assured that it was always off in the suburbs of a science fiction course. Raymond Chandler as a popular and therefore devalued author has fairly recently undergone a rehabilitation as the most literary and thus worthwhile of the hard-boiled detective writers. He is discovered to have been speaking official language all along, if in guttural accents, and is permitted in the hallowed halls as long as he behaves. But Stephen King has not even attained the status of Lovecraft, who at least can be passed off as Golden Age; although scholars of popular culture have begun to turn their attention to King, he is completely unofficial, with no place in the canon. It is plain that double-accentuation can occur in High Literature and popular lit, in Russian and English, in the twenties, thirties, seventies, and eighties, but I wonder if when it does occur it has a tendency to keep the author's works out of the canon. I would enjoy hearing from other scholars who may find examples for or against this. Because he is probably more familiar to more readers than any of the other authors, I will use Stephen King as my exemplar.

Since King's rough-cut narrators generally employ no literary language at all (although there are frequent exceptions), it might seem impossible to find officiality in his writings, but we will see that he has a great deal at his command, and when that loses its impact, he invents his own. He draws attention to language and acts as a mediator, providing a network for various languages to interact (reinventing the heteroglossic world and thus affirming that heteroglossia). King's narrators' speech is highly oral (sentences strung together with "and" or phrases repeated in the redundant stutter of conversation, for instance) and is full of highly unofficial slang, obscenities, and even snips of unofficial culture—bits of rock songs, advertising jingles, and set phrases born on TV. But it would be wrong to believe that this narrative is purely unofficial, lacking any elevated (and thus official) language; it is instead first of all an off-center version of slang, an interpretation that refracts it through a literary lens: "The bulbs couldn't banish the twelve-year darkness; it could only push it back a little and cast a sickly yellow glow over the whole mess" (*Night Shift*, 39). Here, the literary and almost biblical "banish the darkness" is proven inadequate by the conversational "a little" and "the whole mess." This passage is a good example of how in King (and others) official and unofficial languages rub shoulders and in the process may shatter into fragments smaller than a sentence.

In our society, the nonwritten has never had the power of the written word; it is highly unofficial. But in these writings it seems as if unofficial language becomes contaminated with officiality because it is elevated to the position normally occupied by literary language—it is indeed difficult to speak it aloud without excessively monologizing. Oral speech begins to need

demystifying, and this comes in the intrusion of thoughts. These generally utilize typeface to signify and often lack punctuation. It is on the plane
of external versus internal dialogue or narration versus the narrator's
"authorial" comment that some of the greatest tension between official and
unofficial is created. Rather than seconding or ratifying speech, thought
may contradict speech and thus take on the role of the unofficial, revealing
the narrator's speech as inadequate to the situation:

> As I said, there was a slight problem . . .
> *Yes. Horror, lunacy, and death. How's that for a slight problem, kids?*
> (Skeleton Crew, 242)

Here the narrator's blandly official "slight problem" (almost military in its
flare for understatement/lying) is undercut by his own internal other rejoin-
ing with the slangy "kids." An even more powerful example is supplied by
"The Mist," where the internal unofficial other speaks more like itself—not
linearly, not in sentences, but in fragments, in whispers

> [Mrs. Carmody was] [n]othing but an old woman with a few
> stuffed animals in the back room and a reputation for
> *(that witch . . . that cunt)*
> folk medicine.   (*Skeleton Crew*, 141)

For a somewhat more subtle usage, where one insists on one's own
internal, unofficial word over the official word imposed from without, there
is the story of a boy who finds a tiger in

> The bathroom
> *(!basement!)*   (*Skeleton Crew*, 156)

Of course, the internal, unofficial other who insists on "basement" is proven
correct—there really IS a tiger in the boy's room.

These examples illustrate more or less unofficial speech (that is, oral
speech occurring either in dialogue, as it does here, or elsewhere as the narrator's voice) becoming official when used constantly for literary purposes
such as narration. To deflate this now-tainted orality, then, requires another
type of "spoken" speech—thought—so that thought is to spoken as spoken
is to written. It is as if King cannot get enough of unofficiality and must
increase it exponentially.

In King, not only the unofficial language is used for the sake of incorporating someone else's voice; officiality serves the same purpose. It gets the treatment usually reserved in our culture for the unofficial: it is depicted as monstrous, literally or figuratively. In the story of the tiger in the boy's room, official language is used by the authority figure (the teacher) to humiliate one who by virtue of being a child is powerless and who speaks an unofficial language. She demonstrates the violence of which officiality is capable when in front of the entire class she remarks to the boy, "Very well, Charles. You may go to the bathroom and urinate. Is that what you need to do? Urinate?" (*Skeleton Crew*, 156). Later on, the boys use among themselves the unofficial word, "piss," with, of course, no embarrassment.

Official language is also the peddler of dangerously false knowledge that pretends, as usual, to know everything. A version of official language I have elsewhere called Scientific because of its use of science-peculiar buzz-words and syntax occurs in King and normally has lethal consequences, but official language is not limited to this. Religious language proves to be a particularly virulent strain of officiality. It powers "Children of the Corn," where the children adept at religio-speak sacrifice passers-by and their own to a murderous god.

These official languages may easily coexist in the same text. They are well combined in "The Mist," where science, our present religious authority, overwhelms and destroys the world, and old-time religion kills off those who remain. The deadly Mrs. Carmody, who demands human sacrifice to appease the angry gods of scientific blunder, does it in a Revelations version of monologism:

> "—expiation! It's expiation we want to think about now! We have been scourged with whips and scorpions! We have been punished for delving into secrets forbidden by God of old! We have seen the lips of the earth open! We have seen the obscenities of nightmare! The rock will not hide them, the dead tree gives no shelter! And how will it end? What will stop it?"
>
> "Expiation!" shouted good old Myron LaFleur.
>
> (*Skeleton Crew*, 141)

Science and religion, which we would normally see as completely opposed, are revealed as quite similar in terms of their relationship to otherness: if it is not-I, kill it.

In King unofficiality takes over the narrative, dominating the narrator's language and manifesting itself in his truth-telling thought, but unofficiality here is never as impenetrable as it can be elsewhere (for an example in another horror/SF writer, see H. P. Lovecraft's rendering of alien speech as a stream of consonants or the illiterate peasant Russian of Isaak Babel's Cossacks). There are no languages so other as to refuse to yield to our understanding, and King's characters are almost never of the "forbidden" sort that populate the worlds of other writers using this method—a college-educated Jew pretending to be an illiterate cossack, a homosexual avenging his lover's murder, and bad women galore. It seems to me that King does not use these social transgressors because his narrators' speech is already much more *in* unofficiality than most others'; popular culture is celebrated and accepted as a vital aspect of the narrative of our lives. It is unlikely that an untranslatable unofficiality could exist in a world so unofficial, but what is more, King's readers live in this particular unofficiality, which cannot be said of the other writers' works. I believe this accounts for a great deal of King's popularity; he is the native son who speaks the speech never before spoken so proudly or so out loud.

In short fiction (and in general in cultural products) that has an ear for heteroglossia, ideologies in power (official) and those which are disenfranchised (unofficial) interact as particular languages (usually levels within one language, but interactions between two languages such as Russian and French are also possible). The struggle between the two sets of languages bursts apart the narrative of officiality, overtaking the characters' or even the narrator's speech. In this way, the situation of lived reality, which in fact so deviates from its official version, is told or described. The overthrow of a dominant, prestigious language by a subordinate, devalued language is presented in order to demonstrate official ideology's actual inability to gloss the universe, despite its claims to the contrary.

Unofficiality is characterized by its constant attempts to engage in dialogism, to interact, and is generally associated with real knowledge—the truth of the story itself, of narrativity, while official language means bafflement (false knowledge), an inability to listen that results in the inability to create a story that makes sense of the situation. A language combining these two, as does the narrative language of King and other writers, foregrounds the very interaction that occurs in our daily lives but is somehow never given voice.

LINDA BADLEY

Stephen King Viewing the Body

In the early 1970s, when everyone else thought horror was fueled by sex, King targeted the thing Freud had most notably neglected, "the central obscenity, the dark under all our beds, as death" (Gibson, "Foreword" xvi). Two incidents in King's childhood may have provided a basis for his obsession.

When he was two years old his father, Donald King, disappeared—permanently. In the fall of 1959 or 1960, Stephen found a box of his father's old 1940s paperbacks in his aunt's attic together with a sampler of stories from *Weird Tales* magazine, a collection of H. P. Lovecraft stories, and some rejection slips from men's magazines—evidence of Donald King's attempts to write horror and science fiction (*Danse Macabre* 99–102). In recounting his discovery in *Danse Macabre*, King lingers over the "shiny overcoating" on those (Avon) paperbacks, a "cross between isinglass and Saran Wrap" (101), suggesting these objects' talismanic power over him. As in fairy tales and Dickens's novels, King's protagonists are orphans searching for their true parents—and ultimately (as adults) for community. His fiction is a search for the father who walked off and left a box of weird tales in his place, who left his son haunted with stories about absences and hauntings that must be told or lived.

In the second trauma, four-year-old Stephen evidently saw a friend run over by a passing train. Years later, the author wrote in *Danse Macabre*, "my mother told me they had picked up the pieces in a wicker basket" (90). He claims to have no memory of the incident. As a horror writer, he has been picking up pieces of the body ever since.

From *Writing Horror and the Body: The Fiction of Stephen King, Clive Barker, and Anne Rice.* © 1996 Linda Badley.

King has written over and over about this combination: the missing father and the confrontation with the body that "calls" a boy to become (if not a man) a horror writer. It is the kernel that informs King's metafictions and the "King myth" that informs popular culture. The first of these was "The Body," a novella drafted in 1973 or 1974 (Winter, *Stephen King* 207) and published in *Different Seasons* (1982) under the section heading, "Fall from Innocence."

THE BODY IN "THE BODY"

After the death of his football-hero brother, twelve-year-old Gordon Lachance is alienated from his father and finds companionship with three friends. "The Body" follows the gang's journey to find the corpse of a boy who has been killed by a train. This story is equally a Kristevan allegory of the body, a descent into embodiment, the underworld of chthonian nature, followed by an ascent to textuality. The corpse "seen without God and outside science," Julia Kristeva explains, "is the height of abjection. . . . It is something rejected from which one is not separated" ("Approaching" 127). His act of viewing the body marks Gordon's reclaiming of the "powers" of horror:

> For a moment it seemed all right, a more natural deathscene than any ever constructed for a viewing-room audience by a mortician. Then you saw the bruise . . . and the way the corpse was beginning to bloat. . . . You remembered that gassy smell . . . like farts in a closed room. He was a boy our age, he was dead, and I rejected the idea that anything about it could be natural; I pushed it away with horror. ("The Body" 417)

In his revulsion, Gordie pronounces the scene unnatural, detaches himself from the body, and enters the symbolic order of culture and language. In a Stephen Kingish pun Gordie remarks on how the "kid was disconnected from his Keds"—has been literally knocked out of his shoes—"beyond all hope of reconciliation" (405). As the scene's interpreter and the gang's story-teller, Gordie takes on the role of the medicine man (Biddle 96) or sin eater.

In "The Body," the corpse is the last of numerous references—scatological, sexual, and oral—to loss of bodily control. Two embedded stories, representing Gordie's development into Gordon Lachance, the best-selling horror writer, are also allegories of the body. "Stud City," the twenty-year-old Gordon's first published story, betrays its author's immaturity in more than the title. It is "an extremely sexual story written by an extremely inexperienced young man" who had "been to bed with two girls and . . . ejaculated prematurely all over one of them." "Stud City"'s attitude toward women, Lachance admits "verges on actual ugliness—two of the women . . . are sluts, and the third is a simple receptacle" ("The Body" 322). Virginia, Chico's stepmother, represents the sexual aspect of the chthonian mother Gordon defeats in the act of writing. (The more mature Gordon peeps out of two sentences in "Stud City": "Love may be as divine as the poets say, but sex is Bozo the clown bouncing around on a spring. How could a woman look at an erect penis without going off into mad gales of laughter?" ["The Body" 312]).

"The Revenge of Lard Ass Hogan," the story young Gordie tells Vern, Chris, and Teddy, is another Kristevan scenario. As Chris says, it "ain't a horror" but horror's carnivalesque ("Gross but funny" ["The Body" 362]) mask/masque. When in the film adaptation (*Stand By Me*) Lard Ass spouted purple puke "like the combined fountains of Rome," the on-screen hilarity and the theater audience as well reached, according to *National Review*'s John Simon, "gargantuan dimensions. The scene seems to go on forever and gives a wholly new [embodied] meaning to the phrase 'purple passage'" (Simon 60)—as purple *rite* of passage and as communication medium. Lard Ass's passage to maturity means descending into the chthonian underworld ("his whole head disappeared into the pie-plate" [370]) and emerging triumphantly as the hero as artist: (blueberries "flew" from the pie-dish, "staining the tablecloth around him like a Jackson Pollock painting" [371]). His revenge begins in an abjection ritual in which daring to lose control—willfully, publicly, and infectiously—gains him power and perverse respect. Lard Ass is King's comic paradigm of the writer as agonist, who transcends embodiment through the body.

On another front, "The Revenge of Lard Ass Hogan" is *Carrie* in drag. Lard Ass is ridiculed because his obesity makes him soft or abject like a woman, but like the (French feminist) hysteric, he becomes a sorceress. As a metafiction, we should see Lard Ass's triumph as comparable to writing like a woman, from the body, entering the symbolic order through its back door.

The embedded stories are juvenilia King published originally in college magazines (Winter, *Stephen King* 107). As Leonard Heldreth notes, the two stories are in different typefaces (72), suggesting a mastery of several voices. These variations, like King's other typographical enhancements, signal dialogic or polyphonic narrative. It is writing as speech act, postliterate prose. "The Body" only appears to be one of King's more literary stories, a Portrait of the Artist as a Horror Writer. Through a Proustian regression, however, he returns to the oral community of friends and dialogic forms. In King's metafiction storytelling is a "talking cure" but in a literal, social, and Jungian sense. "The Revenge of Lard Ass Hogan" never has a final form, retaining its vitality in oral performance. It is requested (by best friend Chris) and interrupted by audience participation: "There ain't no *Gretna* in Maine" (Vern); "Shut up and let him tell the story" (Chris); "*Whole* pies?" (Teddy) [362–64]).

Paradoxically, the act of writing is "done in secret," like masturbation, twelve-year-old Gordie notes. Writing on the one hand is a private ritual, a regression and return through which one gains self-integration and control, as Leonard Heldreth stresses, and on the other a bonding activity or dialogue that makes the thought of mortality less lonely (74). Isolated by writing, the twenty-year-old Gordon recalls listening to his brother's bedtime stories, and is comforted by that recollection. Fourteen years later the successful novelist knows that people write stories to "*understand the past and get ready for some future mortality; that's why all the verbs in stories have -ed endings. . . . The only two useful artforms are religion and stories*" (395). Gordon's headnote to "The Body" also emphasizes the need for "*an understanding ear*" (289).

KING'S WASTE LAND

King did not confront the body or the subject of death so directly again until *Pet Sematary* (1983), the graphic and disturbing anatomy of the medical perspective he began in 1979. Most of the earlier novels had been adult fairy tales or supernatural epics that buried the real spectre in the subtext. *'Salem's Lot* (1975) attributed the disappearance of an entire town to vampirism, displacing fear of death as fear of the undead. In *The Stand* (1978), in which a superflu destroyed most of the world's population, King took horror to another level of power, acting out a fantasy of invulnerability through destroying and rebuilding the world. "I felt a bit like Alexander or . . . Johnny Rotten," he wrote in *Danse Macabre*. "No more Ronald McDonald! No more Gong Show or *Soap* on TV—just soothing snow! No more terrorists! No more bullshit! . . . I got a chance to scrub the whole human race, and *it was fun!*" (373).

It was far from the earlier admission that "the body" was "a boy our age, he was dead, and I rejected the idea that anything about it could be natural" (417). Through the supernatural coping mechanisms of genre horror, King had "always shied away from . . . the aftermath of death," as he admitted to Douglas Winter in 1984. "The funeral parlors, the burial, the grief . . . the guilt." *Pet Sematary* was about "a real cemetery" (*Stephen King* 132).

As an encounter with mortality, *Pet Sematary* initiated a period of reflection and return and self-analysis. Writing the novel was disturbing, "like looking through a window of something that could be." Determined "to go through with it, to find out everything, to see what would happen," King found the book "ceased being a novel" and became a Sisyphean task (qtd. in Winter, *Stephen King* 131). In 1979, he finished the first draft and put it in a drawer. Two years later he pulled it out and looked at it again. "I thought it was a nasty book" (Winter, *Stephen King* 131).

Pet Sematary was Stephen King's version of *The Waste Land*; it was a cultural diagnosis that indicted his own "white soul." Protagonist and King-surrogate Louis Creed, a doctor at the University of Maine at Orono, has little philosophical or psychological preparation for death. A rational materialist (a lapsed Methodist married to a nonpracticing Jew), he has no formal creed (other than the Hippocratic Oath). When under stress he returns to a fantasy of driving an ambulance in Disney World as the head of Walt's "resurrection crew."

A children's pet cemetery provides an initiation ritual for Louis, his wife Rachel, and his children Ellie (six) and Gage (two). An elderly neighbor and father figure Jud Crandall takes the family there for their "first eyeball to eyeball with death," necessary in "[T]hese days" when "no one wants to . . . think about it" (*Pet* 60). Later, Louis realizes that Ellie knows more about "Ronald McDonald and Spiderman and the Burger King" than "the whole *spiritus mundi*" (Pet 198). The world of religion, myth, and ritual is signified in conspicuous absences or reversals. Time is indicated through references to seasons and holidays, with each commemorated more incoherently as the year goes on, and with Louis's son Gage's death and grotesque resurrection occurring sometime around Passover or Easter. *Pet Sematary* goes over the themes of late modernism, and has similar cultural work to do. King anatomizes mass culture as an evasion of death and life, as simulacrum.

Louis stumbles through his son's funeral in a haze of grief and alcohol, dimly conscious of buying a coffin with his Mastercard, of a fist fight with his father-in-law in the funeral home as grief is displaced in hypermasculine violence (culminating as the two men knock the coffin from the trestle and a small hand spills out), of the "violently green" Astroturf at the graveside, and of a pizza and a painting of a clown at Howard Johnson's. The banality of this death is overwhelming. Louis's coping mechanisms are offered by a youth-oriented mass culture—by rock music (The Ramones), *The Wizard of Oz*, Disney World (his idea, apparently, of heaven), and American naturalism—forces that merge to compose a powerful denial.

Pet Sematary critiques the modern medical perspective, as Foucault does in *The Birth of the Clinic* (1975), as something that mystifies and dehumanizes death at the same time—cloaking it in esoteric language and confining it to sterile sanctuaries. The simulacrum and the hospital collaborate in *The American Way of Death*, as Jessica Mitford put that issue in 1963, and *Pet Sematary* is its post mortem, 1980s style. On the one hand, it is Disney World, ritual as miniaturization and evasion. On the other, it is materialistic and violently alienating.

The pet cemetery is arranged in Druidic rings that allude to Stonehenge (connoting human sacrifice and cannibalism as well as mystery) to suggest the real primitivism behind modern medical "miracles" (King, qtd. in Winter, *Art* 134). It is the outer circle of a Micmac Indian burial ground that sends the dead back in a state of soulless half life, resurrecting with brutal literalness. A succession of accidents, heart attacks, strokes, and deaths—Jud's wife Norma, Louis's two-year-old son Gage, Jud, and Rachel—and resurrections follow.

The turning point is the death of Gage. Louis is a heavy father as a baby boomer with a Peter Pan complex. Obviously at issue is Louis's bioethical creed, his belief in saving the only life he knows, the material. But this desire is based in a patriarchal lust for immortality through the son, expressed first in an agony of sorrow and rage, then ghoulishly, as he disinters his son's corpse and makes the estranging discovery that it is like "looking at a badly made doll" (*Pet* 342). Performing his task, Louis degenerates into a "resurrectionist" from a Victorian shilling shocker or "a subhuman character in some cheap comic-book story" (*Pet* 333). The reanimated Gage appears to have been "terribly hurt and then put back together again by crude, uncaring hands" (*Pet* 388).

The Wendigo, which presides over the supernatural elements in the novel, is a Native American spirit associated with cold, isolation, dislocation, and cannibalism. King appropriates it, associating it with American materialist values and the bioethical dilemmas of the 1980s. The Micmac burial ground where it resides offers a frozen, naturalistic prospect, a high plateau where the stars make him feel "infinitesimal, without meaning" (*Pet* 134), a barren ground where piles of broken stones (as in "The Hollow Men") are the only markers. But the hollowness of Louis's bioethics is truly shown in his habit, when under stress, of taking mental trips to Orlando, Florida, where he, Church, and Gage drive a white van as Disney World's "resurrection crew." In these waking dreams, Louis's real creed is revealed: its focus is on Oz the Gweat and Tewwible and Walt Disney, that *"gentle faker from Nebraska"* (*Pet* 376)—two wizards of science fantasy.

Louis's disintegrating state of mind, which reflects that state of modern culture, is replicated in intensifying textual incoherence and fragmentation. He is increasingly haunted by cartoon visions of Mickey Mouse, Goofy, Gage, and Church, which mix surreally with fragments from Marvell and Eliot and the *Wizard of Oz*. Louis's wizardry is reflected also in the narrative perspective and structure, which flashes back in Part 2 from the funeral to his sun-drenched fantasy of a heroically long, flying tackle in which he snatches Gage from death's wheels. Louis's resurrection schemes reflect a culture-wide Frankenstein and Peter Pan complex, realized in the postmodern monster he has begotten. Wielding his father's scalpel and cannibalizing his mother, Gage is the measure of a generation.

The baby boomers, King explained in *Time* in 1986, "were obsessive" about childhood. "We went on playing for a long time, almost feverishly. I write for that buried child in us, but I'm writing for the grown-up too. I want the grown-ups to look at the child long enough to be able to give him up. The child should be buried" ("The Novelist Sounds Off"). In *Pet Sematary*, King had disinterred and anatomized that buried child. In the novels to come he would bury the child again, this time with formal rites.

Drafted in 1979, when King was teaching creative writing and Gothic literature at the University of Maine at Orono, *Pet Sematary* was the hub of a group of stories that marked a culture's mid-life crisis and a similar turning point in King's career. He would subsequently turn to anatomize the material culture he so often claimed to be speaking for. *Pet Sematary* also foreshadowed his later turn from conventional (*'Salem's Lot*) and fanciful (*Christine*) horror and toward existential themes and experimental, self-aware forms—to the regressive, polyphonic structure of *It* (1986, begun in 1979) and to the metafiction of *Misery* (1987) and *The Dark Half* (1989).

If *Pet Sematary* affirms any source of community, culture, and belief, it is the form and ritual of the children's pet sematary. Its concentric circles form a pattern from their collective unconsciousness, a pattern that mimes "the most ancient religious symbol of all," the spiral (*Pet* 286). *It* makes *Pet Sematary*'s merely hinted consolation into its primary focus and structural device. In *It*, a group of children similarly create a provisional community and a mythology as a way of confronting their fears, as represented in It, a metamonster, the serial-murdering, shapeshifting bogey that haunts the sewers of Derry, Maine. In 1958, the seven protagonists, a cross-section of losers, experience the monster differently, for as in George Orwell's *Nineteen Eighty-Four* (1949), It derives its power through its victim's isolation and guilt and thus assumes the shape of his or her worst fear. (To Beverly Marsh *It* appears, in a sequence reminiscent of "Red Riding Hood," as her abusive father in the guise of the child-eating witch from "Hansel and Gretel.")

In an ominous passage early in *Pet Sematary*, Louis dreams of Disney World, where "by the 1890s train station, Mickey Mouse was shaking hands with the children clustered around him, his big white cartoon gloves swallowing their small, trusting hands" (31). To all of *It*'s protagonists, the monster appears in a similar archetypal form, one that suggests a composite of devouring parent and mass-culture demigod, of television commercial and fairy tale, of 1958 and 1985: as Pennywise the Clown, a cross between Bozo and Ronald McDonald and John Wayne Gacy, the serial killer who performed as a clown. As in *Christine*, *Pet Sematary*, and *Thinner*, the monster is material culture itself, the collective devouring parent nurturing its children on "*imitation*[s] of *immortality*" (*It* 1138). Like Christine or Louis's patched-up son, Pennywise is the dead past cannibalizing the future. Thus twenty-seven years after its original reign of terror, It resumes its siege, whereupon the protagonists, now professionally successful (but childless) yuppies, must return to Derry, like the ex-hippies of *The Big Chill* (1983), to confront as adults their childhood fears. Led by surrogate horror writer Bill Denbrough, who now stutters only in his dreams, and Mike Hanlon, librarian and historian, they defeat It (at last revealed as a huge female spider, the pre-Oedipal mother once more) both individually as an allegory of psychoanalysis and collectively as a rite of passage into adulthood and community.

"WORD MADE FLESH, SO TO SPEAK": THE DARK HALF AND *MISERY*

It was attacked in reviews as pop psychology and a "badly constructed novel" and the puerility was partly intended. (Its inspiration was a beloved image: the entire cartoon cast of the Bugs Bunny Show coming on at the beginning.) *It* would be, he promised, his last horror novel, a nostalgic calling forth of all the monsters at "clearance-sale time. Everything must go" (King, qtd. in Kanfer 83). The book was one important rite in what would be a lengthy passage, a looking backward and inward, regressing and taking of stock. The last chapter begins with an epigraph from Dickens's *David Copperfield* (1849–1850) and ends with an allusion to William Wordsworth's "Intimations of Immortality," from which King takes his primary theme and narrative device, the look back that enables one to go forward. In the 1970s King's fiction was devoted to building a mythology out of shabby celluloid monsters to fill a cultural void; in the postmodern 1980s, he began a demystification process. It was a ritualized unmasking of motley Reagan-era monsters, the exorcism of a generation and a culture. As in *Pet Sematary*, where the monster often appeared as a cross between Oz and Walt Disney, the monster-clown Pennywise came uncomfortably close to resembling most that "gentle faker" from Bangor, Maine. For *It* (the novel) was also an analysis of King's cultural work over the preceding decade.

After *It*'s extensive exploration of childhood, King took up conspicuously adult characters, issues, and roles. In *The Eyes of the Dragon* (1987), he returned to the wellsprings of his fantasy: he wrote a fairy tale for his daughter Naomi, then thirteen. King told much the same story as before but assumed the mantle of the elder and oral narrator. As a fairy tale for adults, *Eyes* summed up and reconfigured many of the oral and mythic elements in King's early work: the presence of a voice, the improvisational tone, the archetypal characters. While he continued to cultivate "voice" or textuality, he sharply restricted character and situation in order to examine writing itself as a mode of knowing and as a speech act. The book introduced King's self-conscious phase, a move away from vast gestures, epic sweep, huge casts, and easy consolations. It picked up where *The Shining*, "The Body," and "Survivor Type" had left off and directly addressed the issues inherent in his peculiar role. Beginning with *Misery* (1987), he would write metafictions that interrogated his own role as horror writer and celebrity. In 1989 he explained that "what I have written about writers and writing in the last five years or so has been a real effort . . . to understand what I am doing, what it means, what it is doing to me, what it is doing for me . . . [to] understand the ramifications of being a so-called famous person" (*Second* 11). *Four Past Midnight*, published in 1990, was a turning point, a "[L]ooking back over the last four years" and seeing "all sorts of cloture [sic]" ("Two Past Midnight" 250).

An earlier, and by far the most dramatic, example of King's deconstruction of "Stephen King" was the creation and subsequent revelation in 1984 of his pseudonym Richard Bachman. He published the five Bachman books over an eight-year period, he has claimed, to limit his official output to two novels a year. Bachman soon grew into an identity with a biography and photographs (he was a chicken farmer with a cancer-ravaged face), dedications, a narrative voice and social vision, and a naturalistic mode in which sociopolitical speculation combined or alternated with psychological suspense. In 1985, when the novels (with one exception, *Thinner*, 1984) were collected in a single volume attributed to King as Bachman, the mortified alter ego seemed buried. Bachman's demise raised the question of what "Stephen King" really was, not only for his readers but also for King. Yet, far from disturbing the interest or the trust of his readers, the revelation enhanced his reputation and sold more books.

As evidence of a dark alter ego, Bachman didn't do King any harm. The squeaky clean family man acquired depth, a dark soul, something more than desirable—indeed necessary—in a shaman. Shortly after Bachman's internment and beginning with *Misery* (1987), King began a series of metafictions whose subject was the King phenomenon itself, especially the writer-reader relationship. *The Dark Half*, which came next, in 1989 (after a decent four-year interval following the pseudonym's decease), was the story of Bachman. The novel was a self-interrogation and an allegory of a relationship that is at least three-fold: between the writer, his imagination or "genius" (his "third eye"), and his public image.

Protagonist Thaddeus Beaumont is a professor and moderately successful literary novelist devoted to his family. But he has been living a secret life of twelve years through George Stark, the pseudonym under which he emerged from writer's block as the author of best-selling crime novels. Stark's genius finds its most vital expression in *his* protagonist, the professional crime boss Alexis Machine. Like King, Beaumont is found out and forced to disclose and destroy his pseudonym and ritualizes the event with a graveside service and *papier mâché* headstone. Destroyed as a fiction (or released from sublimation), the pseudonym bursts out of the grave in physical form. The series of murders that follow (of the people responsible for the pseudonym's "demise") is narrated in Stark's graphic prose style, with Stark's control of the text at this point standing for his power over Beaumont's life, literally to take Thad's wife and children (twins, of course) hostage. What Stark wants is to live in writing, outside of which writers and characters do not exist. King draws on a literature of the double and the detective story, including Stevenson's *The Strange Case of Dr. Jekyll and Mr. Hyde* and Sophocles' *Oedipus Rex*, in which protagonist must discover the demons within himself before he can stop the plague.

The alter ego is a physiological as well as psycho-literary phenomenon: Stark is Thad's cannibalized twin. At age eleven Thad had a series of headaches and seizures, and a surgeon removed from his brain the fragments of his sibling. Stark's origins and their physical juxtapositions suggest that they are Apollonian and Dionysian parts of a whole, a dynamic or dialogue that compels the writer. Thus King literalizes his idea of the visionary "third eye." Tony Magistrale found Stark's separate physical existence hard to suspend disbelief in: "One moment we are asked to view Stark as a secret sharer of Beaumont's most private inclinations; the next minute these two men are as different from one another as a suburban professor and an urban street punk" (*Second* 65). But Magistrale is reading the novel as psychological fiction, with a modernist, Freudian model in mind, where King's models are

Barth, Jung, and Nintendo games.

As a medium, the author's job is to "create a bifurcation in the reader's mind," King told Magistrale. One half "says this is all make-believe, words on a page; the other half is living that life, becoming more and more real. That is power" (qtd. in *Second* 11). Stark is a demonstration of that reality and that power. He is a caricature of the ancient literal-mindedness inherent in postliterate horror. Thus King renders him as a graphic pun and allows him literally to take over. The epigraphs and allusions in the novel are from and to Stark's books. He murders people connected with Thad's decision to bury Stark, most of whom are connected with the literary business—Thad's agent, editor, fan/informer, and a local man who is bludgeoned with his own prosthetic arm. Stark also murders literature, inscribing its corpse with a straightedged razor, meaning a triumph of body in the worst sense—of "stark" and mindless violence, gore, seriality, copycat killers—over literacy and textuality. Stark is a cliché realized through a collective fantasy, projected in part by Beaumont, in part by readers, and hence by culture. Thus King blurs boundaries between Stark and *his* character, Alexis Machine, whose actions are the models for Stark's (or is it Beaumont's?) murders. The ambiguity lent by a third term in this allegory of doubles embodies a larger confusion shared by the reader and the writer between an author, his persona, and his character. The confusion extends to the medium in which Stark thrives best, the shared hallucination of mass mediated space.

King "is tactful in teasing out the implications of his parable," says George Stade. No character says "that reality inevitably leaks fiction, which then floods reality, that reality and fiction feed on and feed each other" (12). Instead, combining comic book flatness with the naturalism of a graphic novel, King gives textuality visceral "life." Of course, Stark describes it best when explaining himself—as "word made flesh, so to speak." The act of will that forces his exit is revealed in the structure of the book. King flouts expectations by reversing his usual procedure, glutting the first half of the book with Stark/Machine's rampages, reconstituting the character of Beaumont in the last half. Beaumont's story falls away as Stark's razor-sharp action emerges; as Stark loses physical cohesion, Beaumont's contemplative metafiction dominates. He performs a series of automatic writing exercises and self-interrogations, alternating between his typewriter or pen and Stark's pencil. In the showdown, Beaumont controls body and mind to regain textual power while Stark writes to remain embodied. Meanwhile Stark's last book, *Steel Machine*, taking shape in pencil, reveals huge gaps and repetitions of the word "sparrows" and "the sparrows were flying"—sparrows being King's metaphor for psychopomps that bear souls to the land of the dead.

The text ends in a "scene from some malign fairy-tale" (423) as Stark is borne away by flocks of sparrows and makes a final imprint as a black hole in the sky.

On the Usenet newsgroup on Stephen King, James MacLeod compared reading the *Gunslinger* books to playing Donkey Kong, a Nintendo game. The Stark half of *The Dark Half* has the berserk momentum of a video game. Stark's character and "logic" come as much from pulp fiction, adult comics, and computer graphics as from psychological or literary sources. He is the action game raging to take over Beaumont's and King's text—or textuality, literacy, and decency altogether.

But as text within text, "Stark" also engages readers in the text's creation, cultivating literacy. Like the metafictional detective stories of Jorge Luis Borges, the computer fiction of Michael Joyce or Stuart Moulthrop, or the old epistolary novel, King's metafictions effect a level of "hypersexual" engagement. Here we have the King of the introductions, notes, and afterwords telling us how and why he does what he does, the experience of "the author" overlapping with his fictions proper. These are merged with the story, however, engaging readers in the production of the text.

Readers are finally encouraged to read the novel as a *roman à clef*. At the outset, in an "Author's Note," King makes sure the Bachman myth informs our experience: "I'm indebted to the late Richard Bachman for his help and inspiration. This novel could not have been written without him." Like Bachman, Stark is the pseudonym declared dead and buried, exorcised as private demon, only to be resurrected as a body irradiated by the "Stephen King Phenomenon." Thus the "real" Bachman gives *The Dark Half* flesh and blood. *The Dark Half* alludes throughout to King: Stark is buried in Homeland Cemetery in Castle Rock, Maine, King's territory. This is the land of the uncanny, that unremembered (all too familiar) territory and, as in *Pet Sematary*, the collective unconscious. The large hole in the turf in front of Stark's fake gravestone remains the central mystery of the novel: it corresponds with the gap or intersection in the text in which meaning is constructed and fictions take independent life.

In the context of the "King myth," *The Dark Half* is a farewell to automatic writing and "action" heroes, comic books, and postliterate prose. At the end of the book Thad says good-bye to the "lovely visions that third eye sometimes presented" (413) and sends off George Stark, a flock of sparrows bearing his decomposing body away. At the same moment, "King," the author who has merged postliterate prose with academic metafiction and "Stark" violence with a moral tale, transcends both Stark and Beaumont. The third eye goes on seeing. The sin eater goes on eating.

The purgation of Stark/Machine, like the revelation of Bachman, is finally cathartic and reassuring for the reader. And in confessing Stark/Bachman, King becomes more saintly in his readers' eyes. Like a number of celebrities (including First Lady Emeritus Betty Ford, televangelist Jimmy Swaggart, and actress-cum-author Elizabeth Taylor), through periodic sinning, public confession, and mass mediated absolution, he becomes "one of us."

King didn't really send off Richard Bachman, of course; he incorporated the alienated, cancer-ridden chicken farmer's perspective into his work. As a pseudonym Bachman had allowed him to be not only pessimistic but more introspective and "literary" and, once introduced as a "part" of King, allowed him to write his series of self-exploratory metafictions: *The Dark Half*, *Misery*, and the novellas "Secret Window, Secret Garden" and "The Sun Dog" (in *Four Past Midnight*, 1990). King has explained that he is often "unaware of what he's really writing until after he is done. It's like drawing pictures in a dark room, and then a sudden illumination shows you what you've been drawing" (Magistrale, *Second* 7). These allowed him to view the relationships of writer, reader, and text in clear relief, focusing more narrowly than before, through two or three characters, on the relationship between writers, readers, and text. *Misery* was conceived as Bachman's book (Beahm 168) but revised and published as King's in 1987. Misery was also the first of his novels to get good reviews.

Misery was about "the powerful hold fiction can achieve over the reader" as personified in Annie Wilkes, a psychotic former nurse addicted to romance novels. After he crashes his car during a blizzard on an isolated Colorado road, best-selling romance writer Paul Sheldon is rescued, drugged, and held prisoner by Annie, "Number One Fan" of his heroine Misery Chastain (of whom he has tired and killed off). This "Constant Reader" becomes Sheldon's terrible "Muse," forcing him to write (in an edition especially for her) *Misery's Return* to life. Like the witch from Hansel and Gretel or the Bad Mother, Annie punishes Sheldon's attempts to get free by amputating his foot and thumb with an ax, "exercising editorial authority over his body" (264). And like Scheherazade, the oral storyteller, Sheldon must publish, perform as demanded, or literally perish.

Misery is unusually cerebral and bitter for King. Among other things, the novel is about the experience of being cut to fit fan expectations. It also attacks America's "cannibalistic cult of celebrity": "[Y]ou set the guy up, and then you eat him" (qtd. in Kilgore 109). *Misery* is a sophisticated satire both on and for the postliterate reader. Before his car accident, Sheldon has attempted to enter the ranks of literary novelists, not only by killing off Misery and his romance series, but also by writing *Fast Cars*, a grimly realistic novel that he feels good about. Annie is dismayed at its lack of "nobility" and then enraged when she reads it: "It's filthy," she says. "It's also no good" (39).

Annie punishes Paul by forcing him to burn his manuscript (his only copy) and write *Misery's Return*, which will bring the nineteenth-century romance heroine back to life. Annie and her obsession represent the pre-literate world associated with Scheherazade as the storyteller in thrall, compared to sexual slavery. With *Fast Cars*, Sheldon has achieved "male" textuality, enters into the symbolic, which liberates the writer from the his-torical-physical context, from presence and audience. (Ironically his "other" fast car has driven him into a snow bank and the arms of Annie Wilkes.) Forcing him to burn his text (his manhood), Annie destroys his (writing's) independent life, and plunges him back into ancient darkness, where he is chained once more to his audience, to his body.

Thus the situation is gendered: textuality and literacy are male, and Paul Sheldon's readers are "ninety percent of them women" (25). The set of oppositions generated by the conflict of Paul and Annie, writer and reader, includes the masculine and feminine. Speechless, helpless, unfocused as a baby at the beginning of the novel, Paul recapitulates child development. "Annie is the mother; . . . the monstrous feminine, the castrating female," presented as all-engulfing (Hanson 150). She is Sheldon's terrible Muse, a female counterpart to Scheherazade's misogynistic Shahyar, and more. Annie comes to embody all that Sheldon's heroine Misery's name suggests. She is the misery traditionally attributed to the female as "the sex." Like "an African idol out of *She*," Annie is a "big but not generous" woman without "feminine curves": she gives Paul "a disturbing sense of solidity, as if she might not have any blood vessels or even internal organs" (7). Here her total objectification identifies her also with the mother in the Kristevan scenario of abjection, where the child's entrance into the symbolic is sig-naled by revulsion from the mother's engulfing body. Thus Annie in her depressive phase, brought on by premenstrual syndrome, softens into more than usual shapelessness, a visual metaphor for the Mother as "the point where meaning collapses":

> This massive . . . strangeness which, if it was familiar to me in an opaque and forgotten life, now importunes me as radically sepa-rated and repugnant. Not me. Not that. But not nothing either. A "some thing" that I do not recognize as a thing. A whole lot of nonsense which has nothing insignificant and which crushes. At the border of inexistence and hallucination, of a reality which, if

I recognize it, annihilates me. (Kristeva, "Approaching" 126)

Annie is the Stephen King "gross-out," suggesting (as Hanson says) that horror is a predominantly male rite of abjection. As she "softens," first bingeing on ice cream, then smearing it on herself, and finally mutilating herself, Sheldon hardens. He literally works out: he recaptures his strength, lifting the typewriter (an ancient Royal) over and over to strengthen his arms. The typewriter and the text symbolize an act of protest against crushing meaninglessness. As in the Kristevan scene, writing emerges out of physical revulsion and an act of separating from the Mother, a struggle Sheldon envisions as a rape ending in the triumph of the symbolic over engulfing flesh. Annie, says Hanson, is a "catalyst" bringing Sheldon out of the darkness of infancy "to the wielding of textual power" (152). The text of *Misery's Return* also rises to the occasion: "Annie was right; the story was turning out to be a good deal more gruesome than the other Misery books. . . . This book, he began to understand, was a Gothic novel, and thus more dependent on plot than on situation. The challenges were constant" (154). Sheldon's definition of the Gothic corresponds with Leslie Fiedler's view of it as masculine protest.

If indeed *Misery* incorporates Bachman's vision, Bachman allowed King to write a politically incorrect novel about gender. Magistrale admits that it is "about the destructive, potentially castrating nature of women." Annie Wilkes is mentally unstable, but she is "one of the few women in King's canon who posseses real power, and she does not know how to handle it responsibly" (*Second* 126).

But *Misery* is also more generally, like "The Body," about writing and the body: the experience of the body, "feminizing" embodiment, and the body as text. King chooses as epigraph to Chapter 2, a proverb from Montaigne, which says that "*Writing does not cause misery, it is born of misery.*" It is as Elaine Scarry suggests in *The Body in Pain: The Making and Unmaking of the World*: one writes to articulate embodiment, the condition of existence epitomized in physical pain, and which can be articulated only indirectly through metaphor or fiction. Expressing physical pain "eventually opens into the wider frame of invention" (Scarry 22).

In the beginning Sheldon is embodied, and the reader experiences the text as his physical struggle for articulation against pain. The seemingly meaningless sounds of the first words of the novel ("umber one fayunn") announce Paul's regression into aphasia, his dispossession of the world.

In the early stages, as he is dozing and waking, he thinks in an allegory of pain. It is "something like a horse race. At first King of Pain was far in the lead and I Got the Hungries was some twelve furlongs back. Pretty

Thirsty was nearly lost in the dust" (34). At last visually conscious, he is just barely able to identify his legs as shapes: "His left knee—a throbbing focus of pain—no longer seemed to exist at all. There was a calf, and a thigh, and then a sickening bunch in the middle that looked like a salt-dome" (35). Only after the renaming of his parts, recognizing and reconstructing himself, can Sheldon complete the making of *Misery's Return*. As the typewriter throws keys, Sheldon writes in the missing characters, and handwritten text threatens to take over the typescript. Yet the text's regression into manual writing corresponds with Sheldon's increasing unity of being and control, his emergence out of pain. (As the typewriter degenerates as a writing tool, it becomes proportionately vital to his reclaiming of physical power, and it becomes the weapon that kills Annie.) The text of the metafiction *Misery* emerges with the agony that produces *Misery's Return*.

Beyond this allegory of writing out of bodily misery, *Misery* suggests that the Constant Reader is the author's text. Indeed, the hallucinatory opening of the novel leaves doubt as to whether the book is other than a dream. And if, as King said, it is about the "powerful hold fiction has on the reader," Annie results from Paul's success in attracting and addicting readers. Misery's last name *Chastain* (suggesting *chain, chastise, chastity*) alludes to Annie's (and the Reader's) repression, which her addiction to romances encourages. In the long run Sheldon needs and serves the terrible Reader/Muse more than he defeats her. Sheldon's writing is like Annie's reading—an addiction, linked with the pain-killing drugs she alternately offers and withholds. The relationship is a terrible co-dependency, a sadomasochistic marathon. Sheldon survives by finding out how "To get her *gotta*." The *gotta* being the drive or compulsion or sickness that compels a person to go on—that makes you *have* "to find out what happened next" (224). "The *gotta* which had kept them both [writer and reader] alive" (226). The irony underlying this battle of the books is that Sheldon's antagonist, like Scheherazade's, is absolutely necessary to his writer's life. When he plots the novel more rigorously than in his previous books (suggesting a triumph of the linear and "masculine"), he discovers that his constant sadistic reader is also his best reader, the one who stimulates the fear of death that (according to Helene Cixous) enables the male to "get it up." Indeed, Sheldon concludes that *Misery Returns*, the product of this sadomasochistic ritual we have shared—and not his "literary" novel *Fast Cars*—was his masterpiece.

The body Sheldon defeats, whether Annie's or his own (or the generic) is "the feminine." Yet Sheldon triumphs only by restoring and reinstating Misery—the romance character and the "female" body, the figure who embodies for Sheldon the misery of writing. Therefore, Sheldon writes not only against the feminizing body; he writes "from the [female] body" in the Cixousian sense, and after an agonizingly long labor gives birth (*Misery Returns*). *Misery* is finally about writing as an encounter with the Anima, whether the female Constant Reader, the "female" body, or the woman in oneself (Frazier 95–97). This encounter means, as in the case of Cronenberg's Brundle, Sheldon must "become" a woman. Thus he is able to invest his heroine with some of his own misery (Magistrale, *Second* 129). Annie is the means for Sheldon's recovery of the feminine he has discarded (in *Fast Cars* and the snow bank) and that is essential, it seems, to his writer's life. Writing requires the "female" flesh it attempts to transcend, and King's novel *Misery* is about the procreative struggle of male word and female flesh for ascendancy over the authorized text.

Misery finally compels readers, male and female, to identify with Sheldon's epistolary misery as a physical struggle, an agony, a battle with drugs and pain, and thus, by implication, with King, who rises to the occasion. But readers are also uncomfortably characterized in Annie. Male or female, we cannot help but note that our activity has a counterpart in Annie's addiction to romances. We turn the pages of *Misery's Return* and *Misery* in sync with Annie as she devours the text. We may, like Clare Hanson, be further disconcerted when the novel culminates in Sheldon's triumphant textuality, imagined as "our" rape.

The jacket copy claimed that King "owe[d] his fans a love letter. *Misery* is it." The flap was consistent with the novel in playing on self-referential elements and provoking readers to think about some rather discomforting things. Richard Corliss compares reading the book with watching the film: King's novel "doesn't stop till your expectations and his energies are depleted . . . wrung out, and he wants you to feel he's exhausted too from some Wrestlemania, this fine fuck." The last sentence of *Misery* comes "from an author who has purged his demon by writing about her" ("By the Book" 38). It is dated "Lovell, Maine: September 23rd, 1984/Bangor, Maine: October 7th, 1986: *Now my tale is told*" (310). Sheldon and King, writer and writer, text and subtext "come" subversively together.

The analogy between the writer's body and the text, and between virility and creative juices, censorship and castration, is hardly new. Overt allusions throughout remind us that the situation is like that in *The Collector* (Paul wonders if John Fowles' first novel is on Annie's shelf.) On page 159, he writes, "Another day lost in the funhouse with Annie," alluding to John Barth's metatext about being in thrall to the Muse. As Barth returned to Scheherazade in his program to revitalize a "literature of exhaustion," Sheldon is revitalized by the Constant Reader, his terrible Muse and

Whore. King's text explores, as Hanson says, itself and in the process "the genesis of all King's fiction, . . . the origins of what he calls his 'Gothic' horror" (149). King contrasts male Gothic-horror with what he apparently views as Female Gothic Romance.

Misery, perhaps the most literate of King's novels, is a middle-aged, gender-troubled, Kristevan version of "The Body." It openly competes with academic metafiction but on King's terms and, within those terms, succeeds. It made its mark as a postliterate version of postmodernism, striking normally hostile critics with its vitality that many other such allegories often lack: "good weight" as well as wit, human interest, vitality of prose style, the "gotta." *Misery* is anything but abstract. Readers experience reading and textuality in visceral and aural terms, experiencing the textual equivalent of the oral agonistic. At the end, cinematic terms like rinse and wipe remind us that Sheldon (and yes, King) is now sitting at a screen, using a word processor. Having regressed and returned, Sheldon transfers his recovered energy over into a civilized—and also clearly postliterate—setting. Most of all, King flaunts his superiority at "writing from the body" in the simplest sense of producing a visceral effect.

But in other ways the metafictions subverted the Stephen King phenomenon. They told how writing is misery, yet to be at a loss for words is to be entrapped within the body. Words aspire to displace bodies, so that the birth of the Author often means the death of the woman (often the wife) in King's stories. And the Author has ultimately little control over his texts. The Reader imprisons the Author, demands, and in effect writes her own romances. Worse, she is a serial killer whose homicidal mania is sublimated in and inspired by the text. The text moves out of the Author's control also as a persona impelled by the phallic power of the pen. Beaumont exorcises Stark, but there is no more evidence that his "literary" novels are good than of the excellence of Sheldon's *Fast Cars*.

King's last metafiction, "Secret Window, Secret Garden" (in *Four Past Midnight*, 1990), undermines the concept of authorship itself. It is Barthes's "The Death of the Author" for postliterate prose. A writer discovers to his horror that he may be a plagiarist, and the uncertainty is the horror, suggesting the postmodern perspective in which all texts are derivative and either consciously intertextual or plagiarized. The open secret in "Secret Window, Secret Garden" is King's recognition that there is no Stephen King.

"Bachman," as the intended author of *Misery* on the other hand, may have expressed genuine horror and a genuinely dark King. *Misery* fits Fiedler's definition of the Gothic as an expression of hypermasculine horror of the feminine, as Hanson argues, and specifically of the feminine as the state of being embodied, without textual Author-ity. *Misery*, moreover, was focused directly on the target. Recent studies of misogyny, homophobia, and fat-phobia in King's novels suggest how squarely his horror is centered in the body's frailty and the horror of the chthonian mother.

Abe Peck of *Rolling Stone* asked King if writing horror was "like Boy Scout camp, sitting around and telling a story," and he replied,

> No, it's a lot more sinister than that. I don't know if we talked about this or not, but at one point somebody said, "What do you think Kubrick wants from *The Shining*?" And I said. "I think he wants to hurt people."
>
> Well, maybe I was just saying what I want. My idea is that you should be able to suck somebody in and really hurt them. (Peck 101)

King's misgivings about *Pet Sematary* even after publishing it suggest that it was "Bachman" who wrote that novel: "It's a terrible book—not in terms of the writing but it just spirals down into darkness. It seems to be saying nothing works and nothing is worth it, and I don't really believe that" (Modderno 144–45). The Bachman books have a similarly alienated pessimism. As Tony Magistrale suggests, Bachman supplied King with a Hyde, a necessary voice to "indulge his darkest fantasies and speculations" (*Second* 63) and "explore a side of himself that is far removed from his image" as a devoted father and husband, and participating citizen of Bangor, Maine. "In the end Bachman served as a means of liberating King's art" (*Second* 65–66).

The Dark Half explored more directly the part of King the writer that wanted to "hurt." Stark is as monstrously hypermasculine as Annie is monstrously feminine. Like Arnie Cunningham empowered by Christine, Stark drives a big oil-burning car with a bumper sticker reading "HIGH-TONED SON OF A BITCH" (430). Stark's hypermasculine "drive" (epitomized in Machine) is linked with writing: the slasher/writer embodies a threefold analogy between penis, knife, and pen[cil]. Like a hard-on, Stark-Machine leads Beaumont headlong through the book until, in the showdown at the end, Beaumont learns to sublimate his aggression in politically correct, literary efforts.

The Dark Half apologized for King's violence and misogyny even as it vented it. However devastating its real implications (which are similar to the message of Oliver Stone's now infamous film *Natural Born Killers*, 1994), *The Dark Half* seemed to say the correct thing and was a safe book. Earlier, and more significantly, "Bachman" had allowed *Misery* to be what Magistrale calls an "unsafe book," an attack via Annie Wilkes on a "composite" of "conflicting forces—from the demands of an expectant audience to the disparaging remarks of academic critics and reviewers*f* that seek to confine the art of Sheldon/King into reductive and therefore safe categories" (*Second* 126). A comment in King's introduction to *The Bachman Books* is in similarly gendered terms: "My 'Stephen King publishers' were like a frigid wifey who only wants to put out once or twice a year, encouraging her endlessly horny hubby to find a call girl. Bachman was where I went when I had to have relief,' ("Why I Was Bachman" ix). But more than that, "Bachman" allowed King to cross taboo lines to project and identify sources of tension and alienation.

One difference between King and Bachman, it became evident, was that Bachman saw through the "white soul" that "Stephen King" as global village bard epitomized. The Bachman books are unrelentingly pessimistic and often disturbing. They depict a debased social landscape: the elements of popular culture that are treated with affection in his mainstream books—for instance, the name-brand mythologies—become the waste land we have seen in *Pet Sematary*. The protagonists are alienated, from the beginnings of the novels, and the future, as Magistrale describes it, "is devoid of love, stable relationships, and any real degree of sociopolitical freedom" (*Second* 63). This is telling when three of the five novels are science fiction: *Roadwork*, *The Long Walk*, and *The Running Man*, two of which compare the future to a game show in which the stakes are life and death. *Thinner*'s protagonist Billy Halleck—a complacent, affluent, obese lawyer responsible in a hit-and-run accident—is reduced by a Gypsy's curse to a shadow of his former self and given a dark vision of "white soul." In the primary metaphor he eats compulsively to fill his empty soul, stopping at fast-food outlets along the highway. Yet he shrinks and hollows out to an image consistent with his truer spiritual state. Regarded as "terminal," he loses faith in the social institutions that once supported him. He ends up thinner: ruined and alienated. The reader is left with a view of a world that is, as in George Romero's film *Dawn of the Dead*, "literally feeding on itself,' (King, qtd. in Winter, Stephen King 205, n. 10). To put the issue mildly, there were no fairy tale consolations for Richard Bachman. *Rage* (1977, 1985) is narrated by an alienated student who shoots his algebra teacher in front of the class. As they sit in stunned silence, he sits down behind the desk. "'This,' [he says] pleasantly, 'is known as getting it on'" (*Bachman* 33).

In June 1993, a high school student named Gary Scott Pennington performed a similar act a few weeks after doing an oral book report on King's novella *Rage* (Reed 44). Annie Wilkes, George Stark, Alexis Machine, and "Richard Bachman" suggest the extent to which King the Sin Eater is haunted by such events, and these characterizations that literally embody violence—social violence and the horror writer's violence—are obviously exorcisms. Their embodiment is also a cautionary tale about phenomena such as Pennington, or Mark Chapman's infatuation with *Catcher in the Rye* before killing John Lennon, or John Hinkley's fixation on Jodie Foster through her role in *Taxi Driver*, or the "Carrie Killer." In *The Dark Half*'s central metaphor of word made flesh, King referred to the "copy cat" killer and acknowledged the collectively projected realities that texts can become, the possibility that the public fascination with serial killers, for instance, actively breeds them. He exposed the danger inherent in his own sin eating, that in absolving society of its guilt by taking on its projections, in healing them, he feeds the collective disease that makes them sick. The healer thus perpetuates the disease. This acknowledgment partly demystified the real-life serial killer "phenomenon" King had helped create. But King's association of himself (and "Bachman" and Bachman's novels) with the serial killer could not help but lend mythic power to the serial killer "phenomenon" in turn. In the process, the serial killer enhanced "Stephen King."

FLESH MADE WORD, OR THE WOMEN'S ROOM: *GERALD'S GAME* AND *DOLORES CLAIBORNE*

As King commented in 1989, "Bachman killed his children before they were out of infancy. I've noticed that in the work I am doing now, if there are any children they tend to be older. . . and all these things seem to be keeping . . . progress with my own life" (Magistrale, *Second* 4–5). After writing as Bachman for eight years, and asserting the conscious control required of *Danse Macabre* and *Pet Sematary*, King was able to step back and write with more "literate" self-awareness. Yet, in spite or because of this increasing self-consciousness, through the postmodern 1980s and now in the anxious, gender sensitive 1990s, he has continued in his role as America's Sin Eater. In his most recent phase, he has moved from metafictional self-exploration to self-expansion. He has engaged in role playing and gender shifting, testing or moving beyond the limits of the horror genre as he formerly defined it, and taking risks. The screenplay *Sleepwalkers* (1991) and novels *Gerald's Game* (1992), Dolores Claiborne (1993), *Insomnia* (1994), and *Rose Madder* (1995) take up gendered issues that are more often the territory of Clive Barker and Anne Rice: among them abortion, religious fanaticism, sadism, masochism, domestic violence, and incest. Three of these books are as King has said, part of a belated effort to understand women by writing from women's points of

view (See Magistrale, *Second* 5), *from* (rather than merely in horror of) the
female body. Testifying to the seriousness of this effort, *Gerald's Game* is dedicated "with love and admiration, to six good women," all originally named
Spruce, among them King's wife and novelist, Tabitha Spruce King. *Dolores
Claiborne* (1993) is dedicated to Ruth Pillsbury King, his mother.

    Gerald's Game is a survivor's story based in a classic Female Gothic sit-
uation: the woman trapped in the house and terrorized by her husband. Over
a seventeen-year marriage, Jessie Burlingame has been coerced into playing
the victim's role in a sado-masochistic bondage and discipline game. At their
lakeside cottage on a warm night in October, already naked and handcuffed
to their bed, Jessie refuses to play Gerald's game. When he persists, Jessie
kicks him in the groin, he goes into shock, collapses, and dies of a heart
attack. The novel consists of her sensations, memories, associations, and
thoughts during the twenty-eight-hour ordeal, during which she recovers
memories of sexual molestation by her father. Connecting Gerald's sex game
with her father's, she begins to understand her oppression. Recollecting further, she engages in imaginary dialogues with long-dead friends, who provide
alter egos to her habitual role as "Goodwife Burlingame." Jessie recovers a
will to live and strength to endure pain—enough to mutilate her wrists and
struggle free of her shackles.

    Misery blamed a sadistic and all-devouring matriarchy for the protago-
nist's victimization. *Gerald's Game*, as its title announces, condemns patriarchy. The latter "corrects" the misogyny implicit in *Misery*, transposing its
situation and setting into Female Gothic and taking the woman's point of
view. Both novels are feats of ingenuity. The setting is the bed, which makes
tortured body language not only exploitable but essential. In both, the gendered body is a prison, trap, torture chamber, and medium. As Sheldon is the
male author shackled to the demands of an insatiable woman/reader/muse,
Jessie's bondage represents the sexual slavery of women. Where Annie turns
from the Constant Reader into an archetypal bitch goddess, Gerald is dead
meat from the beginning, and becomes a reference point for female rage. In
response to Annie's increasing abjection, Sheldon rises to the occasion.
Horror also makes Jessie powerful. The sight and sound of a stray dog (a
bitch?) devouring her husband's body rouses her instinct for survival. From
the opening scene, the male body is abject, positioned as Other. Sheldon is
called on to discard, reconstruct, and resurrect himself through writing;
Jessie recovers her deep resources. The difference is that Sheldon's antagonist is Annie and Jessie's is her context and herself. And where Sheldon must
recover physical and textual power, Jessie must discover hers. She becomes
the Cixousian hysteric whose body speaks unconscious truth. Alone with

her thoughts, without food or water, and for two nights in complete darkness, she becomes preternaturally attuned to sounds and smells, returns to oral/somatic consciousness, undergoes disintegrative regression, recovers memories of past traumas through somatic cues, smells in particular, and undergoes reintegration. This psychosomatic event triggers her assumption of control over her body, a matter of getting outside of her skin, quite literally, of using her body as a tool even while staying in touch with its perceptions.

Jessie's story alludes to novels of women's awakenings that are now required college reading, from Charlotte Perkins Gilman's "The Yellow Wallpaper" to Kate Chopin's *The Awakening* to Atwood's *Surfacing*. In the 1983 *Playboy* interview, King used the words of "that fine poet Anne Sexton" to describe what writing meant personally for him: "I am able to 'write myself sane'" (Norden 44). Jessie's story is also modeled on the incest survivor's narrative that has become a reductionist psychological cliché, one that, as Wendy Doniger notes, "exploits the contemporary American obsession of those who define themselves a victims and orient the rest of their lives around their victimization. . . . Mr. King relies on the victimization scenario for the whole structure of his novel" (3). Such a text made Stephen King not an imitation feminist so much as a poor one.

Gerald's Game was, among other things, a public rite of self-correction, and self-correction sells as well as anything these days. As a massively popular entertainer, King participates in mass culture's co-option, domestication, and (also) inclusion of once marginal causes and groups. If 1970s feminism had given force to Carrie's rage, it also energized *Misery*'s masculinist backlash and provided a female body language for Jessie's recovery in *Gerald's Game*. King's sudden sensitivity in the 1990s to old gender troubles suggests the extent to which feminism—even French feminism—has become a common language and enabling myth.

But in *Gerald's Game* and subsequent novels, King returned to the roots he put down in his first published novel *Carrie* (1974). Like the stories in Angela Carter's *The Bloody Chamber* and Anne Sexton's *Transformations*, *Carrie* was a fractured fairy tale of Cinderella's revenge, whose violence returned to older oral versions that gave women more power. King has called *Carrie* "a book about women" that expressed "a lot of male fears—about menstruation and about dealing with women who eat you up" (Peck 95). In 1983 King admitted that the charge of stereotyping women characters was "most justifiable," and he extended the criticism to his "handling of black characters":

Hallorann, the cook in *The Shining*, and Mother Abagail in *The Stand* are cardboard caricatures of superblack heroes, viewed through rose-tinted glasses of white liberal guilt. And when I think I'm free of the charge that most male American writers depict women as either nebbishes or bitch-goddess destroyers, I create . . . Carrie—who starts out as a nebbish victim and then becomes a bitch goddess, destroying an entire town in an explosion of hormonal rage. I recognize the problems but can't yet rectify them. (qtd. in Norden 47)

In an interview with Tony Magistrale in November 1989, King explained that Carrie was part of an effort, recently reinstated, to "understand women and try to escape the stereotyping that goes on in so much male fiction" (*Second* 5).

Carrie had provided challenges, not the least being the unfamiliar, intimately female nature of the subject matter. King became ill at ease, and he threw an early draft of the first few pages into the kitchen trash basket: "as I arrived at . . . [the opening scene] I suddenly realized that I (1) had never been a girl, (2) had never had a menstrual cramp or a menstrual period, (3) had absolutely no idea how I'd react to one. . . . I had been in a girl's shower room exactly once" ("On Becoming" 21). Tabitha King found the discarded pages and persuaded him to finish the book. Paradoxically, King and Carrie were in precisely the same alien territory for the first time, that of the sex, the female body. Through the feat of empathy that writing it required, *Carrie* somehow became a powerful diagnostic, treating menstrual taboos and the Judeo-Christian origins of misogyny with uncommon boldness for 1974. Carrie is the victim of her mother, who has been inculcated with Judeo-Christian misogyny. Mrs. White demonizes her daughter's body, flesh of her flesh, and therefore constructed under patriarchy in terms of Sin and Death. Carrie is the Female Gothic heroine imprisoned in the "maternal legacy" of the female body (Showalter, *Sister's Choice* 128) perceived as antagonistic to a sense of self, as the following passage could not demonstrate more clearly:

"And God made Eve from the rib of Adam," Momma said . . . [thumping] Carrie with the side of her foot and Carrie screamed. "Get up, woman. Let's . . . pray to Jesus for our woman-weak, wicked . . . souls.

"Momma—". . . .

"And Eve was weak and—say it, woman. Say it!"

"No. Momma, please help me—"

The foot swung. Carrie screamed.

"And Eve was weak and loosed the raven on the world," Momma continued, "and the raven was called Sin and the first Sin was Intercourse. And the Lord visited Eve with a Curse . . . of Blood . . . and Eve found that her belly had grown big with child." (54)

In the end, Carrie has become "a kind of monstrous hero," says Clover—"hero insofar as she has risen against and defeated the forces of monstrosity" and monster in her demonic excess (4).

Dolores Claiborne is equally about a woman who has become a monstrous hero. But Dolores has consistently refused to be a victim. She is not only "the major character" in the story; she "dominates" the book's "landscape" (Magistrale, *Second* 5). And where Carrie's vengeance is the stuff of gossip and legend, Dolores narrates her own story. Terrence Rafferty calls the novel King's "most stubbornly literary" book, "lurching back and forth in time on the waves of the narrator's unruly emotions" ("Under a Cloud" 93). It is a dramatic departure from his ordinarily transparent style and linear plotting (93). Suspected by the police of murdering her wealthy employer Vera Donovan, Dolores explains her role in the death of her husband, Joe St. George, thirty years before. In the process, she accounts for her life, a bleak, narrow existence on Little Tall Island off the coast of Maine. King's strongest and fullest female character, Dolores not only refuses to be a victim; she sees to it that Joe falls down a well shaft—on June 20, 1963, during the total eclipse of the sun—thus ending his molestation of their thirteen-year-old daughter Selena.

Dolores's voice is at first hard to take, and more than one reviewer remarked her scatological garrulity. "I guess you'll have to fix this up some, won't you?" she tells Nancy, the stenographer. "I'm just an old woman with a foul temper and a fouler mouth," Dolores admits, "and that's what happens, more often than not, when you've had a foul life" (5). She opens with a lengthy (twenty-page) series of descriptions of Vera's use of her excretory functions as a form of power and pleasure (the "dirty old bag had her a shit savings account . . . only I was the one who got the withdrawals" [27]) on her "bright" days. The passion and eloquence of Vera's anal retentiveness matches that of Lard Ass Hogan's gargantuan bingeing and purging. However, its purpose is not anything so noble or adolescent as revenge. This book has a different kind of body language. Beyond its effectiveness in an arena of oral agonistic, its purpose may be like that of Angela Carter in *Nights at the Circus* (1984) whose swashbuckling and monstrously heroic narrator employs a

bawdy, blustering, belching, farting, body language as part of her refusal to
be a lady. Another is to show what it is like to be an old woman, one with
"nothin to do but die in an upstairs bedroom on an island far from the people and places she'd known most of her life" (44). Still another is to present
a Female Gothic version of the Kristevan scenario, for Dolores views Vera,
among many other things, as her mother, huge and shapeless in senility. It
reflects, perhaps, King's horror as a child at finding himself alone with his
obese, bedridden grandmother's corpse (described in the story "Gramma"),
his own horror as an adult watching his mother die of cancer (described in
the story "The Woman in the Room"), and his mother Ruth Pillsbury King's
experience as caregiver to her aging parents.

   Gerald's Game's Jessie Burlingame is ambiguous because her sanity and
strength are, after all, in doubt. Her uncertainty is calculated like the point
of view in Henry James's *The Turn of the Screw*. Jessie's final trial in *Gerald's
Game* is the image, apparition, or hallucination of a spectral male figure in a
dark corner. Its existence in the gap of the liminal calls her flashbacks to
scenes of molestation into question and hints at schizophrenia. *Dolores
Claiborne* is a different kind of survivor's story. Its ambiguity is rooted in
sterner stuff. The total eclipse of the sun by the moon, associated with female
power and the body (anima, shadow, womb) provides the moment for
Dolores to lose her husband down a well, described as a light-devouring
black hole. Like Thad Beaumont, Dolores has a dark third eye for her intu-
itive, dangerous side, which provides another image of eclipse.

   Dolores does not lose touch with the natural world or her task, whether
it is to tell her story, rid the world of the scurrilous Joe, or clear away the
"dust bunnies," the "bunch of ghost-turds" (47) whose gray nastiness haunts
and terrifies Vera in her dotage. True to her name, Dolores (Madonna
Dolorosa, dolorous, morose, ill-tempered) Claiborne (clay born, cthonic)
remains steadfastly in the natural world and simultaneously represents the
mother destroyer. Like Vera (whose words, "Sometimes you have to be a
high-riding bitch to survive. . . . Sometimes being a bitch is all a woman has
to hold onto" [*Dolores* 169] provide the motto of the book and who may have
killed her children as well as her husband), Dolores is not *nice*. For that reason—for her resistance to the grieving victim stereotype—we admire her. She
is Annie Wilkes liberated from romance novels, absolved and vindicated.

   The well-made film adaptation scripted by Tony Gilroy and directed
by Taylor Hackford and outstanding for its purposes, improvises what
Rafferty sees as a "warm mother-daughter soap opera," drawing on the same
pop psychology as *Gerald's Game*: we watch as Mother Dolores forces the
churlish, hard drinking Selena to remember her molestation and confront

her victimization. King's book is informed by the more interesting idea, that "women's suffering doesn't have to turn them into victims, and that there's something heroic about the hard shells they develop to protect themselves from a hostile environment" (Rafferty, "Under a Cloud" 94). The novel vindicates the "bitches" of the world, the point being that "without your guts, Dolores Claiborne, you're just another stupid old woman," as Vera puts it (300). The novel reveals the mother-daughter estrangement in flashbacks, leading to Dolores's choice of daughter over husband. But the incest survival plot is a minor part of the narrative, and bad memories, especially for Vera, are all too close to the surface. However melodramatic its ingredients (incest, murder, a suspicious car accident, an eclipse), the novel is a subtle revelation of a relationship, an intensely ambivalent one, between "two bitches livin on a little chunk of rock off the Maine coast," as Dolores puts it, "how they passed the years in that big house, two bitches who ended up spendin most of their time bitchin at each other" (299), and who cared more for each other than for anyone else.

King succeeded in writing a woman-centered novel and also in enhancing, indeed multiplying, his persona. How much his feminism should be trusted, I do not know. Before the 1990s, taken as a whole, King's women have been a horror story. Vera Donovan and even Dolores Claiborne can be viewed in a long line of death bearing mothers. The ultimate horror is the inner-child-devouring female spider that is It's final form and whom Bill Denbrough destroyed with the words, "Try this, you bitch! TRY THIS ONE OUT! DO YOU LIKE IT? DO YOU LOVE IT?" (1093).

The It-Spider's antithesis (or antidote) is Beverly Marsh, whom King has described as just "one of the boys" in the Losers' Club until she must "serve" as earth mother and "symbolic conduit between adulthood and childhood. . . . It is a role that women have played again and again in the lives of boys: the symbolic advent of manhood through the act of sex" (qtd. in Magistrale, *Second* 6). As Mary Pharr notes, this "orgy of flesh and spirit" is "eucharistic," each Loser "finding grace and courage and manhood through Bev's body" (31). What does Beverly find? Her role. As Pharr notes, King's women have long been judged by what Kay Mussell calls the "domestic test" for determining worthiness of romance heroines: they were "good" if they exhibited sexual control, modesty, intuitiveness, selflessness, and caring (Mussell 89–90). They were "bad" if they had opposing qualities, particularly if sexually active (Nadine Cross), or powerful (Annie Wilkes). Dolores and Vera are true exceptions.

King's efforts in writing about women have been a long time coming. In his 1995 review of Louisa May Alcott's *A Long Fatal Love Chase* as an example of the "woman stalked/woman in peril" subgenre, he is not above plugging his latest novel, *Rose Madder* (1995). (The latter, he notes, is also the story of an abused wife who leaves and is stalked by her obsessed husband [17].) Whatever the case, King's nod to feminism has been prompted less by the "alternative" Alcott than by the enormously successful Clive Barker and Anne Rice, who preceded him in explicitly gendered and gender bending "writing from the body."

SHARON A. RUSSELL

Needful Things (1991)

N*eedful Things* is King's last novel to deal with the fictional town of Castle Rock. The town, whose name comes from a Frank Sinatra song of the fifties, is familiar from several earlier works. While King considers *The Dark Half*, "The Sun Dog," and *Needful Things* the Castle Rock trilogy, the town is the setting of novels such as *Cujo*, *The Dead Zone*, and the short story, "The Body." King explains that he is leaving Castle Rock because it is too familiar. He would rather be less comfortable in his writing. Working with a town whose map he can draw discourages him from taking risks (Beahm, *Stephen King Story* 151). Castle Rock is located near Durham, Maine, where his family moved when he was eleven (Beahm, *Stephen King Story* 19). The Durham of King's youth is the model for Castle Rock (Beahm, *Stephen King Story* 27). The two major divisions of the novel are illustrated with woodcut images, and each chapter begins with a small woodcut. Bill Russell did the illustrations for this text and carries on with this style in *Dolores Claiborne*.

Needful Things also brings back an important character from an earlier novel, Sheriff Alan Pangborn of *The Dark Half*. *Needful Things* features a large number of characters who interact as the story progresses. While he experiments with the horror genre in many of his recent works, King returns to his traditional view of horror in *Needful Things*. Supernatural events dominate the plot. While people act realistically, they are motivated by an evil power. King treats the horror genre seriously in *Needful Things*, but he also portrays the interactions of the citizens of Castle Rock humorously.

From *Stephen King: A Critical Companion*. © 1996 Sharon A. Russell.

PLOT DEVELOPMENT AND NARRATIVE STRUCTURE

King opens *Needful Things* with a short chapter called "You've Been Here Before." Here he talks to his readers as though they have just returned to Castle Rock. With a folksy tone he sets the time of year—October. As we sit with him on the steps of the bandstand, he introduces the people who pass and tells a little bit about their relationships, focusing on the aggravations between people. This casual information sets up the personal conflicts which will result in the destruction of Castle Rock. We see the signs Wanda Hemphill, a Baptist, has put up protesting the Casino Nite the Catholics are planning at the Knights of Columbus Hall. The religious leaders of the two congregations, Father Brigham and Reverend William "Willie" Rose, have done nothing to stop the friction between the two groups. We learn about some of the women in town. Myrtle Keeton is worried because her husband Dan, the head selectman, is disturbed about something. Leonore Potter, who takes great pride in her flowers, is considered snooty by the rest of the town.

The narrator then brings us up to date on some of the past history of the town, events covered in previous King fiction. He tells us about Frank Dodd of *The Dead Zone*, Joe Camber and Sheriff Bannerman of *Cujo*, and Pop Merrill of "The Sun Dog." He summarizes other conflicts between Henry Beaufort and Hugh Priest, and Wilma Jerzyck and Nettle Cobb. He informs us that Sheriff Alan Pangborn has lost his wife and younger child and that Polly Chalmers is suffering from arthritis. He ends by telling us that all these events will mean nothing compared to the opening of a new store down the street from where Pop Merrill's junk shop, the Emporium Galorium, used to be. The store's name is Needful Things, and it is about to get its first customer.

After this beginning the novel is divided into three parts: Grand Opening Celebration, The Sale of the Century, and Everything Must Go. It ends with another version of "You've Been Here Before." The action covers eight days, from Tuesday, October 8, to Tuesday, October 15. Each day is clearly marked to help us follow the passage of time. The folksy speaker disappears, and the main body of the novel is told in the voice of a third person narrator who can either remain outside of the characters or move from mind to mind sharing their thoughts with the reader. King picks up the story where the folksy narrator left off. The first sentence not only establishes the focus for this section of the novel but also tells a lot about life in Castle Rock. "In a small town, the opening of a new store is big news" (13). King then introduces the first victim of this new store, eleven-year-old Brian Rusk. A sign announces that Needful Things is a new kind of store where you won't

believe your eyes (13). King shows how various people in town react to the
store mostly through Brian's eyes. When Brian notices that the store is open,
he goes in even though his mother has shown more interest in it.

If we are aware of the horror tradition, we know that Brian should be
careful. The owner welcomes him with echoes of Count Dracula's famous
words, "Come in my friend. Enter freely, and leave some of the happiness
you bring" (22). Dracula says almost exactly the same words to Harker except
for the substitution: "Come freely. Go safely . . ." (Stoker 20). The owner,
Leland Gaunt, claims to be from Akron, Ohio. Brian thinks the jacket he is
wearing may actually be a smoking jacket like Sherlock Holmes wears. This
first meeting with Gaunt establishes the strange nature of his store and its
contents. Brian holds a splinter from Noah's Ark and has an image of actually being on it. We get a better idea of how Gaunt operates when he gets
Brian to tell him what he wants most in the world—a '56 Sandy Koufax card.
When Gaunt locates the card it is not only the perfect card, it is signed for
Brian. Even though Gaunt claims this is just a coincidence, we know these
kinds of coincidences don't just happen, especially in horror fiction.

We are concerned when Gaunt negotiates with Brian for the card. The
price is just below the amount of money Brian has in his pocket. But there is
an additional price. We do not learn exactly what it is, but it involves Wilma
Jerzyck, Brian's neighbor. With this transaction King establishes the pattern
Gaunt will use to involve the whole town in a network of "deeds" leading to
the destruction of Castle Rock. After Brian's purchase King describes the
attitude of a small New England town to a new shop. He explores the relationship between curiosity and a conservative code where certain things are
just not done. He lists the rules which should be followed: you should not be
the first to come or the last to go; you should not show too much interest in
the contents of the shop or the background of the owner; and you should not
bring a welcome-to-town present such as homemade baked goods. But one
resident of the town does not follow its rules.

Polly Chalmers has a history which fascinates the other residents of the
town. Her eccentricity is confirmed when people see her bringing a
Tupperware container containing a cake to the new store right after it offi-
cially opens. When she meets the owner she has the sense she already knows
him even though she is sure she doesn't. She immediately feels the charm of
this stranger. But we sense that King wants us to watch Gaunt very carefully. We may even wonder if there is a little irony in the fact that Polly has
brought him a devil's food cake. We observe the shop through Polly's eyes.
She sees it as a curio shop and notices that there are no price tags on any of
the items. We also learn about the terrible arthritis in her hands, which is

even more of a problem because she runs a sewing shop. As they discuss the
people in the town we find out that Nettle Cobb, who works for Polly, made
the cake. Leland explains that he doesn't price anything because he enjoys
bargaining or "defining worth by need" (48). Even though Polly really likes
him, we are worried. After she leaves the shop his smile, showing "his uneven
teeth, . . . became unpleasantly predatory" (48). We are even more concerned
when he states that Polly will do.

King continues to detail all of the customers who enter Gaunt's shop,
the negotiations, and the purchases. He develops the personality traits of
each character and their reactions. Gradually people leave with their "needful thing" and some unstated agreement to play a little trick on someone, to
do a little deed. Some customers make a good bargain, and Gaunt waits to
trap them into another kind of action. He promises another object to match
the one they have. Once they have discovered how much they want the original piece they will agree to anything to get its mate. Near the end of this section Polly finally agrees to try a charm which will cure her arthritis.

The first section of the novel also puts in motion the events Gaunt has
established with his sales. It covers the longest period of time, from Tuesday
through Sunday. While Gaunt will start a few new feuds between people, he
concentrates on controlling people who already have enemies. He has most
of the people in town in his power by the end of this section. We also begin
to understand the kinds of pranks he asks people to perform and the pattern
of destruction he creates. We also become aware that he is some kind of
monster. The other person to recognize that he is not human is Brian Rusk,
who commits suicide because he cannot deal with this knowledge. Nettle and
Wilma meet and kill each other in the first section. Their horrible fight to
the death is the signal of what is to come. Gaunt is pleased with what he has
accomplished so far. He sees himself as an electrician, cross wiring connections between people. When the wiring is finished he will turn up the volt-
age all the way. Gaunt does this not just out of malice; he is collecting souls
like trophies. But he is also amused by what happens. As he views the town,
he also decides to hire an assistant.

The second section of the novel covers a shorter period of time, from
Sunday to part of Monday. The last section covers from quarter to six on
Monday night through the destruction of the town later that night. Gaunt
hires Ace Merrill, who has just returned to town to avoid people he owes
$80,000 for a drug deal gone bad. On Monday, which is also Columbus Day,
the people of Castle Rock discover unpleasant things about each other. The
various lies Gaunt has caused others to plant being to surface. We watch the
reactions as each prank is revealed and begin to anticipate what will happen.

Some of the events on this Monday don't appear to be that bad. Less likable people seem to bring on their own trouble because they believe what they find and don't actually talk to the other person involved. We can understand that Wilma and Nettle, who were already enemies, might believe the other had done something terrible. But at first we are less sympathetic with people who find forged love letters and believe them.

Gaunt also attacks Alan and Polly in this section. They are lovers and care deeply about each other. Gaunt avoids meeting Alan until the end of the novel. He uses the pasts of these two people to set them against each other. Polly has hidden the cause of her son's death from Alan. Alan still cannot deal with the death of his wife and one son. Alan works to undo the evil Gaunt creates even though he is not aware of the source. He concentrates on the cause of the final confrontation between Nettle and Wilma. The sequence of the events does not work for him, and he begins to suspect that others are involved.

The second section ends with most of the action under way. Gaunt teams up Ace Merrill and Buster Keeton. Buster and Ace set bombs connected to timers all over town. Buster wants to die, and Gaunt convinces him to take his enemies with him. By this point we can see the direction the story is taking. Our main concern is for the positive characters, especially Polly and Alan. King interrupts our observation of Buster and Alan with the more humorous battle between the Catholics and the Baptists over the casino night fund-raiser. The fight is now fueled by Gaunt's intervention. Both sides are attacked by similar bombs at their meetings. King alternates the movements of these two groups with individual acts of destruction.

A state trooper who is investigating the murders in town tries to stop the battle between the two religious groups. Even additional troopers can't halt the fighting. King once again introduces other actions in the middle of this event. Alan returns to town after getting information from Brian's brother. Some people finally realize how Gaunt has manipulated them. Polly rids herself of Gaunt's charm. Meanwhile Ace and Buster are making and setting their bombs. As all of the groups come together, Alan is sidetracked when he believes that a videotape of his wife's death Gaunt has left for him is authentic. King moves everyone into the final confrontations that will end in the destruction of Castle Rock.

As the bombs go off, Polly manages to show Alan how he has been fooled by Gaunt. Alan finally confronts this monster. He uses a magic trick to bring the forces of good to his side. He wants to distract Gaunt by making flowers appear from his watch. The ghosts of previous events in the town appear to Alan during this final showdown. He sees the sparrows from *The*

Dark Half and the dogs from *Cujo* and "The Sun Dog." The Sheriff cannot kill Gaunt, but he manages to grab a bag that contains the souls Gaunt has taken from his customers. When Alan pulls the string to release the flowers, he releases a "bouquet of light" (679) which forces Gaunt to retreat. Polly joins Alan in defending the bag of souls. Gaunt finally changes shape and flies away. The violent storm which has been raging suddenly stops. The few survivors take each other to the hospital.

Alan and Polly leave behind a town which no longer exists. The accumulation of events which has plagued Castle Rock for so many years is over. King has one last message for the reader. The final section of *Needful Things* mirrors the opening. The folksy narrator has returned, but he is in another town, Junction City. A new store is about to open. This time it's called Answered Prayers. King is telling us that he, too, will go on in another location. Castle Rock is gone, but he will find new towns for his horror.

CHARACTERS

Many characters interact in *Needful Things*, but only a few are fully developed. Most of the people in Castle Rock are defined by their needful things and what they are willing to do to get them. Even though we may learn a little about people like Ace Merrill and Buster Keeton, we deal only with the surfaces of these personalities. King deliberately keeps us in the dark about Gaunt, a character who represents absolute evil. Like Barlow in 'Salem's Lot, he is a supernatural creation who looks human but does not share many human traits. We share his view of the town at certain key moments, but he never really exists as a person. The few characters we get to know in detail change as the novel progresses. Brian Rusk, Alan Pangborn, Polly Chalmers, and, to a lesser extent, Norris Ridgewick have both good and bad characteristics and more fully developed personalities.

Sheriff Alan Pangborn

King introduces the Sheriff as he returns from Portland, where he has been testifying in several court cases. We first see him defined by his job. Throughout the novel changes in his personality are connected to his investigations. But King also includes details which begin to give us another view of this man. We see him driving a station wagon which he calls the ultimate unmarked car, a family vehicle. He is also depressed. We soon learn the major reason for his depression, the loss of his wife, Annie, and his son, Todd.

The car holds memories of family events. For Alan it still contains their ghosts. He finds a trick can in the glove compartment. It looks like a can of nuts, but when he opens it a fake snake pops out. His son and wife have been dead for nineteen months, but he still has this can, the last thing his son bought from his favorite store, the Auburn Novelty Shop. He knows he should throw it out, but he can't bring himself to do it yet. Alan is an amateur magician, and Todd shared his father's love of tricks. His skill with magic is also evidence of his grace and agility.

King also introduces Alan's relationship with Polly. Alan decides to call her, just the sound of her voice will make him feel better. He recalls another event from his past, his connection to Thad Beaumont. We find out what happened to Thad after the events in *The Dark Half*. He has a drinking problem and is divorced. The failure of Thad's relationship leads Alan to blame himself for what happened to his own wife. He was too busy with others to see what was happening to her. The autopsy showed that Annie suffered from a brain tumor. Thad Beaumont's brain tumor was also the cause of his problems. When the Sheriff enters the police department we see him interact with First Deputy Norris Ridgewick. Alan operates according to what he sees as right. He can't know that telling Norris to give Danforth Keeton III a ticket for parking in the handicapped space will help create the chaos at the end of the novel. Buster's reaction sets off his personal disintegration and the destruction of the town. We last see Alan on the first day of the novel amusing himself by making shadow puppets on the wall.

The tricks and magic Alan plays with suggest that he has not lost his connection with childhood, an essential trait in a King hero. Alan may be haunted by the death of his wife and son, but he will briefly play the role of foster father for Brian Rusk's brother and uncover important clues about the first murderers in Castle Rock. Alan's role as a detective does not give him personal satisfaction because he cannot solve the mystery of his wife's death. He cannot understand why she was not wearing her seat belt, something she always did. His son was wearing his. He can't figure out if she was planning to commit suicide and wonders why she took their son with her. He blames himself for not seeing that something was wrong, and he also wonders if he could have done something to prevent it. He originally turned to Polly, his wife's friend, to see if she had any information to help him with this problem.

Alan is forced to deal with his ghosts as he attempts to prevent the destruction of the town. He tries to see a pattern in the inquiries he makes about what is happening. King reveals more about his character as we watch him try to solve the town's mysteries. He finally understands when he questions Brian's brother Sean after Brian's suicide. Sean reveals that Brian bought a baseball card he thought was a Sandy Koufax. When Sean saw it was just a dirty old card, Brian discovered the real truth about Gaunt. Sean tells Alan that Brian knew Gaunt wasn't really a man. Alan thinks he knows everything. On the way back to town he worries about why he didn't want his son to buy the trick can with the snake. He finally understands that the can would also appeal to Gaunt. It is a trick based on misdirection. Alan understands that misdirection is the key to the tricks Gaunt has others perform. He understands that magic can entertain, but it can also be used to make people angry with each other.

Alan only thinks he understands Gaunt. When he confronts him, Gaunt has left him a videotape of his wife's accident. Alan cannot stop himself from watching it. Polly forces him to see he has been tricked. Gaunt's version is flawed because in it Annie is wearing her seat belt. When Alan realizes this error he finally can confront Gaunt. He uses the snake in the can and the flower bouquet to win over Gaunt, who believes in magic. For a moment he thinks the snake is real, and it bites him. Gaunt drops his valise, and Alan is able to grab it. When they confront each other Alan creates shadow puppets of the town's past, the town's ghosts, to chase Gaunt. Sparrows from *The Dark Half*, a Saint Bernard from *Cujo*, and the sun dog from the story of that name all appear. Alan understands the importance of magic: it connects him to his dead son, to belief in illusion. He knows his magic is not misdirection, and he defeats Gaunt. As the survivors leave town Alan knows he will never really learn how his wife and child died, but he can finally accept this fact.

Polly Chalmers

Polly Chalmers, too, must come to certain understandings before she can work with Alan to defeat Gaunt. Polly is a different kind of female character for King. His few positive female characters are usually identified with motherly activities; for example, Fran is pregnant for most of *The Stand*. Polly's secret relates to her motherhood. She was a single parent and left Castle Rock to have the child. After her father rejected her she was too proud to accept any help from her parents and eventually moved to San Francisco. She is still too proud to tell Alan what happened to her son. His baby-sitter caused a fire in Polly's apartment which killed them both. Gaunt uses this secret, forging a letter suggesting that Alan is looking into her past by making inquiries of the San Francisco Department of Child Welfare. Polly may feel guilty about her past, but King does not seem to judge her. She runs her own business, is compassionate in hiring Nettle, who was in a mental institution for killing her abusive husband, and has a settled, independent life. Like Alan, she works well with others, especially her employees. Aside from the one secret, she has a mature, adult relationship with Alan.

Her one great problem is her arthritis. Her motive for allowing Gaunt to control her is much more justified than that of the other characters. She is one of the last to deal with Gaunt and only does so because nothing helps the terrible pain in her hands. King also suggests that she is not thinking as clearly as she might because of the pain and the medicine she is taking to deal with it. Gaunt gives her a charm which takes away the pain. But in payment she plants information which turns Ace Merrill against Alan and almost causes her death. She may initially accept Gaunt's forged evidence, but she is finally able to see through it. Through a mental conversation with her Aunt Evvie, another independent woman, she discovers the forgery. When she was alive Aunt Evvie gave her advice and approved of her attempts to free herself from her parents and the town. Polly realizes that in the forged letter she is called Patricia. In San Francisco she used the name Polly. When she frees herself of Gaunt's influence she also finally liberates herself from her past, from her pride and her hurt. Her freedom leads her to understand Gaunt. She is able to make Alan see as well. She knows she has to accept the pain of living, the pain in her arthritic hands. King also suggests that those who form lasting relationships based on trust will survive.

Brian Rusk

Brian is another of the young boys who have important roles in King novels. While Brian shares some of their characteristics, he differs in important ways. He is still at the point where he maintains the beliefs of childhood. In many King novels this ability to retain a sense of wonder is what saves a child from destruction. Unfortunately for Brian, his belief in fantasy makes him a perfect subject for Gaunt, who uses Brian's imagination immediately. Brian senses Noah's Ark in a splinter of wood. He sees the baseball card he is supposed to see rather than the one Gaunt really gives him. Even when he finally forces himself to do the pranks Gaunt demands, he begins to enjoy them the way a child would. But Brian also quickly discovers that part of the joy in having a special card is showing it to others. He senses that this would get him in trouble because he could not explain how he got the card. He moves from enjoying to the more private pleasure of gloating. This reaction alters his personality as he closes up to others.

Brian realizes that Gaunt has trapped him, but he cannot find a way out. He sees no choice but to follow Gaunt's orders. He can't deal with the result of his actions, the deaths of Wilma and Nettle. He has no one who can help him. He is certain that someone saw him, and the Sheriff will be after him. Alan does try to talk to him, but Brian is losing his childhood. He does not react to Alan's flower trick. Brian can't confess, but he doesn't lie either. He tells Alan that a monster caused the destruction at Wilma's house. Alan cannot reach him. Brian's dreams have turned from his crush on his teacher to nightmares about the monster. He knows more than he wants too. "It's like knowing how the magician does his tricks" (463). The knowledge of what is behind the magic belongs to the adult world, and Brian cannot cope with it. Alan does not understand how seriously Brian has been hurt by this knowledge. Sean tries to prevent his brother's suicide, but Brian finally shoots himself. He has moved into the pain of the adult world too quickly.

Norris Ridgewick

While Norris is not one of the most important characters in *Needful Things*, he is one of the few survivors. He has been a deputy for a while and worked with Alan investigating Homer Gamache's death in *The Dark Half*. Our first meeting with him in this book is not very impressive. He does not want to give Buster a parking ticket. We can tell he does not want to confront this man. While Alan likes him, he also makes the shadow hand puppet version of him "skinny and a little self-important" (67). Norris drives Alan crazy because he insists on changing into his uniform in the men's room. But he does stand up to Buster even though it ruins his day. At the end of that day he is trapped by Gaunt when he sees in the shop window a fishing rod like the one he used to have as a boy. He wants it because it represents the good times he had with his father.

Norris becomes involved in the violence in two ways. Like Polly, he cannot avoid performing his little prank. He even is at the point of suicide like Brian. But as he stands with the noose around his neck an inner voice forces him to face the truth. His fishing rod is just junk. He still almost dies. He is certain Gaunt has pushed him. But he manages to free himself in all senses of the word. He destroys the rod and goes after Gaunt. While Norris tries to arrest Ace and Buster, Ace shoots him. Norris survives and redeems himself, managing to shoot Ace before Ace can shoot Polly. Alan tells his First Deputy he can change his clothes in the men's room anytime. Norris still feels that all of the destruction is his fault. But Polly shows him how they are all to blame. The town no longer exists, but the survivors have learned to accept reality.

THEME

In *Needful Things* King explores three familiar themes, managing to develop them in new ways: the relationship between the individual and the community, the importance of childhood, and the destructive impact of an evil presence. While some might only see the novel as an exposé of the greed of a community, not everyone in Castle Rock acts from the same motives or has the same desires. People may promise anything to acquire their needful things, but many of their purchases are not intrinsically valuable. Gaunt exploits people's desires, but these desires are often connected to simple dreams such as owning a certain baseball card or a beautiful piece of glass. The chosen items represent the hidden dreams of the owners and often suggest unfulfilled desires in their lives—a fishing rod like the one a father owned, or sunglasses owned by Elvis. But King is concerned about how far people will go to fulfill their desires. He is concerned that our quest for personal gratification can destroy society.

King is interested in both individual actions and the organization of the community. By taking apart Castle Rock he investigates what held it together. In *The Stand* King looks at what happens after a civilization is destroyed. In *Needful Things* he details the process of destruction. King uses Gaunt and his store to test the rules of society. He details the laws covering the behavior of the town toward a new store. But these codes are not strong enough to save the community. Kings shows how these codes break down. We quickly believe the worst of each other and act rather than talk. In part, we are trapped by our own needful things. We want to believe we can get what we want without paying the full price. Civilization is just a thin coating over our more violent impulses. Only a few of Gaunt's customers can see how they have been manipulated. King is not very hopeful about our ability to live together.

When the social structures of Castle Rock begin to fall apart, King shows how ineffective the traditional supports of a community can be. All the organizations we trust to maintain society become involved in the destruction. The Sheriff's office becomes a source of contamination when Norris falls under Gaunt's spell. Buster's actions compromise the city government, and the churches generate much of the hostility in town. When individuals begin to attack each other there is no higher organization to prevent the

violence from escalating. King does not see much hope for society. In the end
the town is destroyed and only a few individuals remain. Society's failure to
control evil means that Gaunt survives to continue his work elsewhere. Alan
can save the souls of his town, but we don't know if individuals in the next
town will be able to save themselves. Alan can trick Gaunt because he has
special powers of is own. He understands the power of magic and misdirection. Polly is able to get Alan away from the false video because of the force
of their relationship. But King leaves us wondering what might have happened if these two people had not been successful. And they cannot save
everyone. Many of Gaunt's victims are good people who just wanted to fulfill one of their dreams. The failure of the community in *Needful Things*
allows Gaunt to partially succeed. He does not get their souls, but he does
destroy Castle Rock. In King's world the punishment does not always fit the
crime, and bad things can happen to good people. But society's rules do not
protect good people who make bad decisions.

In *Needful Things* King changes his view of childhood. Even children
are taken in by Gaunt. Their innocence is no protection. Brian sees the reality of his actions too late. He has lost the protection of being a child. In other
King novels children survive because they believe in the monsters adults
deny. Brian's childhood dream of owning a special baseball card betrays him.
King may be suggesting that collecting baseball cards has become tainted by
adult greed and materialism. Baseball cards have become big business. Brian
is too young for the adult world. He has confused childhood desires with
adult dreams of getting something for nothing. He cannot confide in Alan.
He commits suicide, an act associated with adults, because he does not see
any other solution.

Society's failure in *Needful Things* extends to the parent/child relationship. Alan does not really get a chance to form a new father/son
relationship with Brian and save him. Gaunt's actions either play on failed
father/son relationships or destroy potential relationships. Characters are
drawn to Gaunt's shop by the promise of either improving or regaining
a connection with a father figure. Brian's father started his collection. Brian
has worked hard to get many of his cards, but the Sandy Koufax card
is beyond his reach. A purchase from Gaunt's shop does not improve his
relationship with his father because the terms of purchase make it impossible for Brian to share it with anyone. Items from Gaunt's shop isolate people because they cannot admit what they have done to purchase their treasures. Norris and Brian finally realize that things cannot substitute for
true parent/child relationships. They feel so guilty about their actions that
they no longer want to live. The destruction of family connections is

just one kind of evil that Gaunt brings to Castle Rock.

Gaunt embodies a kind of evil which exists outside of normal human interactions. He is a monster, but he uses human needs and emotions as the tools of his destruction. In *Needful Things* King is saying good-bye to more than Castle Rock. He examines the nature of the relationship between good and evil in a small New England town. The opening description of the town explains its social structure and examines members of Castle Rock and the motives for their actions. King assigns different values to the choices people make in Gaunt's shop. The objects they select reflect their lives. Some people operate out of greed and pettiness. They choose things which support their fantasies. King finds these adults ridiculous and even dangerous. While Cora Rusk indulges in her fantasy relationship with Elvis, Brian, her son, commits suicide. Some shoppers are pathetic. Gaunt tempts Nettle with a piece of carnival glass. She once had gone crazy and killed her abusive husband when he broke pieces of her collection. King suggests that our attachment to things as a substitute for real relationships is sad, leading us to overvalue things and become paranoid about losing them.

Gaunt's evil is successful because he knows how to take small human defects and connect them to create mass destruction. No one really enjoys their purchase from Gaunt. His bargains are too costly. People can't show their objects to others. In most cases, if they shared the joy in their purchase, they would find out how they had been cheated. Gaunt controls the way they see their objects. They can't see the reality behind their bargains. Many of their treasures are really junk. False things cannot replace real relationships, as many people discover. They also realize that they have made bad bargains they can't revoke. Only a few people successfully break away from Gaunt's control. Alan escapes from the power of the videotape, and Polly returns her charm.

Alan is able to defeat Gaunt because he is not impressed with the man or his power. Alan's character unites many of the themes in the novel. He has lost his son and cannot save Brian. He is a representative of law and order who cannot prevent the destruction of the town. But Alan survives and triumphs because he learns how to accept his losses. His dead son's trick works on Gaunt. His successful relationship with Polly overcomes the power of Gaunt's tape. Their combined goodness turns Alan's magic tricks into real snakes and shafts of light which overcome Gaunt's evil. Gaunt is not destroyed, but he leaves town without the souls he came for. The survivors know they will have to live with the consequences of their actions. There will be no more Castle Rock. But they value what they have learned. They see the effect of the evil Gaunt represents, and they understand their own complicity in the destruction. This knowledge is their punishment for agreeing to Gaunt's terms, but it also gives them the power to avoid such choices in the future.

ALTERNATIVE READING: GENRE

Needful Things is another example of how King explores the limits of the horror genre in his recent fiction. In *Misery* he uses realism to create a different kind of horror—one without supernatural origins. In this novel we must witness the horror of human evil. *Gerald's Game* and *Dolores Claiborne* are also realistic novels. In *Needful Things* King examines our relationship to the supernatural. He looks at the horror genre and its relationship to the evil which comes from within us and that which has a source outside of us. Many of King's horror novels deal with evil which originates outside of the individual: the aliens in *Tommyknockers*, the clown in *It*, the ghosts in *The Shining*. Often the horror comes from inside a character. In *Needful Things* the evil begins outside of the individual, but humans carry out the destruction. Gaunt uses human malice and greed to accomplish his destruction.

In the horror genre, we expect a conflict which will involve some aspect of the supernatural. We also assume that there will be a certain amount of violence connected to this conflict and that the conflict will include a confrontation between good and evil. Like other King novels, *Needful Things* has all these elements of the genre. Gaunt is like many supernatural horror figures in his fiction. He controls people through a kind of hypnosis, appearing to them when they think they are alone. He knows things about people that no one else knows. He operates out of a sense of pure evil. Humans amuse him, and he plays with them. At the end of the novel he reveals his true nature. As he leaves town in defeat he goes through a series of changes. We don't always see Gaunt, but his car turns into a buckboard driven by a dwarf and then a medicine-show wagon with the sign "Caveat Emptor," buyer beware. As he leaves, the souls he has captured escape from the valise, and the town and its people are no longer poisoned. The fighting and the storm stop.

King expands the genre by including more than just the horror which comes from outside. He is also interested in the way we contribute to the horror we experience. Gaunt exploits the needs of the citizens of Castle Rock. He may have an unfair advantage because of his supernatural powers, but he cannot be effective without their help. The destruction he helps them create may have started because of his supernatural powers. But Castle Rock is destroyed by human violence. King uses Alan's interest in magic to help explain what is happening. Magic works because the audience is tricked into believing. The magician misdirects us. When Alan understands this concept he understands how Gaunt operates. But magic is so powerful that we may fall under its spell even if we know there's a trick. Alan falls under Gaunt's spell until Polly helps him see Gaunt's mistake. Alan's magic is human in origin, but it becomes transformed when he meets Gaunt. Contact with Gaunt releases the supernatural in others. Gaunt believes in the power of magic, and his belief turns human magic into the supernatural.

In *Needful Things* King explores the relationship between the supernatural and natural worlds. He is concerned not just with the horror we usually find in the genre. He is worried about the natural horror which results from the way humans treat each other. He looks back on the past of Castle Rock. Some of the town's problems have a supernatural origin, as in the monster dog released by the photographs in "The Sun Dog." Other conflicts in Castle Rock may combine natural and supernatural forces. In *The Dead Zone* special powers lead to the discovery of a serial killer. In this novel individuals are responsible for the human horror. Cujo is just a poor rabid dog who attacks the humans and causes the death of a child. The supernatural is not really important in *Cujo*. Thad Beaumont does not wish his evil half to come alive in *The Dark Half*, and Thad needs help from supernatural forces to overcome him. In *Needful Things* a single evil being sets the townspeople against each other. Gaunt accomplishes some of his goal by using the evil in us all. King still employs supernatural elements to explore the horror genre in this novel. But he also suggests that human horror is more destructive than any which comes from outside of us. Castle Rock has been the scene of both natural and supernatural horror. King has used this town as a setting to examine the many kinds of evil possible in the horror novel. He finally destroys the town by combining the power of a supernatural evil with the destructive power of the average human being.

EDWIN F. CASEBEER

The Art of Balance: Stephen King's Canon

Stephen King is the most popular horror novelist today (and also the most popular novelist). He is the only writer ever to have made the Forbes 500; his annual income exceeds that of some third-world countries. His works are a significant percentage of the book industry's annual inventory. The average American recognizes his name and face. Yet, paradoxically, his novels also top the lists of censored authors. Perhaps that is because he creates fiction and cinema about that which we would rather avoid: modern meaninglessness, physical corruptibility, and death. Do the fictional situations he presents argue for a decline in our culture's energy for life, a descending depression and despair that lends enchantment to the graveyard, the kind of apocalyptic view that often ends centuries and heralds new human hells? Or is his appeal understandable in a way that affirms our culture and its willingness to deal with its dilemmas?

If we begin with Stephen King's status among his immediate peers—the horror novelists—the reasons for his broad appeal are clear. He has taken command of the field by writing representative masterworks: the vampire novel (*'Salem's Lot*), the monster novel (*The Dark Half*), wild talent fiction (*Carrie*), zombie fiction (*Pet Sematary*), diabolic possession fiction (*Christine*), and realistic horror fiction (*Misery*). His presence in the field extends to its very boundaries.

But King is actually a genre novelist; that is, he writes in all of the major popular genres now marketed to the country's largest reading population: horror, fantasy, science fiction, the western, the mystery, and the

From *A Dark Night's Dreaming: Contemporary American Horror Fiction.* © 1996 University of South Carolina.

romance. While he works in pure forms (*'Salem's Lot* as a vampire novel, *Cycle of the Werewolf* as a werewolf novel. *The Talisman* as a quest fantasy, and *The Running Man* as science fiction), he often mixes genres. An early example is *The Stand*, particularly its first published edition, which begins as one form of the science fiction novel (the apocalyptic), evolves into a second form (the utopian), and concludes as a fantasy which blends elements of the quest like Tolkien's *Lord of the Rings* trilogy with Christian apocalyptic fantasy like *The Omen* trilogy. Similarly, his *Dark Tower* trilogy combines apocalyptic science fiction with Arthurian quest fantasy, itself subordinated to the western, and then introduces science fiction's alternate worlds concept. The standard detective mystery does much to shape *The Dark Half, Needful Things*, and *Dolores Claiborne*, while the Gothic romance and the feminist novel are essential features of *Misery, Gerald's Game*, and *Dolores Claiborne*. The resulting breadth gives his fiction a much wider appeal than might come to a "pure" horror writer.

But King's appeal is even broader than that of a genre writer. From the beginning of his career, he was responsive to those horror writers of his decade, like Ira Levin, who moved from the traditional confines of the *fantastique* to establish analogies between the world that we all occupy and the horror novel's traditional settings, situations, plots, and characters. King, too, grounds fantasy in realism. In fact, his earliest published work, *Rage* (published under the Richard Bachman pseudonym), is a capable realistic novel. Motivated by his own boyhood and his involvement with his children, King's early novels demonstrate strong characterizations of preadolescent boys and small children. In the ensuing years, he has added to his palette, and now is taking up the challenge of realistic female protagonists.

King's appeal thus broadens even further: this realism opens up a subtext that addresses urgent contemporary concerns. From his youth, he has been a man of his generation; a man with deep political awareness and involvement. As has been elaborated critically by such works as Tony Magistrale's *Landscape of Fear* and Douglas Winter's *The Art of Darkness*, King has created many novels which allegorically address current social dilemmas: the corruption of school and church (*Rage, Carrie, Christine*), the government (*The Long Walk, Firestarter, The Running Man, The Stand, The Dead Zone*), the small town (*'Salem's Lot, It, Needful Things, Tommyknockers*), the family (*The Shining, Cujo, It, Christine*), and heterosexual relationships (*Gerald's Game, Dolores Claiborne*). Thus, King's work offers more than mere escape fiction or "adrenaline" fiction; it urges readers to confront squarely and disturbingly the horror in their own lives. The resulting depth connects him to an audience drawn to literature more "serious" than horror or genre fiction. His model has inspired enough followers to cause horror fiction to move to the front of bookstores and the top of the *New York Times'* bestseller list. It is not so much that the reading public has developed a perverse taste for horror as it is that, emulating King, horror writers have broadened and deepened their art enough to address us all on issues of consequence.

Paramount among these issues is death. As James Hillman pointed out in *Revisioning Psychology*, contemporary Western culture is the first extensive culture which has had to consider death as an ending, rather than as a transformation. Instead of believing in a transformation into an angel or devil, animal, or star, today's rationalists regard being as matter and unanimated being as refuse. Founded upon such materialism, the contemporary state and school have reinterpreted reality so as to provide for the here and now, and have maintained a polite skepticism about other realities. King repeatedly dramatizes, from an evolving perspective, the dilemma in which we find ourselves: we are without resources before the imminence of our own deaths and the catastrophe of the deaths of those we love. Adopting (such as in *Carrie*) a contemporary existentialist attitude (where the only constants are isolation, decay, and death), King explores such values (acts, creations, children) as may survive death or those entertained by other cultures (as in *The Stand*). In other novels (such as *The Talisman* and *The Dark Tower* series) King will entertain the possibilities suggested by post-Einsteinian physicists (the multiverse, the reality of process and the nonexistence of time, space, and matter). As in *It*, King looks at possibilities suggested by the psychoanalytic architects of reality, particularly the Jungian theory of an archetypal dimension underlying matter—a dimension that can be apprehended and molded by the artistic imagination. Although King sometimes ends his novels in nausea (*Pet Sematary*) or nothingness (*Carrie*), normally he views the human condition in terms of possibilities and affirmations. Again representative of his generation—and his American community (small-town New England)—those affirmations are based upon what is possible for the individual, particularly the individual not blinded by rationalism. He displays deep distrust for any human configuration larger than the family.

Although King's thematic reach is wide and deep, ascertaining his position on any given issue is not simple. This ambiguity also underlies his broad appeal, for vastly different readers may arrive at vastly different conclusions about his agenda. King seems, in a novel like *The Stand*, to be able to appreciate the validity of the opposed positions of a small-town Christian, Republican American with a high school education and a sophisticated, liberal, and urban existentialist. In a way, like Shakespeare, he does not conclusively resolve a plot or commit irrevocably to the agenda of a specific character or group of characters involved in the conflict. But his noncommitment is so submerged that readers normally assume (as they have with Shakespeare for centuries) that he agrees with them; he economically gestures toward the possibility of gestalt, not a specific gestalt. On the contrary, his chief artistic talent—the talent that has kept all of his work in print throughout his career and is likely to keep it in print—is his ability to balance opposing realities. The reader must resolve the issues. If we supinely regard King as simply a popular artist and expect a canned resolution, we often will find his resolutions unsatisfying. If we invest the energy in tipping his balance toward ourselves, we will behold in the artistic experience an affirming and illuminating mirror of our problems and our solutions.

Such a mirror develops not only from King's choice of situations of great concern to us, but by his technique of characterization. Here again, he achieves balance, gains breadth and depth of appeal. In one sense, King is a highly accomplished realist with a keen eye for the nuances of image and voice; but, in another, his characters are archetypal with origins in myth and folktale. Characters fall into two large groups—the sketch and the multidimensional. One of his true talents is the sketch: he is able to populate novels like 'Salem's Lot, The Stand, and The Tommyknockers), with hundreds of briefly executed, vivid characters—each efficiently caught in a telling and representative moment that is often grotesque and generally memorable. King can make credible, as in The Stand, a plot that quite literally involves a whole country. He sketches characters from the South, New York, New England, the West, from the rural and urban blue-collar class, the middle class, the criminal and indigent, the police, the army, the entertainment world, and the clerks and functionaries of cities and small towns from all over America. These characters, placed in highly detailed topographies, create for us the realistic element of his fantasies so central in enabling us to accept their supernatural premises. As King said in an interview with Magistrale: "The work underlines again and again that I am not merely dealing with the surreal and the fantastic but, more important, using the surreal and the fantastic to examine the motivations of people and the society and the institutions they create."

King's realistic techniques for creating the primary multidimensional characters significantly differs from those producing the sketch. Generally speaking, he avoids the customary expository visual portrait of a primary character; he prefers to develop the character internally. Thus by beginning in the character's sensorium, we can project more quickly and directly into it than we might if the objectification of a physical description was between us and it: existing as the bound Jessie Burlingame in Gerald's Game, we see, hear, touch, taste, and smell her experience of her world; and from these physical experiences we enter into and share her psychological presence. Generally, we find that psychological presence to be archetypal—the anima. Like any popular artist working with the stereotypical, King is always on the border of creating Jungian personae and plots emanating from the cultural unconscious. Therefore, however individually a multidimensional character may be textured, it feels very familiar as we settle into it.

But King goes a step further, particularly in his more epic novels, by exemplifying the theories of such neo-Jungian thinkers as Hillman: (1) the human psyche is basically a location for a cast of personae in dynamic relationship with one another; (2) the one-persona psyche—humanity's current and dominant commitment to unity, integration, and control—is pathological (the excesses of the rationalistic materialist); and (3) the universe and its inhabitants can only be seen clearly through multiple and dynamic perspectives. Thus, except in novellas and short stories, King generally prefers multiple points of view. Here he is influenced by modernists (such as Faulkner) and by cinema: perspective follows setting—and if the setting contains different characters, he still develops multiple points of view. In the larger novels, typically King pits a group of comrades against a common threat, a dynamic for which he found precedent in both Tolkien's *The Ring* trilogy and Stoker's *Dracula*. Though the details produced by setting and sensorium conceal the fact, each comrade is a persona—a specialized and archetypal figure such as the child, the old man, the lover, the teacher, the healer, etc. As the plot progresses and each persona contributes its vision, the remaining personae subsume these perspectives and evolve into a single (hero or heroine) or dyadic (lovers or parent/child) protagonist with the capacity to defeat or stalemate the antagonist, which itself is often a persona embodying death, decay, or meaninglessness.

Just as often, however, the antagonist is the monstrous. King has a particularly complex attitude toward such a persona. Like Clive Barker, King is able to see the positive side of the monstrous—its incredible energy and commitment, its individuality, and its ability to function in the unknown. Unlike Barker, he is not ready to embrace the monstrous and let it transform him. Again, balance prevails. In *Danse Macabre*, King analyzes the function of author and antagonist in novels. For him, the authorial is not the autobiographical; the "King" is another persona—the folksy, small-town Maine citizen of the commercials, of the prefaces, and of the authorial asides. The persona of the author agrees with the norms of the community. But the antagonist (as monster) is that shadow aspect of us which finds its reality in the individual, the bizarre, and the grotesque. This antagonist seeks to tyrannically control or to destroy rather than to belong, which is dynamic rather than centered and driven rather than ordered. We contain both and we come to the novel to experience both. Their conflict will never be settled, for it is the essence of what they are: opposites that define one another. Although Thad Beaumont, the protagonist of *The Dark Half*, wins his conflict with George Stark (the monster within him) we learn in *Needful Things* that he has lost his love, his art, and his family—he has settled back into alcoholism. In summary, the traditional horror novel, such as Bram Stoker's *Dracula*, excises or conquers the antagonist; the postmodernist horror novel, such as Clive Barker's works, transforms the protagonist into the antagonist, or vice versa; and King's novels balance these processes.

The end result of such a dynamic perception of character and structure is that the novel becomes psyche: that is, it is the location of archetypal personae and their dynamics. It is the interface between the psyches of writer and reader, a template of the soul, a mirror in which we see ourselves most clearly in terrain we least care to explore, the nightworld of death and monstrosity. Seen from the above perspectives, King becomes a modern shaman employing magic (the fantasy image, childhood imagination) to lead his culture into self-discovery where it most needs to look while maintaining commitment to love, family, and community—for King is also a husband, father, and highly visible "social" presence. Again he balances: he is of the tribe and he directs the tribe. No wonder we read him; no wonder we approach him with caution.

Because of his inclination to balance consecutive novels by opposing them to one another, these propositions apply more to the broad characteristics and processes of the canon rather than to individual novels. But his novels also fall into categories in which the same striving toward the balancing of opposing forces is evident: the community, the child, the writer, the woman, and the quest. These categories not only provide a more useful way of approaching King's fiction specifically than would a chronological or genre discussion, but they also focus the preceding theoretical discussion. Each category is a broad, shared foundation with the reader upon which and through which King can consistently design and redesign his social allegories and the psyche's archetypal templates that so consistently and profoundly link him with his audience.

King's writings about the community establish him as one of the country's major regionalist writers whose influences can be traced to the New England Gothic writers, Thornton Wilder's *Our Town*, and the novels of William Faulkner. The community which King most often chooses to present is one inspired by the town of his childhood—Durham, Maine.

Sometimes the town is Jerusalem's Lot of the *'Salem's Lot* stories, Haven of *The Tommyknockers*, or Castle Rock—the setting of such works as "The Body," *Cujo, The Dead Zone, The Dark Half*, and *Needful Things*. A citizen of his region, King believes that the most politically viable unit is one small enough to hear and respond to individual opinion; as in *The Stand*, cities like New York regularly appear in an advanced state of disruption and the federal government responds only to the reality of its paper and its power.

Although community is more feasible in a small town than in a large city, in King's small towns it is rare. More frequently, their citizens (as in *'Salem's Lot,—The Tommyknockers*), and *Needful Things*) are caught up in materialistic pursuits that lead them into conflict with their neighbors. This conflict results in a community held together by conformity rather than cooperation, with narcissism and the closed door, fealty to no code but self-gratification, and apocalypse simmering beneath the surface. Yet—to stress King's seeking of balance in this category—there appears the option of a better way of life. The Boulder Free Zone of *The Stand* comes closest to such a utopia: it is small, it accords a place to each according to need and talent, and it attends to the individual. But King is ambivalent about such a grassroots democracy; the true reason for the survival of the Free Zone is the emergence of an elite presiding coterie composed of exceptional individuals with exceptional social conscience. When events demand the sacrifice of most of these people and the Free Zone becomes too large for rule by their dialogue, Stu Redman and Fran Goldsmith (the surviving hero and heroine) conclude that their community now is simply recycling the former decadent and materialist world. They opt for a more viable social unit: the family. And they leave the Free Zone for the locale of King's own family, Maine.

To understand King's strong focus on the family and the child requires recognition that during his career he has been a husband and father of two boys and a girl. During their childhood, he generally worked at home, but brought his family with him on the rare occasions when he left Maine. Thus, his family is often major material; he need only look up from the word processor to find grist. And as his own children have aged, so has the presence of the child diminished in his novels. The category of the child arises for a second reason: in his own development, King has had to reencounter himself as child and boy in order to remove the blocks to his becoming a man: "The idea is to go back and confront your childhood, in a sense relive it if you can, so that you can be whole." Also in this category are early novels such as *Rage* (begun while he was in high school), *The Long Walk*, and *Carrie* (written by a young man dealing with problems posed by family and organized adult society).

Among King's most endearing characters are small children such as Danny Torrance of *The Shining* and Charlie McGee of *Firestarter*. In their characterization, he avoids the potential sentimentality that often sinks such efforts by manipulating sentences that seamlessly weave together the diction and phrasing of both child and adult, thus conveying the being of the one and the perspective of the other. The second paragraph introducing Danny provides an example: "Now it was five o'clock, and although he didn't have a watch and couldn't tell time too well yet anyway, he was aware of passing time by the lengthening of the shadows, and by the golden cast that now tinged the afternoon light." The first subordinate clause is childishly run-on in structure and uses Danny's diction, while the second main clause is complex-compound within itself—its subordinate elements are parallel and its diction is the polysyllabic format typical of the narrator in King's lyric mode. Such a combination of styles and perspectives works so well because King adheres to the romantic belief that the child is the father of the man. It may be that children are superior in wisdom and psychological talents to adults simply because the latter are corrupted by psyches shrunken by materialism and rationalism—but they are superior. Thus, Danny is one with time and space, almost godlike in his perception of those dimensions in the haunted Hotel Overlook, while Charlie's power over the material world establishes her as an angel of apocalypse when she incinerates the Shop (King's version of the CIA).

King's adolescents can also be superior to his adults. In fact, the major reason for grouping the adolescent with the child is that, normally, King's adolescents are prepubescent: they have no explicit sexual identity and are still more child than adult. It is in such adolescents that we see his attempt to achieve yet another kind of balance—between the two stages of life. While the child has intimations of immortality, the adult has knowledge of death. Thus, the Castle Rock novella "The Body" (made into the excellent film by Rob Reiner entitled *Stand By Me*) initiates its four boys by leading them not into a sexual encounter, but into another rite of passage: their first encounter with death as the corpse of a fifth boy. Similarly, in *It*, a group of boys encounters and prevails over the protean incarnation of every human's deepest fear, and in *The Talisman*, co-written with Peter Straub, a trio of boys (an archetypal id, ego, and superego) transcend the force of this reality to enter a reality in which death is unempowered. Sometimes, as in *Carrie*, *The Stand*, and *Christine*, death and sexuality are negatively related: as Carrie becomes sexual, she becomes monstrous and an angel of the apocalypse. The sexual foreplay of Nadine and Harold in *The Stand* is a clear symptom of their degenerate state. As Arnie becomes sexual, Christine corrupts him—even

Arnie's benevolent alter ego, Dennis, discovers that his first love turns to ashes. In his most recent novels, King demonstrates a mature and central sexuality; but in the novels of this earlier period, in which he is reencountering his boyhood, sexuality leads to adulthood which leads to diminished psychological resources and death.

Coincidental with King's emphasis on the child and the boy is his emphasis on the family (often in a pathological phase). One of the earliest and most powerful of these novels is *The Shining*, which, long before systems theory, dramatized the point that the pathological individual is a symptom of the pathological family and that both must undergo treatment. Jack Torrance's obsessions and his wife's posture as victim are inheritances from their parents which bind them together and threaten Danny. In *Christine*, Arnie's pathological family environment leads to his destruction and theirs, while Dennis's family supports and creates him in its image. It provides the reader with a wide range of family dynamics, both successful and unsuccessful, and relates such to the girl and boys who are the protagonists. The most powerful of the numerous family novels is the tragic *Pet Sematary*, which develops for the reader a realistically ideal family which is demolished by its own estimable values when its child is senselessly killed. The question posed by the novel is whether the family can survive the death of a child. The answer is no. In this system, the death of a child kills the family.

A subject as close to King as the child and the family is that of the writer—a character who dominates as either protagonist or antagonist in a wide range of short stories, novellas, and novels (most significantly *'Salem's Lot*, *The Shining*, *It*, *Misery*, *The Tommyknockers*, and *The Dark Half*). The novelist-protagonist who dominates *'Salem's Lot* is more a product of King's youthful ideals than his experience. Like King, Ben Mears (a "mirror") undertakes a novel which will allow him to productively relive his childhood. But Ben's conflict with the vampire Barlow enlarges him to mythic proportions: as the personae about him converge and provide him understanding, faith, wisdom, and imagination, he develops a godlike perception and power. Metaphorically, when he encounters and conquers the vampire that is feeding on the town, he becomes the archetype of an elemental "good . . . whatever moved the greatest wheels of the universe." The following novel, *The Shining*, establishes balance by becoming an exact opposite to its predecessor: the alcoholic Torrance (a playwright this time) is the monster. King sees this particular writer as a failure because he stops writing—Torrance's writing block leads to psychosis. Among the complex communities of *The Stand*, a similar opposition is in the contrast between Larry (the successful musician) with Harold (the unsuccessful writer): although his success nearly destroys him, Larry literally enacts a second crucifixion that saves the world; abnegating art for dark vision, Harold still manages some dignity before succumbing to demonic forces. Both figures physically resemble King: Larry has King's height and current physique and Harold has the height and King's adolescent physique. Although the hero is blond and the villain dark-haired, both have hair the quality of King's. In *It*, where the child's imagination is the only weapon of the adult against the death and meaninglessness of the eponymous evil, the novelist Bill Denbrough (who this time resembles Peter Straub) regains this state most easily and thus is a vital element of the protagonistic band.

Balancing again, King writes two novels—*Misery* and *The Tommyknockers*—which countervail such optimistic authorial characterizations. In *Misery* the primary subject is the negative relationship of the reader and the writer: the reader is the writer's enemy. Readers regularly read the genre writer rather than the literary artist—in *Misery*, this is the Gothic novelist. Since the readers' choice enforces conventions and confines the writer's creative talent, in a sense the audience "writes" the genre novel. Apparently tiring of these limitations, King personifies his tyrannical audience in the archetypal figure of Annie, who literally limits the aspiring literary artist, Paul Sheldon, to genre fiction by drugs, bondage, and torture. Despite such a negative response to whether readers are the motivation for writing, King gives the issue a serious and detailed treatment: his writing of a Gothic romance novel within a realistic novel and his exploration of the psychological processes of writers and their relationship with those of readers is a fascinating and original effort. And, again, he negates his own negation by undercutting Paul's distaste for genre fiction by his admiration for this bloodily extracted romance, even though its creation mutilated him.

While *Misery* suggests that the literary artist's social influence is more negligible than that of a genre novelist by creating a character with a conflicting literary agenda, *The Tommyknockers*, approaches the same issue by creating two authors: (1) the genre novelist, Bobbi Anderson, whose dark vision unleashes an alien presence which enslaves her community; and (2) the literary artist, poet Jim Gardener, whose self-sacrifice saves that community. Both are competent and dedicated writers who hold one another's work in esteem. But both are fatally flawed. Bobbi's kind of writing leaves her psychologically open to outside control (from audience and alien): she becomes the conduit which unearths and directs a cosmic darkness to the human community. Jim is armed against such possession, but isolated from the community by an art aspiring to the ideal. He has the vision to see through the darkness—he can and does die for the community, but it will never buy his books. As in *Misery*, King's final position on the writer's value is extremely pessimistic.

After writing *Misery* and *The Tommyknockers*, King entered a hiatus. For him, writing had become an existential act. He had the money but he felt controlled and depleted by the audience that he did have and despaired of the existence of any other kind of audience. Why continue to write? Developmental theory, such as Gail Sheehy's *Passages*, suggests that other processes were affecting King. He was passing through a chronological period from the age of 38 to 42 in which a man or woman working in the public area generally experiences extreme conflict as life takes a new direction: he or she reaches the end of a horizontal direction in which new territory and material are claimed through a process of conflict (a masculine direction), and a vertical direction where depth rather than width is sought through the development of nurturance and personal relationships (a feminine direction).

King emerged from his hiatus with an ambitious contract for four books—he wrote five (the last two of which were novels solely about women). But before he undertook this feminine direction, he closed the canon to children, Castle Rock, and writers. Children had by this time become lesser characters. The people of Castle Rock, given a slight nudge by a minor demon, destroyed themselves in the apocalyptic cataclysm ending *Needful Things*. The resolution of the issue of the writer in *The Dark Half* was more complex. The opposition of popular writer and artist in *Misery* and *The Tommyknockers*), is here internalized in *The Dark Half*: warring for the soul of a writer are his personae as literary artist (Thad Beaumont) and as genre novelist (George Stark). The artist wins, but the victory is pyrrhic. Closer examination reveals that Beaumont's friends, wife, and children are psychologically akin to his nemesis. We find out in the sequel, *Needful Things*, that not only has the artist lost friends and family, but also the will to write. He is an alcoholic and the circle is closed. King leaves the issue behind him unresolved: it is what it is.

In *Gerald's Game* and *Dolores Claiborne*, King picks up a gauntlet. Long criticized for unidimensional female characters in such articles as Mary Pharr's "Partners in the Danse: Women in Stephen King's Fiction," he apparently decided that a new direction for growth both as human and as artist would be appropriate in accepting the challenge to create convincing women. Written simultaneously, the novels are most productively regarded as two poles in a meta-narrative process. At the one pole is the heroine of *Gerald*, Jessie Burlingame—economically and socially privileged, childless, and in her own eyes significant only as her husband's sexual object. At the other pole is Dolores, a figure apparently based on King's mother (to whom he dedicates the novel)—economically and socially underprivileged, a mother, and in her own eyes significant in herself. Through their telepathic awareness of one another and through their experience of the same eclipse as a central incident in their lives, King establishes the commonality of these two very different women: it lies in the fact that they are whole only in those years before and after men entered their lives—the period of the eclipse. In *Gerald*, King dramatizes the entry of Jessie into an eclipse through the seduction and domination by her father; she exits the eclipse by killing her dominating husband, Gerald. The subsequent fragmenting of her victim persona into a community of sustaining female personae provides her with the resources to free herself from a literal bondage. In *Dolores*, the titular figure is a mother and wife who exits the eclipse by murdering a husband who also seeks to sexually exploit his daughter. In either case, the women experience one horror in common: the entry of men and sexuality into their lives. By erecting such contrasting poles as Jessie and Dolores, and yet maintaining both as sympathetic characters with a shared dilemma, King writes paired novels sympathetic to a wide spectrum of women and evades an easy condemnation of his women characters as unidimensional.

Overall, King's canon is a quest. But his battle cry is not "excelsior!" The direction is downwards and the path is a spiral. Many of King's characters experience life as a quest: Ben Mears of *'Salem's Lot* questing for self and conquering the vampire; *The Tommyknockers*' Gardener questing for death and finding self; the comrades of *The Stand* marching against the Dark One and founding the New Jerusalem; the boys of *It* killing fear; and the boys of *The Talisman* killing death. The gunslinger of *The Dark Tower* series is, however, probably most typical of King: he seeks to understand what the quest itself is. His enemies become his friends, his guides his traitors, his victims those he has saved, and his now a then. Paradox; transformation; balancing the dualities, an emergent, tenuous, ever-fading, and ever-appearing balance—these are the duplicitous landmarks in the terrain of King's work and his life. Both are open enough and fluent enough to mirror us and ours as we seek to make our own accommodations with modern monsters, personal meaninglessness, social chaos, physical decay, and death.

Chronology

1947 Stephen King is born on September 21 in Portland, Maine, the second son of Donald Edwin King and Nellie Ruth Pillsbury King.

1949 His father abandons the family.

1950–57 Nellie, Stephen, and an older brother, Donald, live with various relatives in Durham, Maine; Malden, Massachusetts; Chicago; West Du Pere, Wisconsin; Stratford, Connecticut; and Fort Wayne, Indiana. Nellie supports her children by working at a succession of low-paying jobs.

1958 The family settles in Durham, Maine, where Nellie King cares for her parents. King will later fictionalize the town as Castle Rock, Maine.

1965 King's first short story, "I Was a Teenage Grave Robber," is published in *Comics Review*, and he writes his first novel-length manuscript, "The Aftermath," about the survivors of an atomic-bomb explosion.

1966 While a senior in high school King begins what will later become a novel, *Rage*, a study of madness and adolescence during the Vietnam War era. He receives a scholarship to the University of Maine at Orono, where he majors in English. He writes a column, "King's Garbage Truck," for the student newspaper, *Maine Campus*.

1967–69   King publishes the first fiction for which he is paid: "The Glass Floor" appears in the Fall 1967 issue of *Startling Mystery Stories*. King criticizes the traditional approach to literature of the university's English department and is allowed to teach a seminar, Popular Literature and Culture, while an undergraduate.

1970   After graduating from the University of Maine King is unable to find a teaching job. He works in a gas station and a laundry, experiences he will use in his fiction.

1971   King marries novelist Tabitha Jean Spruce on January 2. They will have three children. King is a teacher at the Hampden Academy in Hampden, Maine, and writes at night. *The Running Man* is rejected by publishers.

1972   King writes *Carrie* during the summer and discards it; Tabitha retrieves the manuscript and urges him to continue.

1973   The sale of the paperback rights to *Carrie* in 1973 enables King to become a full-time writer. King's mother dies of cancer, before her son is recognized as a writer. He will dedicate two books to her, including *Dolores Claiborne* (1993), and he fondly describes her in *Danse Macabre* (1981). King discusses his literary debt to the tradition of horror fiction in a published essay, "The Horror Writer and the Ten Bears"; writes "Second Coming," which will become *'Salem's Lot*.

1974   His first novel, *Carrie*, is published and sells over 3.5 million copies, establishing King as a best-selling author. Writes *The Shining*; begins a novel, "The House on Value Street," inspired by the 1974 kidnapping of newspaper heiress Patty Hearst.

1975   *'Salem's Lot* is published; the paperback edition tops the *New York Times* best-seller list. King's publishers are concerned that he will saturate the market; in response, King adopts a pseudonym, Richard Bachman, under which he will publish several novels.

1976   King writes *The Dead Zone* and *Firestarter*.

1977   *The Shining* is published and is the first of King's books to reach
            the *New York Times* hardcover best-seller list. *Rage*, his first novel
            published as Richard Bachman, receives little critical attention.
            Writes *Cujo*; a novel rooted in everyday experience; it antici-
            pates the naturalism of his later fiction. Meets Peter Straub in
            London; they begin collaboration on *The Talisman*.

1978   Writer in residence and instructor of literature and creative writ-
            ing at the University of Maine at Orono. Publishes *The Stand*
            and *Night Shift*. Begins *Christine* as a short story.

1979   *The Dead Zone* is published and sells well. *The Long Walk*, pub-
            lished as Bachman, receives little notice. Writes first draft of *Pet
            Sematary*.

1980   *The Dark Tower: The Gunslinger*, inspired by Robert Browning's
            "Childe Roland to the Dark Tower Came" (1868–69), published
            in five installments in the *Magazine of Fantasy and Science Fiction*
            (1980–81). *Firestarter* published.

1981   *Cujo*; *Danse Macabre*, a nonfiction study of King's relationship to
            the horror genre; and *Roadwork*, as Bachman, published. Begins
            writing *It*.

1982   *The Dark Tower: The Gunslinger*; *Stephen King's Creepshow*;
            and *Different Seasons* published.

1983   *Pet Sematary* published; critics note that, with this novel, King
            transcends the traditional horror genre. *The Running Man*, pub-
            lished as Bachman; *Christine*; and *Cycle of the Werewolf* also
            appear. Begins writing *The Tommyknockers*, *The Talisman*, and *Eyes
            of the Dragon*.

1984   *Eyes of the Dragon*, originally conceived as a children's story for
            his daughter; *The Talisman*, an American epic fantasy; and
            Thinner, as Bachman, published. Writes *Misery*.

1985   *The Bachman Books* and *Skeleton Crew* published.

1986   *It* published.

1987   *Misery*, considered his best novel; *The Dark Tower II: The Drawing of the Three*, a quest novel; and *The Tommyknockers* published. Begins writing *The Dark Half*, a story about the relationship of a writer as his pseudonym.

1989   *The Dark Half*; *Dolan's Cadillac*; and *My Pretty Pony* published.

1990   *Four Past Midnight* published.

1991   *The Dark Tower III: The Wastelands* and *Needful Things* published.

1992   *Gerald's Game*, critically praised for its psychological insight, published.

1993   *Dolores Claiborne* and *Nightmares and Dreamscapes* published.

1994   The novel *Insomnia*, and a nonfiction account by the "Rock Bottom Remainders," a rock group of best-selling authors that includes King, published.

1995   *Rose Madder* published.

1996   *The Regulators*, as Bachman; *The Green Mile*, a six-part novel; and *Desperation* published.

Contributors

HAROLD BLOOM is Sterling Professor of the Humanities at Yale University and professor of English at New York University. He is the author of numerous volumes of literary criticism, including *Shelley's Mythmaking*, *The Visionary Company*, *The Anxiety of Influence*, *A Map of Misreading*, and *Agon: Towards a Theory of Revisionism*. His forthcoming study, *Freud, Transference and Authority*, attempts a full-scale reading of all of Freud's major writings. A MacArthur Prize Fellow and a member of the American Academy of Arts and Letters, Professor Bloom is general editor of five series of literary criticism published by Chelsea House.

CHELSEA QUINN YARBRO is both novelist and critic. Her works include the historical horror novels *A Candle for D'artagnan*, *Crusader's Torch*, and *A Flame in Byzantium*. Her science fiction writings appear in *Beyond the Gates of the World* and *The Harriers*. *Michael for the Millennium: The Fourth Book in the Michael Teaching*, on spirit writings, is her most recent book.

BEN P. INDICK has written several articles on the fiction of Stephen King and the tradition of horror fantasy. His works include *The Sage of Sauk City: August Derleth* and *Ray Bradbury, Dramatist*, published in *Essays on Fantastic Literature*. He has contributed essays to *From Fiawol to Gafia: All About Fandom*, edited by Joe Sanders; *Fiction Factory and Noble Fantasist: The Fiction of L. Ron Hubbard*, edited by William Widder; and *Fantasy in the Theatre: Staging the Impossible: The Fantastic Mode in Modern Drama*, edited by Patrick D. Murphy.

KATHERINE K. GOTTSCHALK is Director of Freshman Writing

Seminars at Cornell University. Her recent publications include "Paralyzed in the Present: Susan Fromberg Schaeffer's Mothers, or Daughters" in *Mother Puzzles: Daughters and Mothers in Contemporary American Literature*, and "Training TA's Across the Curriculum to Teach Writing: Embracing Diversity." She is coeditor of and an author included in *Teaching Prose: A Guide for Writing Instructors*.

KAREN A. HOHNE is a professor at Moorhead State University. Her critical focus is upon the interaction of language and ideology in literature. She is coeditor of a collection of essays on feminism and Bakhtin.

LINDA BADLEY is Professor of English and popular culture at Middle Tennessee State University. She has published articles on fiction, film, poetry, and gender studies. Her latest book is *Film, Horror, and the Body Fantastic* (1995).

BERNARD J. GALLAGHER is a professor at Central Methodist College. His most recent essay, "Breaking Up Isn't Hard to Do: Stephen King, Christopher Lasch, and Psychic Fragmentation," was published in the *Journal of American Culture*.

TONY MAGISTRALE is associate Professor of English at the University of Vermont. His numerous books on the works of Stephen King include *Landscape of Fear: Stephen King's American Gothic* and *The Moral Voyages of Stephen King*; he is editor of *The Shining Reader*, a collection of critical essays on *The Shining*.

JAMES EGAN is Professor of English at the University of Akron. He has published many articles on horror fantasy and dystopian themes in the works of H. P. Lovecraft and Stephen King.

CLARE HANSON is a Lecturer in English and Humanities at the College of St. Paul and St. Mary, Cheltenham, England. Among her published works are *Katherine Mansfield*, with Andrew Gurr; *Short Stories and Short Fictions, 1880–1980*; and *Virginia Woolf*. She is editor of *The Critical Writings of Katherine Mansfield* and *Re-Reading the Short Story*.

JONATHAN P. DAVIS graduated from North Central College in Naperville, Illinois. He has written about sports for the *Chicago Tribune* and is currently working on his first fiction manuscript.

JEANNE CAMPBELL REESMAN is an author and editor, with Earle Labor, of a critical volume entitled *Jack London*, and with Leonard Cassuto, *Rereading Jack London*. Her recently published articles include *"The Savage Path"*: *Nightwood and the Divine Comedy* and book reviews in the *Journal of English & Germanic Philology* and *American Literature*. She is the author of *American Designs: The Late Novels of James and Faulkner*.

SHARON A. RUSSELL is Professor of Communication and Women's Studies at Indiana State University. She is the past head of the Detective and Mystery Fiction section of the Popular Culture Association and a member of the International Association for the Fantastic in the Arts. She is editor of two forthcoming volumes: *The Dog Didn't Do It: Animals in Mystery* and *A Guide to African Cinema*.

EDWIN F. CASEBEER is Professor of English at Indiana University, where he teaches courses in Shakespeare, popular culture, and American Studies. He has published several essays on Stephen King, most recently in *The Dark Descent: Essays Defining Stephen King's Horrorscape* and *A Casebook on The Stand*.

Bibliography

Alexander, Alex E. "Stephen King's *Carrie:* A Universal Fairytale," *Journal of Popular Culture*, 13 (Fall 1979): 282–88.

Barker, Clive. "Stephen King: Surviving the Ride," *Fantasy Review*, 9:1 (January 1986): 6–8.

Beahm, George. *The Stephen King Story: A Literary Profile*. Kansas City: Andrews & McNeel, 1991. 27–29.

Beeler, Michael. "Stephen King: *The Stand,*" *Cinefantastique*, 25:3 (June 1994): 24–31.

———. "The Book vs. the Miniseries," *Cinefantastique*, 25:2 (1994): 10–11.

———. "The Horror Meister," *Cinefantastique*, 25:2, 12–13.

———. "Working with Stephen King," *Cinefantastique*, 25:2, 16–17.

Bernard, Maxine M. "The Religious Significance of Names in the Horror Fiction of Stephen King," *Connecticut Onomastic Review*, 3 (1990): 16–19.

Bleiler, Richard. "Stephen King," *Supernatural Fiction Writers: Fantasy and Horror, Vol. 2, A. E. Coppard to Roger Selazny*. New York: Scribner's, 1985.

Blue, Tyson. *The Unseen King*. Mercer Island, WA: Starmont House, 1989.

Booth-Bangor, Cathy, and Kanfer Stefan. "King of Horror," *Time* (October 6, 1986): 74–83.

Brown, John. "The Impossible Object: Reflections on *The Shining,*" *Cinema and Fiction: New Modes of Adapting, 1950–90*, eds. John Orr and Colin Nicholson. Edinburgh: Edinburgh University Press, 1992: 104–21.

Burns, Gail E., and Melinda Kanner. "Women, Danger, and Death: The Perversion of the Female Principle in Stephen King's Fiction," *Sexual Politics and Popular Culture*, ed. Diane Raymond. Bowling Green, OH: Popular Press, 1990: 158–72.

Canby, Vincent. "Pseudonym Comes to Life in a Stephen King Tale," *New York Times* (April 23, 1993): 10C.

Cheever, Leonard. "Apocalypse and the Popular Imagination: Stephen King's *The Stand,*" *Artes Liberales*, 8:1 (Fall 1981): 1–10.

Collings, Michael R. "Dean R. Koontz and Stephen King: Style, Invasion, and an Aesthetics of Horror," *Sudden Fear: The Horror and Dark Suspense Fiction of Dean R. Koontz*, ed. Bill D. Munster. Mercer Island, WA: Starmont House, 1988. 45–65.

———. *The Films of Stephen King*. Mercer Island, WA: Starmont House, 1986.

————. *Infinite Explorations: Art and Artifice in Stephen King's It, Misery, and The Tommyknockers.* Mercer Island, WA: Starmont House, 1986.

————. *Stephen King as Richard Bachman.* Mercer Island, WA: Starmont House, 1985.

————. *The Stephen King Concordance.* Mercer Island, WA: Starmont House, 1985.

————. *The Stephen King Phenomenon.* Mercer Island, WA: Starmont House, 1986.

———— and David A. Engebretson. *The Shorter Works of Stephen King.* Mercer Island, WA: Starmont House, 1985.

Dameron, J. Lasley. "Edgar Allan Poe, Stephen King, and Other Contemporaries," *Odense American Studies International Series,* 6 (1993): 1–21.

Davis, Jonathan P. *Stephen King's America.* Bowling Green, OH: Popular Press, 1994.

Dettelbach, Cynthia. "In the Driver's Seat: The Automobile in American Literature and Popular Culture," *Contributions in American Studies,* 25. Westport, CT: Greenwood Press, 1976.

Docherty, Brian, ed. *American Horror Fiction: From Brockden Brown to Stephen King.* New York: St. Martin's Press, 1990.

Egan, James. "Antidetection: Gothic and Detective Conventions in the Fiction of Stephen King," *Clues: A Journal of Detection,* 5:1 (Spring–Summer 1984): 131–46.

————. "Sacral Parody in the Fiction of Stephen King," *Journal of Popular Culture,* 23:3 (Winter 1989): 125–41.

————. "Apocalypticism in the Fiction of Stephen King," *Extrapolation* 25 (1984): 214–27.

Ehlers, Leigh A. *"Carrie:* Book and Film," *Ideas of Order in Literature and Film,* eds. Peter Ruppert, Eugene Crook, and Walter Forehand. Tallahassee: University Press of Florida, 1980. 39–50.

Gallagher, Bernard J. "Breaking Up Isn't Hard to Do: Stephen King, Christopher Lasch, and Psychic Fragmentation," *Journal of American Culture,* 10:4 (Winter 1987): 59–67.

Gibbs, Kenneth. "Stephen King and the Tradition of American Gothic," *Gothic,* 1 (1986): 6–14.

Gorner, Peter. "Stephen King's Horror Comes Down to Earth," *Chicago Tribune* (November 18, 1992): 5:3.

Gray, Paul. "Master of Postliterate Prose," *Time* (August 30, 1982): 87.

Hansen, Ron. *"Creepshow:* The Dawn of a Living Horror Comedy," *Esquire,* 97 (January 1982): 72–73, 76.

Heldreth, Leonard G. "Rising Like Old Corpses: Stephen King and the Horrors of Time-Past," *Journal of the Fantastic in the Arts,* 2:1 (Spring 1989): 5–13.

Herron, Don, ed. *Reign of Fear: Fiction and Film of Stephen King.* Los Angeles: Underwood-Miller, 1988.

Hohne, Karen A. "The Power of the Spoken Word in the Works of Stephen King," *Journal of Popular Culture,* 28:2 (Fall 1994): 93–103.

Holland-Toll, Linda. "Contemporary Tragedy: Stephen King's *Pet Sematary,*" *Studies in Weird Fiction,* 16 (Winter 1995): 28–33.

Indick, Ben. "Stephen King as an Epic Writer," *Discovering Modern Horror Fiction,* ed. Darrell Schweitzer. Mercer Island, WA: Starmont Press, 1985.

Janeczko, Paul. "An Interview with Stephen King," *English Journal,* 69 (February 1980): 0–10.

Kent, Bill. "*Dolores Claiborne*," *New York Times Book Review* (December 27, 1992): 7–15.

King, Stephen. "Son of Best Seller Stalks the Moors," *New York Times Book Review* (June 6, 1993): 59.

———— and Kenneth K. Sereno. "Conversational Appropriateness as a Conversational Imperative," *Quarterly Journal of Speech*, 70:3 (August 1984): 264–73.

Lehmann-Haupt, Christopher. Review of *Misery*, by Stephen King, *New York Times* (June 8, 1987): 13.

Magistrale, Anthony. "Art Versus Madness in Stephen King's *Misery*," in *The Celebration of the Fantastic: Selected Papers from the Tenth Anniversary International Conference on the Fantastic in the Arts*, eds. Donald E. Morse, Marshall B. Tymn, and Bertha Csilla. Westport, CT: Greenwood Press, 1992. 271–78.

————. "Free Will and Sexual Choice in *The Stand*," *Extrapolation: A Journal of Science Fiction and Fantasy*, 34:1 (Spring 1993): 30–38.

————. "Native Sons: Regionalism in the Work of Nathaniel Hawthorne and Stephen King," *Journal of the Fantastic in the Arts*, 2:1 (Spring 1989): 76–86.

————. "Stephen King's Vietnam Allegory: An Interpretation of *Children of the Corn*," *Cuyahoga Review*, 2:1 (Spring–Summer, 1984): 61–66.

————. *Stephen King, the Second Decade: Danse Macabre to The Dark Half.* New York: Twayne, 1992.

———— and Joseph A. Citro. *The Dark Descent: Essays Defining Stephen King's Horrorscape.* New York: Greenwood Press, 1992.

Martin, Sue. " 'Stand' Corrected," *Los Angeles Times* (July 15, 1990): 12.

McGuire, Karen. "Of Artists, Vampires, and Creativity," *Studies in Weird Fiction*, 11 (Spring 1992): 2–4.

Murphy, Patrick D. "The Realities of Unreal Worlds: King's *The Dead Zone*, Schmidt's *Kensho*, and Lem's *Solaris:* Selected Essays from the Sixth International Conference on the Fantastic in the Arts," reprinted in *Spectrum of the Fantastic*, ed. Donald Palumbo. Westport, CT: Greenwood Press, 1988: 175–83.

Mustazza, Leonard. "The Power of Symbols and the Failure of Virtue: Catholicism in Stephen King's '*Salem's Lot*," *Journal of the Fantastic in the Arts*, 3:4 (1994): 107–19.

Nicholls, Richard E. "Avaunt Thee, ReCreant Cyborg," *New York Times Book Review* (September 29, 1991): 7–14.

————. "*Rose Madder*," *New York Times Book Review* (July 2, 1995): 11.

Patrouch, Joseph F., Jr. "Stephen King in Context: Academic Programming at Chicon IV," *Patterns of the Fantastic*, ed. Donald M. Hassler. Mercer Island, WA: Starmont House, 1983.

Pollin, Burton R. "Stephen King's Fiction and the Heritage of Poe," *Journal of the Fantastic in the Arts*, 5:4 (1993): 2–25.

Pourteau, Chris. "The Individual and Society: Narrative Structure and Thematic Unity in Stephen King's *Rage*," *Journal of Popular Culture*, 27:1 (Summer 1993): 171–78.

Price, Robert M. "Fundamentalists in the Fiction of Stephen King," *Studies in Weird Fiction*, 5 (Spring 1989): 12–14.

Punter, David. "Stephen King: Problems of Recollection and Construction," *Lit: Literature, Interpretation, Theory*, 5:1 (1994): 67–82.

Rafferty, Terrence. "Under a Cloud," *New Yorker* (April 3, 1995): 93–95.

Reed, Kit. "Will You Please Be Quiet Please?" *Washington Post* (December 13, 1992): 5WBK.

Reino, Joseph. *Stephen King: The First Decade: From Carrie to Pet Sematary.* Boston: Twayne, 1988.

Rodriguez, Rene. " 'Insomnia' Proves Master of Macabre Struggling," *Terre Haute Tribune Star* (October 9, 1994): 3B.

Senf, Carol A. "Donna Trenton, Stephen King's Modern American Heroine," *Heroines of Popular Culture*, ed. Pat Browne. Bowling Green, OH: Popular Press, 1987. 91–100.

———. "Stephen King: A Modern Interpretation of the Frankenstein Myth," *Science Fiction: A Review of Speculative Literature*, 8:3 (1986): 65–73.

Schopp, Andrew. "Writing (with) the Body: Stephen King's Misery," *Lit: Literature, Interpretation, Theory*, 5:1 (1994): 29–43.

Schweitzer, Darrell, ed. *Discovering Stephen King.* Mercer Island, WA: Starmont House, 1985.

Skal, David J. "The Dance of Dearth: Horror in the Eighties," *New York Review of Science Fiction*, 52:1 (December 1992): 10–16.

Slung, Michele. "In the Matter of Stephen King: *Armchair Detective: A Quarterly Journal Devoted to the Appreciation of Mystery, Detective, and Suspense Fiction*, 14:2 (Spring 1981): 147–49.

Somtow, S. P. "A Certain Slant of 'I': *The Stand* by Stephen King," *Fantasy Review*, 9:9 (October 1986): 11–16.

Spignesi, Stephen J. *The Complete Stephen King Encyclopedia.* Ann Arbor, MI: Popular Culture, Ink, 1993.

Stein, Leon. "A Holocaust Education in Reverse: Stephen King's *The Summer of Corruption: Apt Pupil*," *Journal of the Fantastic in the Arts*, 5:2 (1993): 61–80.

Steuwe, Paul. Review of *Christine. Quill Quire*, 49 (June 1983): 37.

Stewart, Robert. "The Rest of King," *Starship: The Magazine About Science Fiction*, 18:1 (Spring 1981): 45–46.

Taylor, James E. "Plantinga's Proper Functioning Analysis of Epistemic Warrant," *Philosophical Studies*, 64:2 (November 1991): 185–202.

Terry, Clifford. "Frightful Things' from Stephen King," *Chicago Tribune* (August 27, 1993): 7A

Travers, Peter. "Stephen King Divided," *Rolling Stone* (May 13, 1993): 113–14.

Underwood, Tim, and Chuck Miller, eds. *Kingdom of Fear: The World of Stephen King.* New York: Plume: New American Library, 1986.

———. *Bare Bones: Conversations on Terror with Stephen King.* New York: Warner Books, 1988:44.

Review of *The Wastelands: The Dark Tower Book III*, in *Atlanta Journal and Constitution* (January 5, 1992): 12K.

Whitehead, Colson. "*The Stand*," *The Voice* (May 10, 1994): 49.

Will, George F. "The Lure of the Lurid," *Washington Post* (December 10, 1989): 7C.

Winter, Douglas. *Stephen King: The Art of Darkness.* New York: Signet, 1986.

———. *The Reader's Guide to Stephen King.* Mercer Island, WA: Starmont House, 1982.

Wohleber, Curt. "The Man Who Could Scare Stephen King," *American Heritage*, 46:8 (December 1995): 82–90.

Wood, Gary. "Stephen King, the Horror Franchise," *Cinefantastique*, 25:2 (1994): 22–23.

Wood, Robin. "Cat and Dog: Lewis Teague's Stephen King Movies," *Gender, Language, and Myth: Essays and Popular Narrative.* Ed. Glenwood Irons. Toronto: University of Toronto Press, 1992. 303–18. Previously published in *CineAction!* 2 (Fall 1985).

Acknowledgments

"Cinderella's Revenge: Twists on Fairy Tale and Mythic Themes in the Work of Stephen King" by Chelsea Quinn Yarbro from *Fear Itself: The Early Works of Stephen King*, edited by Tim Underwood and Chuck Miller, intoduction by Peter Straub, foreword by Stephen King, afterword by George Romero. © 1982, 1993 by Underwood-Miller, Inc.

"King and the Literary Tradition of Horror and the Supernatural" by Ben P. Indick from *Fear Itself: The Early Works of Stephen King*, edited by Tim Underwood and Chuck Miller, introduction by Peter Straub, foreword by Stephen King, afterword by George Romero. © 1982, 1993 by Underwood-Miller, Inc.

"Surviving the Ride" by Clive Barker from *Kingdom of Fear: The World of Stephen King*, edited by Tim Underwood. © 1986 by Underwood-Miller, Inc.

"Reading Between the Lines: Stephen King and Allegory" by Bernard J. Gallagher from *The Gothic World of Stephen King, Landscape of Nightmares*, edited by Gary Hoppenstand and Ray B. Browne. © 1987 by Bowling Green State University Popular Press.

"Technohorror: The Dystopian Vision of Stephen King" by James Egan from *Extrapolation*, 29:2 (Summer 1988). © 1988 by The Kent State University Press.

"Inherited Haunts: Stephen King's Terrible Children" by Tony Magistrale from *Landscape of Fear: Stephen King's American Gothic* by Tony Magistrale, with an annotated bibliography compiled by Marshall B. Tymn. © 1988 by Bowling Green State University Popular Press.

"The Shape Evil Takes: Hawthorne's Woods Revisited" by Anthony Magistrale from *Starmont Studies in Literary Criticism 25: The Moral Voyages of Stephen King* by Anthony Magistrale. © 1989 by Starmont House, Inc.

"Stephen King: Powers of Horror" by Clare Hanson from *American Horror Fiction:*

From Brockden Brown to Stephen King, edited by Brian Docherty. © 1990 by Editorial Board, Lumiere (Co-operative) Press Ltd.

"Stephen King and the Tradition of American Naturalism in *The Shining*" by Jeanne Campbell Reesman from *Starmont Studies in Literary Criticism #30: The Shining Reader.* © 1990 Starmont House, Inc.

"Stephen King's Dark and Terrible Mother, Annie Wilkes" by Katherine K. Gottschalk from *The Anna Book: Searching for Anna in Literary History*, edited by Mickey Pearlman. © 1992 by Mickey Pearlman.

"Childhood and Rites of Passage" by Jonathan P. Davis from *Stephen King's America* by Jonathan P. Davis. © 1994 by Bowling Green State University Popular Press.

"Dialects of Power: The Two-Faced Narrative" by Karen A. Hohne from *The Text Beyond: Essays in Literary Linguistics*, edited by Cynthia Goldin Bernstein. © 1994 by The University of Alabama Press.

"Stephen King Viewing the Body" by Linda Badley from *Writing Horror and the Body: The Fiction of Stephen King, Clive Barker, and Anne Rice* by Linda Badley, from the series *Contributions to the Study of Popular Culture*, Number 51, Greenwood Press, 1996. © 1996 by Linda Badley.

"Needful Things" by Sharon A. Russell from *Stephen King: A Critical Companion* by Sharon A. Russell, from the series *Critical Companions to Popular Contemporary Writers*, Greenwood Press, 1996. © 1996 by Sharon A. Russell.

"The Art of Balance: Stephen King's Canon" by Edwin F. Casebeer from *A Dark Night's Dreaming: Contemporary American Horror Fiction*, edited by Tony Magistrale and Michael A. Morrison. © 1996 by the University of South Carolina.

Index